A Magical Journey to India

A MAGICAL JOURNEY TO INDIA

Print ISBN-13: 978-1-957581-05-7
Ebook ISBN-13: 978-1-957581-06-4

Cover photo: Ramakrishna Temple at Belur Math,
photo credit: Brandy Williams

Interior photos by Brandy Williams and Alex Williams

Durga Puja In Kolkata and *A Visit To Kamakhya Temple And The Mahavidya Shrines* were originally published as separate works by Mnemosyne Press in 2022 and are included here by permission.

Mnemosyne Press

Dedication

To Alex

TABLE OF CONTENTS

Book Two: Durga Puja in Kolkata

ACKNOWLEDGEMENTS

I write this book as a scholar practitioner. As an independent scholar I have written on Pagan history. As a practitioner I am a Witch, a Pagan, a Ceremonial Magician practicing theurgy, and a Tantric initiate and Shri Vidya student. The travelogues are filled out with background information about the people, places and events which I experienced. I have filled these in with research conducted before, during, and after the pilgrimage.

In writing this account I am inspired by Laura Amazzone. Her work *Goddess Durga and Sacred Female Power* opens a portal into the liberating power of the Mother Goddess. In particular her description of her visit to Kamakhya was heart-felt and informative. I am deeply grateful for her knowledge, wisdom and courage.

Thank you to Ted Gill, partner in so many ways, for his ongoing support of both me and Alex. My deepest thanks and love to my travel companion and partner Alex Williams whose grace and insight have steadied me for all my adult life.

Introduction to the Collection

When we retired I asked Alex "What do you want to make sure you do in this life?" He said, "I want to go to Kamakhya Temple." So we went to India on a magical pilgrimage in October 2019.

When I started researching the trip I had no idea where to start. The country is a subcontinent – it's huge! The tourist web sites shunted me to the Taj Mahal. None of them spoke to the magical pilgrim. I wasn't going for a vacation or to take pictures of wonderful sights, I was drawn to a spiritual experience.

The advice of other travelers wasn't particularly helpful to me. The people I know who had traveled to India had all gone as tourists, even people in the magical community. They'd tell me about their camel rides in the desert and visits to temple courtyards. Pretty much every visitor I talked to had a spiritual experience, but it was a matter of luck, personal to them and non-repeatable by anyone else.

Drawing on our religious and magical resources, Alex and I called on the gods to guide our choices. Ultimately we chose to tour West Bengal, Assam, and Varanasi. As the journey unfolded we realized that these choices were truly magical. West Bengal and Assam lie in the heart of the mother land, the country in which the religion of the mother persists. This was important to us as Pagans and Tantrics. In Kolkata we traced the footsteps of the westerners who had come before us and learned the stories of the accomplished scholars and saints who deliberately constructed a bridge between cultures. Varanasi is India in miniature; there we were able to connect to everything we hadn't been able to shoehorn into our limited time.

This constructed our pilgrimage in three distinct phases, each reflecting one of the gunas, the qualities of embodied life.

- **Tamas** is the energy of inertia, the heavy quality which slows us down, hampering us when we want to move but also allowing us to rest and sleep. West Bengal is dedicated to Kali, the Mother of the tamasic experience.
- **Rajas** is the active energy which allows us to move and exercise power but can overstimulate us. Guwahati centers on Kamakhya, the lively energy of the Mother of Life.
- **Sattvas** is the spiritual energy elevates our earthly experience but is rarified and hard to maintain. Varanasi is the city of Shiva, the necessary balance to the power of the Mother, reflective and tranquil, the sattvic quality of stillness.

The Pilgrim as Tourist

Magical people are used to going incognito. I've traveled around the globe as a pilgrim masquerading as a tourist. I went to Greece to touch the temples where the gods lived. I went to Egypt to see with my own eyes the texts on the walls that shaped my personal practice. Like many of my friends I stood among the ruins on these trips to sneak in a bit of practice under the watchful eye of a suspicious guard.

I've had to masquerade as a tourist because the ancient religions practiced in these countries was suppressed. Pagan practice has survived and is reviving, but the dominant religions in these countries are Christianity and Islam which are still hostile to Paganism.

India is different. Mughal rulers introduced Islam and British colonialists brought Christianity, but neither succeeded in suppressing Hinduism. While the temples in Greece and Egypt are in ruins the temples of India are alive and thriving. Even the archeological sites attract religious practitioners.

What this means is that a pilgrim can just go ahead and worship in public along with everyone else. You don't have to hide the fact that you are there to connect with the gods and seek their blessings because everyone around you is doing the same thing.

The freedom to worship is one of the reasons that a trip to India is life-changing. In the west Pagans and other magical sorts live among people who are indifferent or hostile to our religion and rituals. We can only dream about what it was like for our ancestors to join in the festival processions to the temples. In India we can experience this for ourselves. We may be outsiders, but we are included in the crowd along with everyone else.

Since the gods are everywhere and anyone can be a pilgrim, what does it matter where you go? In some ways it doesn't. That's why people have spiritual experiences everywhere, because the gods are everywhere. That still leaves the pilgrim at sea to plan an itinerary. In all the vastness of the subcontinent, where should you go?

Pagans and Hindus

Pagans and Hindus have an affinity. We are comfortable with female deity and multiple deities, with incense and bells and offerings of food, with all the noisy and colorful and deeply devout apparatus of ritual.

One way to approach a pilgrimage to India is to connect with one or more of the Devis and Devas, the goddesses and gods. You can seek out the temple of that deity in each place you visit. After the trip I realized that our planning decisions had been guided by the goddess Kali. She led us to Kolkata to her temple there and to experience the city-wide festival of Durga Puja. She pulled us into the temple at Kamakhya which enshrines the yoni of the goddess. Finally she insisted we must visit her consort Shiva in the city of Varanasi.

Another approach is to seek out the Shakti Piths. These are temples with a long history of goddess worship. They have been linked together by the story that each of them enshrines one of the body parts of the goddess. Many devotees make the point that all of India is a Shakti Pith and the land herself is the body of the Goddess.

Shakti Piths are scattered all over the country so almost everywhere you go you will have the opportunity to visit one. That said, the vast majority of these temples cluster in the northwest and eastern coast, in the country of the Mother.

Esotericists and Tantrics

Just as Pagans have an affinity with Hindus, magicians and esotericists have an affinity with Tantrics. The rituals of Tantra have a mystique: they are ancient, powerful, and secret, and those who practice them gain almost unbelievable powers. Magicians pore over texts and try to unlock their knowledge.

These texts capture the historic and contemporary practices of Tantric country. It starts in the north in the country of Nepal and the disputed province of Kashmir, runs through Assam and West Bengal, and dips south to Odisha and Andhra Pradesh. While Shakti piths are sprinkled throughout India, a preponderance of those temples cluster in these provinces. The religion of the Mother is still strong in these places and offers opportunities for encounters with ancient practices.

Alex and I visited two major Tantric centers. Kamakhya Temple in Assam is a major and ancient center of Mother worship. The priests there conduct ongoing Tantric rites in the temples and in their homes. It's the most energically powerful place I've ever been.

The other major site we visited was Kalighat temple in West Bengal. It is located in the city of Kolkata which is a center of esoteric activity. There we walked in the footsteps of Arthur Avalon, Annie Besant and Aleister Crowley, teachers who have inspired our spiritual practice. Kolkata also introduced us to the native saints of the city, Ramakrishna, Vivekananda, Sarada Ma, and Sri Aurobindo. We learned how much western esotericists and westerners in general owe to their life works.

Structure of the Collection

This volume includes four books detailing the three stages of our journey: tamas, the earthy energy of West Bengal; rajas, the fiery power of Kamakhya Temple; and sattvas, the serenity of Varanasi.

The first book, "An American Magician in Kolkata", describes our travels in Kolkata and the surrounding countryside. It centers on our encounter as western magicians with the spiritual teachers of West Bengal.

The second book, "Durga Puja", overlaps the first chronologically but focuses specifically on the festival. It's a complex topic and deserves its own treatment.

The third book, "A Visit to Kamakhya and the Mahavidya Shrines", intersperses travelogue with detailed research. Both "Durga Puja" and "A Visit to Kamakhya" were previously published as stand-alone texts.

The fourth book, "Varanasi", documents a moment of transition for the city and the conclusion of our own journey.

This travelogue is the guide I wanted to have before I bought the plane tickets. If I had known a little more about the history of India's interaction with the west I would have known immediately that these places were significant to magical people. My years of Tantric practice have illuminated the significance of the Shakta Hindu Tantra of West Bengal and Assam. Luck and the gods directed us. In turn I hope that these notes will help you to make informed decisions if you decide to make a trip yourself, and inspire you to learn more about these lands and their people on your own journey of understanding.

Book One:
An American Magician
in Kolkata

Introduction

I had three reasons to travel to India: Aleister Crowley, Tantra, and Alex Williams.

When Alex and I met we snapped together like magnets. What happened between us sexually was an order of magnitude different than anything else we had experienced. It changed the energies of our bodies. We found ourselves circulating power, melting into each other, experiencing a sense of presence within our joined selves. I was a Witch and he was a ceremonial magician so we were accustomed to channeling energy, but nothing in our training or practice had prepared us for this. We weren't alarmed, it was exhilarating and nourishing, but we wanted to understand what was happening and direct it if we could figure out how.

We knew that Tantra had something to do with sexual practices. Alex had a bit of instruction to work with. In his younger days in Atlanta he had visited one of Muktananda's Siddha Yoga ashrams. Subsequently the master appeared to him in a dream and gave him a Shaktipat, a kundalini energy jolt, which imparted to him both energy and devotion. Alex chanted to Shiva until the chant became automatic. In the first year of our marriage he taught me rudimentary pranayama. I chanted "Om Namah Shivaya" while I thinned apples in the orchard.

Alex's experience couldn't take us much farther than that. In 1981 it was difficult for farm workers in rural Washington to connect to Tantric teachers. We could have picked up and gone to India, for example to Muktananda's ashram, but this seemed beyond our financial and emotional reach. I was wary of Tantric gurus anyway as they had a reputation for exploiting women. As a young sexually active woman I had already had several run-ins with sexually predatory "spiritual leaders" and I wasn't particularly interested in adding to the set. Alex and I also shared a reluctance to turn over our lives to a guru, any guru.

Without a physical guru we turned to books. Our library contains shelves of English-language Tantric texts. Most are academic, some are theoretical, and a few gave us ideas about practice. Some of these addressed the movement of energy in the subtle body, in particular the rise of the serpent power kundalini along the spine through the chakras which is a spiritual awakening. Most also carried warnings that engaging in exercises to rouse kundalini was dangerous without a teacher.

The exception to that rule was sex. Kundalini naturally roused and lifted her serpent head during sexual union as the energy channels of two bodies merged and supported each other. Several books detailed how this worked. Alex and I applied ourselves to learn these skills and learned how to channel the sexual energy we generated.

Now that we had it, what were we to do with it? We rapidly reached the limit of what we could learn about Tantra from books. There was a gap between academic knowledge and our practice. We understood Tantra as an ancient and deeply sophisticated spiritual system and we longed for instruction that would turn the energy we experienced in a spiritual direction.

Witchcraft gave us the earth: the seasons of the year, connection with other living creatures, spellcraft shaping the gifts of the earth for our protection and healing and growth. Ceremonial magick, specifically the Golden Dawn system, gave us an explanation of the soul's journey on earth. Aleister Crowley's religious philosophy Thelema filtered these things through the lens of sex, directing the energy of sex in magick that was focused on the male magician. In the end we used our education and experience to craft our own system, understanding the soul's love for the divine through our love for each other.

After a few years of practice we started teaching. I wrote up our sex magick system and continued to write about magick. We formed a coven with a ceremonial flavor, Coven of the Mystical Merkabah. We became active in the national Witchcraft community, then in the Thelemic fraternity Ordo Templi Orientis. I founded an order of my own, the Sororal Order of Sisters of Seshat, a woman-centered counterpoint to the male-centered focus of the O.T.O. (We define woman as anyone who says she is a woman).

When we were both old enough to retire we finally connected with Tantra in its own right. A friend who was a Witch and Thelemite gave us an initiation into a Tantric line which came with energy but no instruction. The experience prompted me to revisit my Tantric studies. I found that today there are a lot more books that offer genuine instruction and it is now possible to receive instruction and initiation by video conference. I found a lineaged teacher who has guided us ever since and gives us mantra initiations and practices.

I was 62 and Alex was 70 when we finally made our pilgrimage to India. We'd been married and practicing sex magick for almost forty years. In our youth we had considered traveling to India but it seemed out of our reach. In our age it became possible for us. Our marriage and our magic had taken us from the apple orchard to the city, from farm hands to retired corporate workers, from untraveled locals to experienced world travelers. We finally had the time, the money, and the ability to make the journey. It felt like an end and a beginning.

Tantric practitioners are notoriously private about their practices. I don't name our teacher in America or our guide in Kolkata as they have not given me permission to do so and they are both careful with their public presentation. I also don't describe the practices as they have explicitly requested that we keep these private. I'm not an academic, I am a practitioner, and my fealty is to the work and to the people who share it with me. Today any sincere seeker can find teachers and genuine practices.

We didn't go to India seeking a Tantric initiation, we already had that. We didn't go to India seeking a teacher, we already had her. We went to India through a pure longing to experience the Mother in her places of power. Starting our trip in Kolkata was a fortunate decision. West Bengal is one of the centers of Shakta Tantra.

The Western Magical Tradition has three great roots. First there is the magic of Egypt, Kemet, whose great temples were universities and hospitals and churches all at once. Next there is the magic of the Greek philosopher-priests who traveled to Kemet to study at the temples and then went home to teach their practices. Finally there is the magic of India which came to Kemet and to the Hellenistic world 2500 years ago. When the western world turned its back on magic we lost the memory of these roots and only rediscovered them in the mid-1800s with the revival of magical practice.

Alex and I went to India to explore the origins of Tantra. What we found in Kolkata, to our surprise, was the origin of the esotericism we had been practicing all along.

A Magician and a Tantric Step Into a Car

Our guide looked at me in horror. "Madam! You are a magician? Here we think this is very bad!"

The tour had been going so well until then. On our first day in Kolkata Alex and I were met at the airport by a driver who didn't speak much English. He drove us to the Oberoi Grand and unloaded us into a lobby featuring marble columns and an impressive chandelier.

Our guide greeted us at the door, a native of Kolkata who worked for an American tour organizer. He settled us on a white couch, delivered glasses of lemon-flavored water, and brought out a bevy of desk clerks who presented us with check—in paperwork. Once the formalities were concluded he draped Assamese scarves around our necks like we were celebrities and said "Welcome to Kolkata!"

We started the tour by walking to the India Museum. It was only a few blocks down the street so our guide decided to lead us by foot. This was definitely a throw-them-in-the-deep-end experience. The sidewalks of Chowringhee Road were lined with stalls selling saris, bangles, bags, bottled water. Pushing our way through the crowd was like squeezing ourselves into a tube of toothpaste – there wasn't a lot of room and everything was kind of slick. When we popped out into the street to avoid the crowd our guide discovered why his pasty white Northwesterners had brought the hats he had forbidden us to wear as we baked in the fierce afternoon sun.

The museum bills itself as the oldest and largest in India. Walter Granville's Italianate palace wraps three stories of hallways around a central courtyard. Alex and I and our guide had jointly decided to ditch the parts of our itinerary that surveyed colonial buildings, so this was the only British Raj architecture we would experience.

Our guide distinguished firmly between Calcutta, the imperial capital, and Kolkata, the city which he loves. I was acutely aware that the British occupation of India in general and West Bengal in particular made my experience easy and comfortable: everyone speaks English, restaurants serve meals with forks, and I was treated with a deference I had not personally earned. The statue of Queen Victoria in the museum stamps the British claim of ownership on Bengalese culture. I hissed at it.

We wandered through spacious rooms admiring extensive collections of statues, textiles, paintings, antiques, coins, stuffed birds. We grabbed some relief from the heat in the air-conditioned mummy room where the dead are kept dry and cool. In the Bharhut Gallery our guide planted us in front of an intricately carved two-thousand-year-old bas-relief and delivered an extemporaneous lecture on Buddhist history and belief tied to the images in the stone. He attracted a crowd of children and adults who listed with rapt attention.

The American tour organizer who arranged the trip had read through my author web site and encouraged me to bring our guide one of my books. On the morning of the second day our guide and I waited for some minutes in front of the hotel for the driver to bring the car around. I took the opportunity to present him with my book. I had chosen *For the Love of the Gods, the History and Modern Practice of Theurgy, Our Pagan Inheritance.* "You wrote this?" he said. Digesting the subtitles he murmured "So that's your assumption, interesting." He showed it to the doorman who said, "Madam?" and looked impressed. I was secretly pleased. Yes, the woman is an author.

Our guide settled Alex and me in the back seat, took the front passenger seat and sent the driver on our way. Then he turned the book over and read the bio. "*Brandy Williams is a ceremonial magician who has been practicing and teaching magic for more than twenty-five years…*" He spun around in his seat in horror. "We have heard this is black magic!"

For context, it was early in the morning and I was jet lagged. I was also experiencing Kolkata traffic for the first time. In a width of road that America would make into two marked and regulated lanes, Kolkatans managed to squeeze two cars, a motorcycle with a passenger hanging onto the driver, a rickshaw, and a bus. They accomplished this feat by driving bumper to bumper at about 20 miles an hour. This means the traffic was moving slowly enough that pedestrians mingled freely with the cars, weaving their way through the meandering vehicles. They drive on the right side of the road, as in Britain, and cars driving the opposite direction would take a bite out of the oncoming lane, so at times a car or a bus was coming straight at us. The honking formed a constant backdrop to every conversation.

In Calcutta in 1902 Crowley fielded this same comment sitting at dinner with English acquaintances. In *Aleister Crowley in India* Tobias Churton reports that Crowley's hosts told him the servants had identified him as a magician. His hosts asked if this was true. Crowley admitted it was, but he was astonished the servants would know this about him, since he had done no magic in Calcutta. He quickly turned the conversation to the "native telegraph" that passed information across the country faster than the pole-and-wire variety. Later Crowley noted in his diary that his Hindustani teacher approached the reputed magician with a request to kill an inconvenient aunt. Churton comments "Crowley told him that only reasons incomprehensible to the uninitiated could possibly persuade him to kill strangers."

Our guide said earnestly, "Suppose this driver is a bad man and you decide to kill him with your magic. You have taken away the years he would have lived. His karma for those years becomes yours!"

I thought, what is it with magicians and killing people? What I said was "There are two kinds of magic, thaumaturgy and theurgy." Until recently western scholarship distinguished between religion and magic. Religion or theurgy is spiritually developed and focuses on prayer, magic or thaumaturgy is primitive and superstitious and tries to wield power to get real world results.

Our guide's comment triggered the defense mechanisms I've built up in a lifetime of living as a public esotericist in Christendom. Witch, Pagan, magician, all register on the Western public as evil sorcerer. With our guide I took the tack that I take with people living in the Christian-dominated world: I made a bid to place ceremonial magic in the religion category. "This book is about theurgy, recognizing god in yourself. This kind of magic is not respected." Immediately I felt like a fraud. This was all true, but I don't only practice theurgy, I also practice thaumaturgy, and teach it too – *Practical Magic for Beginners* passed its tenth printing while I was having this conversation.

Then I realized that I wasn't talking to a Christian Englishman. I was talking to a native of Kolkata and a Tantric practitioner. I volleyed back. "We hear that Tantra is not respected here, that TV shows make you the villains."

Our guide said "Yes, very much so. One kind of Tantric did black magic and now everyone thinks we all do."

While Western culture makes every Tantric a sex magician, Indian popular culture makes every Tantric an evil sorcerer. June McDaniel details these local suspicions in her survey of Tantra, *Offering Flowers, Feeding Skulls*.

> There are many informal definitions of Tantra in West Bengal, and many of them revolve around Tantra's bad reputation: a Tantrika is a person who hypnotizes people, who drinks alcohol and takes various drugs, who sleeps with girls who are underage and low-caste.

I asked our guide if he'd read McDaniel's book but he hadn't heard of her. I surmised she hadn't interviewed him. To reassure our guide I needed to establish ceremonial magic as cognate with Tantra, which it is - ceremonial magicians can actually get a little snooty about practicing theurgy and not stooping to the homely everyday uses of thaumaturgy. I earnestly discussed the spiritual focus of Tantra and the spiritual focus of theurgy and how people misunderstand both of them. Finally our guide was satisfied that I did not intend to kill our driver and said "We are in agreement."

It was a relief to pass this hurdle since we were spending two weeks in our guide's company. But why did the word "magician" conjure up specters of people-killing for a Kolkatan Tantrika? Were he and I so different in practice? How could I make a meaningful connection with him across our cultural divide?

An English Education

When College Street showed up on our proposed itinerary I didn't think twice about the name. I thought it was just a street name like Main or First or State. This illustrates exactly how little I knew about Kolkata, or Bengal, or India.

College Street

Our driver dropped us off a block away and drove off to park the van. As we turned the corner I took in one of the great vistas of the literate world. I've toured the city-street-spanning bookstores of the world, Foyle's and The Strand and Powell's City of Books, and I've stood on the banks of the Seine scanning the bookseller stalls. College Street dwarfs them all: the Boi Para, Colony of Books, is the largest secondhand book market in the world.

As a lifelong bibliophile I've dreamed of finding an antique book of nearly-lost knowledge in a tiny bookstall, some magical secret that would change my life. I lurched instantly for the nearest vendor to jump in and browse. Our guide reeled me in, explaining these were mostly textbooks for students and promising a stop at an English language bookstore later. I couldn't help but scan the titles as we walked along the street.

Above the sidewalks the balconies and windows of the multistory buildings advertise College Street businesses. One sign leapt out at me, Motilal Banarsidass Publications, a name I had seen on the copyright pages of many of the books in our Tantric collection, especially the key works by Arthur Avalon. "Publishers?" I said to our guide. He laughed. There are a thousand small and large publishers around College Street turning out titles in Bengali, Sanskrit, Hindi, English. The second stories and back rooms of the buildings still house letter presses, etching presses, gold foil stamping machines. The whole atmosphere is an intoxicant to a writer.

As we were squired down the street by a native son we were schooled in what College Street means to India. Our guide plopped us in front of a gigantic statue of David Hare. I was immediately suspicious of the stiff British burgher, but our guide told us that the statue had been paid for by the citizens of Calcutta in gratitude for founding the first college on the street. When I investigated David Hare later I learned that he did not initiate the idea of a college, he acted in support of Raja Rammohun Roy who organized the people to make it happen. The collaboration of Hare and Roy established the institutions which would assimilate Indian students into English culture, the stated goal, and nurture the revolutionary fuel that would ultimately throw off English rule, an unintended consequence.

This was my first encounter with a repeated pattern: behind every English citizen famous for their work in India there is a native citizen who made the work possible.

Our guide gave us a rough outline of the struggle toward self-rule as he stood in front of the gates of Presidency University, formerly the Hindu College, the very first school on the street. Sanskrit College was established next, and our guide made it our next stop too so we could admire the soaring Greek Revival columns. These are massive buildings projecting authority and importance, just the thing to instill confidence in young scholars claiming power over their own future.

After that we swung into the iconic tour of College Street. We admired the public swimming pool. We ducked into the Paramount for a sharbat which turns out to be not ice cream but a sweet drink. Green coconut or dub sharbat is the house special and we sipped ours underneath yellowing photos of famous Bengalis. Our guide explained that the Paramount was founded in 1918 as a front for students plotting to overthrow the British. We were thrilled.

No trip to College Street is complete without a stop at the Indian Coffee House. Our guide brought us coffees and stepped away for a moment. When he returned he noticed that my coffee had turned white. We'd been warned not to drink local beverages and he'd had to assure us that the sharbats were safe. "Milk?" he said, surprised. Sheepishly I revealed my secret, a bottle of powdered creamer secreted in my purse, which made him laugh.

As we sipped our coffees he invited us to contemplate the generations of earnest intellectuals who came to this place to savor the pleasures of adda, free-ranging conversations that last for hours. The Indian Coffee House is so important to Kolkatans that when the Coffee Board shut it down due to lack of business a worker's collective stepped up to run it. Coffee shops, like schools and printing presses, turn out to be essential to free thought.

So far our College Street tour had followed the standard tourist template. Our stop at the Putiram Sweet Shop took us deeper into the history of the street. Our guide led us past the tempting sweet counter to the back of the store, settled us onto benches, and came back with trays of soup and flat breads. This, he said, was a lunch that was tailored to widows. The custom of child marriage left some young women widowed before they went to college. Because of the strict dietary conditions placed on widows they couldn't eat just any food like the other students. Where would they get their lunch? The tradition-approved fare served here had allowed generations of young women to attend school. This is a story I have not been able to document elsewhere so it's interesting to have it from a local source. Today the dietary requirements for widows are no longer strictly observed and Putiram is famous only as a place to get sweet treats.

Theosophy and Tantra

Walking back to the car we passed a sign that took my breath away. *Bengal Theosophical Society*! At one time I was a card carrying American Theosophist, more by way of supporting a feminist organization than committing to the style of practice. The society was founded Helena Petrovna Blavatsky, the first teacher in the modern era to combine yogic metaphysiology with western esotericism. Theosophy introduced the western world to chakras and the energy body.

I knew the society was based in India with a headquarters in Adyar. The connection to Kolkata surprised me. In my post-trip research I learned that Annie Besant had walked College Street herself. She had a political career centered in Kolkata and devoted herself to the service of India, although on her own colonialist terms, imposing her own ideas on the people she meant to serve rather than crediting their own narratives. This is also a flaw in Theosophy.

Besant's life story illuminated for me Mahatma Gandhi's connection to Kolkata. Gandhi knew Besant through Theosophy and succeeded her in politics. Kolkata was the site of his political career and the city where he was killed for promoting peace between Hindus and Moslems. When we focus on Calcutta as the historic British capital we miss Kolkata's importance in shaping Indian independence.

The founders of Theosophy, Helena Blavatsky and Annie Besant, took the knowledge they received about Hindu and Tantric religion and practice and used it as raw material to shape their own philosophy and practice. Kolkata has a strong connection with this stream of knowledge. It has an even stronger connection with the stream of knowledge about Tantra that made its way to the west. As we walked down College Street our guide turned to me and said, "Do you know the works of Arthur Avalon?"

"Sir John Woodroffe," I replied. "I've read his books." It's hard to overestimate the impact of that work. If you've ever heard of kundalini you've experienced that impact first hand. He wrote under a pseudonym, Arthur Avalon. *The Serpent Power* and *Shakti and Shakta* were the first works that made Tantric philosophy available in English.

Our guide was pleased that I was familiar with him. "Did you know he was a Tantric initiate?" He said Woodroffe had an initiation from a Bengal master and everything he wrote about he had achieved. "Don't doubt it." I was thrilled. Western magical folk tend to assume he had an initiation on the basis of his work but he doesn't make the claim himself. Here I was on the ground in Kolkata with a Tantric initiate learning this first hand.

When I got home I discovered to my great delight that this connection is now documented. Kathleen Taylor had exactly this experience, she learned about Woodroffe's initiation on the streets of Kolkata. She'd actually gone looking for the information; when she was searching for a doctoral topic she found to her surprise that no biography had been written about Woodroffe and set about to remedy this.

For a century esotericists who study the books have assumed that Woodroffe took a pseudonym to protect his reputation from being associated with Tantra. However he wrote politically incendiary works under his own name and openly claimed the work of Arthur Avalon. So what was he protecting?

Taylor gives us the other half of the story. Woodroffe had an collaborator. Atilal Bihari Ghose was the Tantric teacher and Sanskrit scholar who shaped their joint work. Ghose had the knowledge, Woodroffe had the respectability to present it. Western scholars before Woodroffe had labeled Tantra as disreputable, dangerous and not worthy of study. It was only when a prominent Englishman produced these serious works that Tantra entered the world stage as an ancient and profound spiritual practice.

In retrospect it seems obvious that Woodroffe would have to have had a collaborator. How could an Englishman translate Sanskrit texts and write about Tantra with such authority? Hopefully Taylor's work will shift some of our admiration for the work from Woodroffe to Ghose. There is no better example of the debt the western world in general and esotericism in particular owes to the intellectual culture of Kolkata than the works of Arthur Avalon.

A Magical Secret

Our final stop on College Street was the English language bookstore that our guide had promised us. I browsed shelves that seemed to hold books I could find anywhere in the world, mostly contemporary accounts of life in India. Frankly I was disappointed. Of course I was glad for the chance to visit a bookstore but it didn't live up to the romantic notion of finding an ancient magical secret in a forgotten tome.

I had to buy something. I chose a shrink-wrapped used copy (why shrink-wrap a used book?) of a book titled *India in Love, Marriage and Sexuality in the 21st Century*, written by Ira Trivedi and published in New Delhi by Aleph Books. The book was mildly interesting, the kind of thing I read along with a score of others when I'm researching gender and women's studies. I took it home and shelved it along with all the other books we picked up on our travels.

I didn't actually break the shrink wrap until I started to write this piece. I thought that I should at least look at the book before writing about it. At first the tome seems to be contemporary reporting I thought it would be. In her introduction Trivedi promises to look at the changes to marriage and sexual activity among the younger generations of India. So I was quite surprised when she began chapter one with a first-hand account of her trip to Kamakhya Temple. There, to my complete astonishment, I found the secret of sex magick I'd been looking for my entire magical career.

Here's her story. After her visit to the Kamakhya cave she spent some time chatting with a tea vendor. He turned out to be an eighth generation

Tantric priest in training. He commented that the temple gets visitors from the west seeking to learn about Tantra, "although unfortunately Tantra in the West is associated almost exclusively with 'Tantric sex'."

I admit that I have contributed to this. When Alex and I unleashed sexual energy in each other we lacked was a clear manual about how to structure our sexual experiences in a spiritual context. So I wrote the book I needed, *Ecstatic Ritual, Practical Sex Magic*. As a magician I'm quite proud of it. It joins a very small group of books written by women magicians on any subject, it contests the sexual exploitation of women in some writings, and it speaks to sex between all genders. As a Tantric practitioner I'm embarrassed that I knew so little about the origin of the practices when I wrote it, and ashamed that I didn't credit kundalini yoga as the source of chakra practices, although I'm glad that I didn't mislabel sex magick as Tantra as so many writers do.

Kamakhya Temple drew us to India. Alex deeply longed to visit the sacred cave of Goddess and we went to Kamakhya in the second phase of our pilgrimage, described in a later chapter in this book. After the trip I took a deep dive into literature describing the rituals there. I learned that hereditary priestly families practice Tantric sex rites privately between husband and wife. One of these practices makes sexuality a literal sacrament: semen is mixed with menstrual blood and then consumed by the magician.

This practice filtered out into western sex magick. The founders of Ordo Templi Orientis learned it and then swore initiates to secrecy when they taught the practice. Aleister Crowley built an entire magical system around this operation.

Crowley's writings firmly place the sacramental operation in the male magician's hands. Crowley explains that sperm is the active element in the operation while the menstrual blood only provides passive nourishment for the elixir. The magician's mind and intent direct the operation. Crowley admits that women can try the operation but expresses doubt that they can be successful since the power of intellect and the power of sperm belong to the male magician. I've labored under that approbation for my entire magical career.

Back at Kamakhya, Trivedi reports the rest of her conversation with the eighth-generation Tantric priest.

He explained to me that Tantric rituals were a lot more than just sex. In fact, sex was just a means to an end, a means of awakening latent energies in the body and of attaining spiritual liberation; female power or shakti was at the centre of all their worship and rites. For example, powerful female yoginis would drink a cocktail of semen and menstrual blood and use sexual rites to awaken the kundalini shakti.

There at the home of Tantra the priests and yoginis hold onto this knowledge: the active power is Shakti, Devi, Goddess, represented by the woman's body. Female yoginis have the knowledge, the intent, the power, and perform the operation for their own benefit. Women can perform sex magick on our own behalf. We can own our power. I can own my power.

I should not have doubted the guide who always steered me in the right direction. He took me to the bookstore in Kolkata where I found that the famous secret of sex magick belongs to women after all.

The British Raj

When Alex first suggested Kolkata the first thing that came to mind was "black hole of Calcutta". I'd heard the city was dirt poor and that Sister Theresa had set up a healing ministry there, and that was the extent of my knowledge. I said, "What's interesting there?" Alex said the city celebrates Durga Puja. I had just begun my journey with this amazing goddess so I agreed to go.

When I started to read about the city's history I learned that the "black hole" was actually a dungeon where British soldiers were imprisoned by the Islamic Mughal ruler in 1756 in a brief battle for control of the city (the British won). I also learned that Sister Theresa denied treatments to her patients on the grounds that suffering makes you closer to God. She channeled the massive donations she received not to her patients but to the Vatican which in return obligingly declared her a saint. The Ramakrishna Mission actually does heal and feed people and provides job training but they don't receive the big bucks from western donors.

The European powers treated India as a source of resources to be mined. They justified their actions on the grounds that theirs was the superior civilization - they would trade their benevolent rulership and modern education in exchange for the food and labor they took. Even today we flinch from the full realization that they were actually brutal invaders whose policies starved and enslaved millions. Calcutta may have been the capital of the colonial administration but Kolkata was the heart of the revolution that finally won India's self-rule.

Touring College Street grounded my book learning about the British Raj in the sights and sounds of Kolkata today. I resented the imposition of colonial rule on behalf of the people of India. I was surprised to discover the ways in which Kolkatans engaged with European languages and cultures and ideas and made them their own. They took the Anglicization of everyday culture and volleyed back with the Indianization of spiritual culture.

As the journey unfolded I began to realize that this exchange went both ways. Esoteric ideas which we think of as our own were actually born in Kolkata and deliberately sent out to the west. Kolkata responded to the anglicization of India with the Indianization of western spirituality. It also became clear that the city takes in the visitors who approach sincerely and folds them in as her own.

Kalighat at Durga Puja

We had timed our visit to Kolkata to experience the festival of Durga Puja. This is the largest Goddess festival in the world. It's a mark of how disconnected we are from the Indian roots of our esoteric heritage that very few western Goddess worshippers, Witches, Pagans and magicians even know that it exists. I made notes during the trip with the distinct feeling that this was more like fieldwork than tourism. I followed up with research once I got home to understand and contextualize what I'd experienced. I wrote up the result as *Durga Puja in Kolkata* published separately and included in this volume in a later chapter. Here I'll include a few notes about how that experience fit in with the overall trip.

On our first day in Kolkata we toured the museum, the second day we toured College Street, all normal tourist activities. On our third day in

Kolkata the sightseeing trip finally turned into a pilgrimage. We stepped into the stream and joined the festival crowds ourselves on a visit to our first Shakti pith. The story goes that Shiva mourned his first wife Sati so fiercely that he neglected his other duties, so Vishnu cut up her body and distributed the pieces across India in the sites that became the Shakti piths. Each temple maps onto a body part, at Kalighat it is her right big toe.

For me there was a distinct click as we entered the temple grounds, a place where the energy started. I felt the emotional impact of the Mother slam my heart. My eyes filled with tears. I thought, *this is what we came for.* The experience definitively answered the question *why travel if you can see a photo or a film?* The answer is because only through physical presence can you feel the power of the land herself.

This was our first temple experience and I was grateful to have a guide to help us through it. Reading about it had left me with a lot of questions that could only be answered by actually doing it. Temples in India require visitors to take off their shoes which means that you need a place to put them. Every temple is surrounded by vendors and shopkeepers who will all watch your shoes for you whether you buy something from them or not. Also, the major temples tend to be crowded, especially during festivals like Durga Puja.

Alex had looked forward to this as a highlight of his trip. He is deeply drawn to Kali. However Kalighat at Durga Puja turned out to be a disappointing experience for him, the crowds were fierce and the priests jostled him in his microsecond at the heart of the shrine. My heart ached for him.

Our guide made the most of our visit. He gave us a tour of the grounds including a shrine to Krishna. He also supervised a shopping trip around the vendors where we discovered a need for local money. Hotels and tourist stores take cards but temple vendors only take cash. This was something we had not adequately prepared for. The guidebooks had all said confidently that money could be withdrawn from ATMs. They failed to warn us that cash transactions are common and you're going to need quite a lot of it. The hotels will change paper currency but hate to make credit card advances. Every morning that we stayed in Kolkata I braved the streets to make the rounds of the local ATMs before they tapped out. It took me the entire fortnight we were there to collect the cash tip for our driver and guide.

Our guide arranged a stop at an ATM on the street next to a chai shop. He had another goal in mind as well, he took Alex to a neighborhood temple dedicated to Kali. This little local shrine lacked the crowds and the priest was helpful and supportive. Alex could take as much time as he needed to connect with the goddess who is the mother of his heart. It soothed my heart to see him so happy.

East Meets West

Each day as our driver expertly piloted the van along the trunk road through the snarled cacophony we passed signs posted proudly in the meridian: HOME OF RAMAKRISHNA. HOME OF SARADA MA. HOME OF VIVEKANANDA. HOME OF NIVEDITA. On College Street we'd confronted the influence of the British empire on Kolkata. I was prepared for this since the western narrative of Indian history focuses on the colonization of a less powerful people by a more powerful military force. On the ground I learned that this is only one side the story. What we miss in the west in general, and Paganism and esotericism in particular, is the ongoing influence of Kolkata on the world and the conquering power of a spiritual tradition.

Ramakrishna, Sarada Ma, Vivekananda, Nivedita. Of these four Vivekananda was the only familiar name. In 1993 I attended the Parliament of the World's Religions. The gathering brought 8000 people together to teach, learn, sing, and celebrate the spectrum of human religious belief. Representatives from many faith groups signed the document "Towards a Global Ethic – An Initial Declaration" calling for an end to religious war. Deborah Ann Light signed as a representative of three Pagan groups in attendance, Covenant of the Goddess, EarthSpirit and Reclaiming.

I attended the Parliament as emeritus president of Covenant of the Goddess (C.O.G.). I presented "Wiccan Devotionals" which described the path of devotion in the Witchcraft tradition as I understood it at the time. Because the summit commemorated the centennial of the 1893 Parliament I prepared for the event by digging up a book on the proceedings of the 1893 congress. This was my introduction to Vivekananda's work.

Pagan and esoteric historians point to the Theosophical Society as the bridge between India and the English-speaking world. However it was not their aim to present Hindu or Tantric practice, instead they used what they understood of that practice to create Theosophy. Vivekananda traveled at great personal cost to represent Vedanta as a native practitioner. If you practice yoga, if you've heard of karma, if you think of Hinduism and Buddhism as legitimate world religions, you've been influenced by Vivekananda's message.

I didn't understand the basis for that message until I visited Kolkata. Our guide made sure that we learned about Vivekananda's teacher Ramakrishna. He also made sure that we knew how much both Ramakrishna and Vivekananda owed to the women who supported their work.

Dakshineswar

Our guide planned an entire day to immerse us in Ramakrishna's milieu. We spent the morning at Dakshineswar. Alex was excited. He had been drawn to Kolkata when he saw an online image of the statue in the Kali temple there. He had experienced darshan from the image on the screen and longed to experience it in person.

Actually darshan requires a bit of an explanation. It may seem strange to westerners who are used to viewing deity statues in museums as artifacts of a dead religion -we admire them as art, nothing more. In contrast Hindu religion is very much alive. Hindu and Tantric devotees experience a connection with deity by interacting with statues which embody the living power of divinity. Darshan is a blessing, a connection with the divine, in which you see the deity and the deity sees you. Alex had sought Kali's darshan at Kalighat and the neighborhood temple, but this was the day he would seek darshan from the avatar of Kali who had called him.

We spent a morning at Dakshineswar. We had to leave our bags and phones in the car, so all my pictures were snatched from the car window before we parked. Our guide picked the first garland vendor he saw and purchased long strings of orange carnations while Alex and I stowed our shoes.

Our guide led us through the orchards and gardens on the grounds to a tree caged behind a padlocked gate. He said there were five skulls buried beneath the tree. Elizabeth Harding's book *Kali: the Black Goddess of Dakshineswar* lists the skulls: snake, rabbit, frog, fox, and human. Tantric practitioners meditate while sitting on five-skull sites. The Pancha Munda Sadhana is a secret practice passed from guru to student, generally respected in West Bengal but frowned on in other parts of India. Our guide noted that the site was previously open to anyone who wanted to meditate there. Locking it away was a new and unwelcome change.

Before we entered the temple proper we paid our respects to Rani Rashmoni. The white pillars of her shrine frame a statue looking serenely out on a landscape of greenery and bright flowers. Our guide made sure we understood that this woman had funded the entire complex. Without Rani Rashmoni there would be no Kali temple, Ramakrishna would not have had a home, and Vivekananda would not have been able to launch the mission to the west. Rani Rashmoni's shrine sits on the grounds outside the temple proper as both her caste and her gender dictate. Our guide commented that this did not give her the honor she truly deserved. Alex offered the consoling observation that the location makes her shrine accessible to everyone.

Dakshineswar Kali

Entering the temple requires passing through a security gate. The lines separated women from men to be scanned and searched, although on that day we were all simply waved through. Once through a security guard sorted people out into various lines and put our guide and Alex in a different line than me. It was the first time I had been separated from Alex, but I felt comfortable surrounded by women and they paid me no special attention. After a bit our guide came to fetch me, saying husband and wife should not be separated.

At the Kali temple there was no premium entry and the lines were long at festival time. Alex and I merged seamlessly into the flow of devotees. I had the chance to admire the variety of colorful patterns on the women's Durga Puja saris. All three of us had time to settle our hearts, to chant, to prepare ourselves for the encounter.

It took Rani Rashmoni eight years to build the main temple, done in Bengal Architecture style with nine elaborate spires. The temple sits on a platform surrounded by flights of stairs which give separate views to the inner sanctum. A thousand-petalled lotus flower made of silver supports the statue which houses the living presence of the divine. The goddess here is Sri Sri Jagadiswari Kalimata Thakurani, an avatar of Dakshinakali, stepping on Shiva with her right foot as he lies on the ground. He is white, inert, she is black and lively, the red tongue of her power leaping out from her mouth, blessings pouring out from her hands and her wild eyes.

Our line viewed the inner temple from the side. We went up to the railing all in a rush, gave our garlands to the priest, received a packet of red flowers in return, had a glimpse of the black face of the goddess, and rushed down the stairs again.

Here the power was not in the land or immemorial custom as in the Shakti piths. I connected instead to the quiet perseverance of devotion: the people waiting patiently in the lines, the village girl turned wealthy widow who made the gift of a temple despite rejection, the desire to touch the divine that brings us all to the feet of the mother wherever we can find her.

Living Quarters for Saints

While we were still inside the temple proper our guide took us to the room where Ramakrishna had spent his life. People crowded around his simple bed and peered at the photographs on the wall which show him surrounded by his devotees. The visitors seemed in awe, happy to be so near to the presence of the holy man, standing where he had stood.

In the days before railways Dakshineswar provided a place to stay for travelers and pilgrims who would meditate in the gardens and forests. Ramakrishna spent time with these travelers. He took an initiations from a Brahman Vaisnavite Tantrika, another initiation from a Vedantic monk, meditated with a Sufi mystic, listened to a devoted Christian read the

Bible and had a vision of Jesus. Through these encounters Ramakrishna came to believe that all faiths, Hinduism, Islam, Christianity, Buddhism, lead to the same realization. All faiths are one faith. It is this teaching which is his greatest impact on the world.

While we were still in Ramakrishna's room our guide pointed out two women in one of the pictures, Gauri Ma and Gopal Ma. He said firmly that women were critically important to the Ramakrishna mission. When Ramakrishna died he had only initiated two people, his wife Sarada Ma and Gauri Ma, so all the initiations in Ramakrishna's lineage trace back through these two women.

When we left Ramakrishna's room our guide steered us to the neighboring tower called Nahabat or music tower and showed us a tiny room on the ground floor. This, he said, was where Sarada Ma had lived. He explained that Ramakrishna had married her in his home village before taking the sannyas vows and living a life of renunciation. She followed him to Dakshineswar. She made a place for himself in his life by cooking for him and for his disciples until his death. After his death she was the living connection to his lineage.

We'd already seen the home where she'd spent her final days. The day we toured College Street our guide swung by a modest two-story home tucked away in a residential neighborhood. It's run by the Ramakrishna Mission as memorial and a place for poor people to receive lunch. Our guide led us into the cool interior of the house, up a steep set of stairs lined with people waiting to be fed, and into Sarada Ma's bedroom, where devotees meditated before her photograph. Two things impressed me immediately: she inspires devotion, and feeding people is her legacy.

Kali and Shiva

Our guide frequently made the point that every Kali temple requires a Shiva shrine. The red-hot dance of the goddess requires Shiva's cooling influence so as not to destroy the universe. Even though the Dakshineswar Kali statue in the main temple stands on a motionless Shiva, the temple complex also includes a set of Shiva lingam shrines. After we visited Sarada Ma's tiny room our guide asked if we would like to see them. Alex said yes; later he confessed to me that he could tell we could catch a view of the river from there.

Twelve identical Bengal Architecture domes sit on a raised platform. We dutifully trudged along the row, standing outside the open doors to admire the massive stone lingams set in their stone yonis. Here there were no priests or offerings. Everyone on the platform seemed to just be doing what we were, walking along the row. I silently chanted a Shiva mantra and made a little respectful bow to each.

When we reached the end of the row we all leaned on the railing on the river side of the platform. As Alex had suspected we had an admirable view of the river. Far below us a line of people waited to step onto a boat carrying pilgrims across the river. This was the boat to Belur Math, our next destination. Our guide had thought that we would take the boat, but when he saw the length of the line and surveyed his flagging charges he announced that we would go by car.

On our way out of the temple we did some sacred shopping. After Kalighat I'd learned to keep cash in a small cloth purse that made it past the security lines. Our guide helped Alex procure a framed photo of the Kali and Shiva statues in the temple; when Alex got home he installed it as the main image on his home altar. Alex and our guide also spent some time selecting a conch. Our guide blew on them until he found one that sounded to his satisfaction. Then he handed it to Alex who surprised him by producing a sound the first time. Alex is a flute player and has never met an instrument he couldn't make sing.

Belur Math

After a lunch break at a western style restaurant on the highway our driver piloted us into Belur Math, headquarters of the Ramakrishna Mission. We walked onto the grounds past a wall painted with the sign EAST MEETS WEST. This is a nod to Vivekananda's mission to bring the spirituality of India to the rest of the world.

Our guide steered us toward the temple which was still closed for the lunch break. It was difficult to take in at first. I've toured the cathedrals of Europe, the mosques of Cairo, synagogues and Buddhist temples in Seattle, and of course the Hindu temples in Kolkata. Each has a cohesion. I couldn't fit this building into any pattern precisely because it was deliberately constructed to echo all of them. Our guide parsed the architecture for us: the main hall was built like a Christian church but topped with a mosque-like dome. Columns supported the roof as in Buddhist temples. The garbagriha or inner sanctum was built in the Hindu style. However this temple does not house a deity. Instead it hosts a marble statue of Ramakrishna, a man, pointing the path to embodying the divine.

We spent the afternoon wandering around the spacious grounds. Crowds of people sat quietly on the grass under the trees waiting for the temple to open. When it did our guide confidently sent us off to view the statue. When we returned immediately he looked up from his phone and said "What is the problem?" We pointed to the hours-long line wrapping the building. I suggested that we could look in at the statue through a side window. Even this brief glimpse required waiting in a line for our turn! That bought our guide the time he needed to spend on something other than us.

Dakshineswar and Belur Math are dedicated to Ramakrishna, the man who realized his own divine nature and demonstrated that this realization could be achieved through any religion. Just as Dakshineswar wouldn't exist without Rani Rashmoni, Belur Math would not exist without Vivekananda. After his teacher's death he was inspired by a vision to take the teachings of Vedanta to the western world. He called this the "Mission to the West". He sought approval from Sarada Ma and received her blessing for the mission. Vivekananda managed to travel to the Parliament of the World's Religions in 1893, a great story in itself, where his articulate and spirited speeches won respect for the religions of India. On his return he bought the land for Belur Math as a home for Ramakrishna's order and to house Ramakrishna's ashes.

The Ramakrishna Mission at Belur Math was also the longtime home of Sister Nivedita. Margaret Elizabeth Noble met Vivekananda on one of his Mission to the West tours of England. She followed him to Kolkata where she became a dedicated nurse, teacher, and advocate for the people of West Bengal. Later she became a key supporter of Sri Aurobindo.

There is one more presence who is important to the story of the Mission to the West. Yogananda grew up in Kolkata and spent his youth wandering in the gardens of Dakshineswar and Belur Math. He connected with one of Ramakrishna's disciples there. He went to Varanasi and found a guru, then returned to Kolkata to create his first ashram near Dakshineswar. Yogananda's teachings rooted in Kolkata, blossomed in America, and followed through on the promise to bring India's spiritual wisdom to the materialist west.

Kolkata proudly proclaims itself as the home of Vivekananda, Ramakrishna, Sarada Ma, Nivedita. A few of my friends in the Witch, Pagan and magical communities are aware of Vivekananda. No one, not even the ones who also study Tantra, have heard of Ramakrishna or Sarada Ma or Nivedita. We're not aware of the spiritual family or cultural context that surrounded Vivekananda. We don't know the ways in which colonial exploitation impacted his country and the ways in which the Indian people triumphantly survived and prospered. It took a visit to Kolkata itself for me to finally learn about them.

Home of Saints and Revolutionaries

Every day involved a lot of driving with a lunch stop at various western-style restaurants. This gave us a quite a bit of time with our guide. One day at lunch he said, "I am reading your book. I have completed the section on Egypt."

I thought, if I can explain to him what has happened to the word magic, that it has come to be synonymous with baneful action in common language but also means a spiritual path, I might make an incremental rapprochement between his community of practice and mine. So I said, "What do you know about Plato?"

"He was a great politician," he said cautiously.

"And philosopher," I said.

"Yes yes," he said. "We studied Plato, Machiavelli, and Hume."

Alex and I contemplated this in silence for a moment. "Plato to Machiavelli with no stops?" I said faintly.

Alex commented helpfully, "Plato is like Gandhi, Machiavelli is like Nehru."

"Later in my book," I said, "you will read about the Golden Chain of philosophers. They had their own spiritual practices. They meditated on the gods. When the Christians banned those practices their philosophy was separated from the practice and the gods became demons." He winced. "Then in the nineteenth century Western academics used the word religion to mean Christian faith and science to mean factual truth. Magic was pseudo-religion and pseudo-science, and what you do and what I do was called magic."

"Hypatia was a great mathematician," he ventured.

It was my turn to be surprised. "You know Hypatia?"

"Of course. Mathematics is the highest Tantra. Yantra," he explained.

"Hypatia is a link in the Golden Chain," I told him.

"You see?" he said cheerfully. "It is the same."

Every night we returned to the Oberoi Grand. It was a study in colonial-style opulence with a balcony overlooking the gardens, an ornate wooden writing desk I wanted to take home with me, daily laundry and turn down service. The dining room boasted no fewer than a dozen servers at any given time. I've never been waited on in such grand fashion and I was distinctly uncomfortable with the experience.

Sri Aurobindo

On our last night in Kolkata our guide took us to the Sri Aurobindo Institute established in the house where he was born. The gardens house a shrine which contains some of his relics. It's a peaceful place and I spent a few moments in contemplation there.

I didn't know anything about Sri Aurobindo before this visit. In my post-trip research I learned that he combined Kolkata's revolutionary fervor with spiritual accomplishment. Educated in England, he returned to Kolkata to an outwardly successful career as an administrator and teacher, while secretly joining a revolutionary cell. Vivekananda's student Sister Nivedita joined this cell. This was one of the sparks for her separation from the Ramakrishna Mission as she became more involved with the revolution. Sri Aurobindo was caught and imprisoned by the British authorities, and when he was released he turned over his organization to Sister Nivedita and fled British-run India. He settled in French-run

Pondicherry. There he founded an ashram where he taught his own interpretation of spiritual yoga.

On our visit to the Sri Aurobindo Institute Alex and I were thrilled to discover that the bookstore was still open after dark. It was well stocked with books in English. We accumulated many pounds worth of texts, including pocket biographies of the saints of Kolkata which fueled our later research.

In the bookstore our guide presented us with a gift, a copy of Sri Aurobindo's book Savitri. He recommended this to us as an important read. It turned out to be a retelling of the folk story of a woman who bargained with Death to save her young husband's life. In Sri Aurobindo's hands the story becomes an allegory of the soul's theurgic journey. It's the kind of book that takes a lifetime of study. It has comforted and guided me in many ways since it settled in my hands.

In the Countryside

After a week in Kolkata our itinerary took us out into the countryside. The idea was to see the villages where artists and musicians live and get in touch with the roots of the artistic flowering in Kolkata.

An hour out of town on the highway we reached Konnagar. In our trip planning I'd found a temple on Google Maps and insisted on visiting. It's dedicated to Sri Raj Rajeshwari, a form of Lalita Tripurasundari, and as a student of Shri Vidya I was drawn to the temple. As soon as I stepped on the grounds I found myself bathed in light. I discovered to my great delight that the temple had a collection of 64 yoginis. I took the time to gaze at every one wishing I could photograph them. The stop didn't feature on our tour of Kali sites or the Durga Puja tour or our guide's own plans, but it was the happiest moment I personally spent in a temple in Kolkata. The moral here is to listen to your heart. Also West Bengal is filled with many wonders.

Nadia District

There were two Kali temples on our itinerary, both located in Birbhum District. That's a long drive from Kolkata so we stopped for the night in the Nadia District in a heritage hotel outside the village of Krishnanagar.

Driving through Krishnanagar we ran directly into the local celebration of Durga Puja. The countryside around Kolkata supplies drummers, musicians, porters, and other artisans and workers to the city who provide much of the labor for the festival. The villages delay their own rituals for a few days to allow those workers time to return home join the celebrations.

There's only one road through Krishnanagar. The day we drove through was the day that the villagers were processing their Durga statues to the Jalangi River nearby. Our car was swept up in the parade. Trucks carrying the statues blared music into the street, followed by groups of boisterous young men jostling each other, then young women dancing in their Durga Puja finery, then the more sedate older women and men. A ride that would normally be twenty minutes turned into two hours. The car was completely surrounded by people for the entire time. The energy was celebratory but non-inviting, clearly for locals only. When we'd passed through our guide exhaled and remarked to our driver that he was glad the townspeople had been peaceful and friendly to us. I'm not sure he noticed the glares some of the men gave to the foreigners in the back of the luxury car.

Heritage Plantation

Eventually we turned down a long driveway and pulled up at a magnificent colonial-era estate. The Balakhana Heritage Manor boasts a wrap-around stone veranda with majestic columns. Our hostess showed us to an air-conditioned room and let us settle in before inviting us out for tea. We joined our host and our guide ensconced in wicker chairs looking out on the gardens.

Our host gave us the history of the place. It had been an indigo plantation owned by his zamindar (wealthy merchant) family. They'd lost it during the transition from colonial to home rule but it had been returned to them fairly recently. Of course the indigo trade had died with the invention of modern aniline dyes. To support themselves and the estate the family turned to tourism and opened their home to visitors. The extensive grounds surrounding the mansion featured tamarind trees and many lovely flowers but no tracts of indigo. So many guests had been disappointed that our host imported one indigo plant and placed it on the main walkway. We dutifully admired it, but I secretly thought it was small and drab for a plant with such a famous history.

I hadn't known much about the indigo trade before visiting West Bengal. I'd thought of it as romantic. My pre-trip research revealed the brutal reality of colonial conquest. British plantation owners drove native workers to hard work in the indigo vats, then traded the dyed cloth for enslaved people from Africa, who were then shipped to the plantations of America and the Caribbean to grow cotton, sugar and rice. This three-cornered trade drained wealth from three continents to fund the lavish English lifestyle.

Indigo wasn't the only resource the British drew from West Bengal. They controlled the production of food, rice in particular, and shipped it out of country. This is one of the causes of the famine which killed 30 million people in 1770. It was shocking to me that I didn't know that before. Thirty million people! Another four million people in West Bengal starved to death in 1943 when Britain was putting all its resources into the war effort. Even today there are apologists excusing Churchill's inhumane wartime policies.

While we were talking an older woman in drab clothing came by to sweep the veranda. Neither our host nor our guide acknowledged her. I recognized her as a servant and was a little taken aback at the casual classism. June McDaniel explains that in Bengal the traditional four Hindu castes are reduced to two, Brahmin and Shudra, priest-class and servant. Despite the many sub-castes it's in the main a flattened class system. The relationship was apparent on the stone veranda with the owner of the mansion taking tea and the servant sweeping around him.

A pair of dogs joined us and planted themselves on the cool stone alertly scanning the gardens. The streets of Kolkata and the surrounding villages are home to scores of Indian Pariah dogs which live on the streets. This pair also lived out of doors but were cared for by the family in return for chasing wildlife away from the house. I looked out into the gardens listening to the chatter of birds and other sounds I couldn't identify. The forests of West Bengal are home to dozens of varieties of birds, plus snakes, crocodiles, turtles, rhinos, elephants, jackals, pandas, monkeys, and a surprising diversity of wildcats, including the famous Bengal tigers. It was one of those travel moments that's thrilling to remember but a bit alarming at the time. I was happy to have a pair of dogs patrolling the veranda for us.

Balakhana Heritage Manor is in the class of lodging designated as a homestay where guests stay in a room in the family's home and eat with the family. At dinner we all sat together around the massive wood table. Our host urged us to try the teas of India, our hostess talked about making mulberry jam. After dinner they showed off a curio cabinet of family treasures which included a block of indigo dye.

We slept peacefully in our air conditioned room. We'd chosen to visit in the early fall to avoid the summer heat, but the daily temperature in the 90s was significantly hotter than the cool Northwest weather we are used to. Air conditioning was a lifesaver for us.

At breakfast our host asked where we were headed next. Our guide said we were touring two lesser known Shakti piths, both Kali temples, Attahas and Kankalitala. Our host asked if he guides large groups out there. "No!" our guide exclaimed. "Next thing you know people will show up in black robes muttering rituals. They mean to cause harm."

"Do they really exist?" our host said. Our guide assured him that they did.

Later in Assam at Kamakhya Temple I had a chance to see black robed practitioners first hand. One day I was watching the crowd flowing up the lane to the main temple entrance, women in bright saris and men in jeans. Then a group of men in black robes slunk by carrying trishuls they'd hammered out themselves, moving soundlessly through the crowd like sharks swimming among the minnows.

Another time I was waiting for a temple to open when a black robe walked by. His eye was attracted to me – I was the only white woman at the temple the week I spent there – and I caught him giving me the once-over. There's a type of practitioner attracted to women; as the phrase goes, "He wants your Shakti". I wasn't an easy target though. I was chanting the Devi Kavacam every night. There's a passage in that text where eight protective goddesses rattle their battle weapons. When his eyes hit me I felt the devis wake up in my energy field, shake their weapons and hiss. He dropped his eyes and kept going.

I can't help but think that these are the kinds of Tantrikas who might actually practice black magic. Not every Tantric practices in that way, but some do.

Attahas Temple

After breakfast we loaded back into the car. We endured a couple of hours of really bad washboard roads to reach our pilgrimage site of the day, Attahas Temple. As we drove up to the temple our guide howled in protest at the Disneyesque statues of Shiva and family which newly adorn the front drive. He objected that the energy of the place was dissipating – you need serious practitioners to sustain the energy of a major temple.

Attahas is a Shakti pith, a place where a part of the body of Sati fell. Attahas has the lower lip. The temple houses a small black statue of Goddess, variously named Kali, Durga, Parvati or Phullara. Our guide procured an offering basket for us from the local vendors. We lined up for our turn to duck down under the archway for a quick darshan with the Goddess and to get a forehead dab of kumkum from the priest there. When he touched me I felt the energy of the place and wanted to cry with the fierce emotion.

Afterwards our guide showed us around the grounds. The local forests are famous for the variety of birds and butterflies that show up there in the wintertime. Our guide showed us to a five skull site. Unlike the one at Kalighat, this one is out in the open and clearly in use, both from the ribbons hanging from the trees and from the energy of the place.

Birbhum District

We spent three days in the Birbhum District. This is the area where June McDaniel talked to her informants to write her study of West Bengal Goddess religion *Offering Flowers, Feeding Skulls*. It was fascinating to re-read the book after I'd traveled through the region myself. Knowing a bit about the towns and the customs, talking with local people, experiencing the temples, provides a context that reading just doesn't cover.

Shantiniketan

From Attahas we had another hour on bad roads to reach our next destination, the Garden Bungalow in Shantiniketan. Even though it's located in a well-appointed suburb there was security on the grounds and the staff opened a substantial locked gate to let our car pass through.

Where the Oberoi Grand is a hotel and the Balakhana Heritage Manor is a homestay, the Garden Bungalow lands between. It's billed as a homestay but reads more like a hotel with a separate dining room where meals are served to the guests.

On arrival we were ushered into another zamindari-style building with a columned porch and a great hall. The rooms are named romantically – the King's Chambers, the Poet's Recluse, the Painter's Retreat. We ended up in the Painter's Retreat which had antique furniture, an en-suite bathroom, air conditioning and wi-fi, combining modern conveniences with a countryside atmosphere. Red dirt paths wandered invitingly around three acres of manicured gardens.

In the afternoon our guide took us on a walk around nearby Shantiniketan, the house of peace (Shanti, peace and niketan, house). This university started life as an ashram founded by Rabindranath Tagore's father Debendranath Tagore. Rabindranath turned the facility into a school with an emphasis on the arts.

Rabindranath Tagore is one of West Bengal's most famous and accomplished citizens. He's known as a poet, the first non-European to win the Nobel Prize for literature, and he wrote the national anthems for both India and Bangladesh. He's less well known as an artist but made drawings all his life. They've been collected in a massive four volume set, Rabindra Chitravali, published by Pratiksha Press. The day we toured College Street our guide had stopped by the press so we could leaf through the books. When we returned home we ordered the set. The images are dream-like renderings of people, animals, trees and landscapes.

The school at Shantiniketan emphasizes the importance of nature. On the day we visited the school was closed which allowed us to wander the grounds without disturbing students. Our guide pointed out an open-air classroom, a circle of stone chairs surrounding a tree; teachers here are actually assigned a tree to teach their classes, establishing a relationship that is more guru-student than institutional.

Our guide led us on a tour of the major pieces on campus. Some are statues, some are paintings on the walls, some are actually the buildings themselves. The Kalo Bari, Black House, was made of coal and mud tar. It was designed by Nandalal Bose, Surendranath Kar and Ramkinker Baij and features Harappan and Egyptian reliefs. Another building features Bose's Asian-influenced murals retelling the birth of the local poet-saint Chaitanya and other stories.

We marveled at Ramkinker Baij's major sculptures of Gandhi and Buddha. However two of Baij's massive sculptures particularly interested our guide. Instead of great world leaders or poets or saints they depict ordinary people. Mill Call depicts two women running to work at the textile factory. The second sculpture, Santhal Family, is considered to be Baij's most significant work, showing a tribal couple walking with their children and dog and carrying all their possessions, migrating as many tribal people have done to work in the tea or coal fields.

The tribal peoples are outside the caste system and have historically been exploited. In the last few decades they've fought for and won the right to occupy and utilize their ancestral forest lands. As we drove through Birbhum District our guide pointed out a group of tribal women gathering brush in the forest. These women have a deep connection with the land in general and trees in particular and hold some of the most ancient Goddess traditions.

At least it seems they do, although we don't have that information from the women directly. In *Offering Flowers, Feeding Skulls*, June McDaniel reports the tree goddess practices of village women. I took the time to look up her sources and realized that she didn't make contact with village women herself. She cites the work of mid-twentieth-century Bengali scholars. They in turn drew on administrative notes from mid-nineteenth-century British colonial bureaucrats who sent Bengali clerks out to the villages to transact business and collect information about folk customs. The Bengali clerks would ask the men in charge of the village about the practices and dutifully take the report back. So McDaniel's information is a century and a half old and filtered through several layers of male interpretation.

Tribal women in West Bengal work today with the government and NGOs to improve irrigation and agricultural practices, gain access to health care, and educate their children. However their voices continue to be mediated through governmental agencies and academic reports. As technology brings the world closer we can hope that they will gain control of their story as well.

Kankalitala

There was one more stop on our tour of Shakti piths in the Birbhum District. We woke early in the morning for our trip to Kankalitala. Our guide expected the trip to take an hour but it turned out to be a quick 20 minute drive on a newly paved road. Our guide found to his dismay that the area around the shrine and the bathing pond had also been paved. There were sadhus meditating at the pond. Our guide noted that they don't visit the shrine itself, they just come to meditate, and their meditation adds to the energy of the place.

As we waited in line for our moment in the shrine we saw a goat dragged toward a sacrifice yoke. We'd seen the yokes at all the temples but this was the first time we saw the animals. Our guide explained that a mantra is whispered in the kid's ear and the goat is told if he gives up his goat's life willingly he will be reborn as a human next life. The sacrifice has to be willing and it has to be male. Then the sacrificed goats are made into stew. The objections of the goat tugged at my heart, but I've eaten meat my whole life and have no grounds to object to a goat stew that starts out as a temple sacrifice.

As I gazed into the shrine while the priest dabbed my forehead with kumkum I felt again the pulse of energy. Once through the line I felt a pull off toward the side. Our guide tried to lead me to the crematorium for a lecture-tour but I veered off toward a small shrine with a painting of Kali and an urn decorated with flowers. Our guide smiled and said

"This is the real place." I asked if I could practice, and he said go inside. So I sat there and chanted to Chandi.

All through the trip I had hoped to find a place to chant. It'd thought it would be an overwhelmingly emotional experience. Interestingly it didn't turn out to be. It just felt normal. I chant wherever I am; that day I chanted at a Shakti pith, and I did feel her with me, but she's always with me. The energy flow actually went the other way, I was glad I had a chance to add a bit of energy to the place.

On our way back to the car we encountered a kumari puja. Kumari is a form of the goddess as a young girl, and at Durga Puja young girls are worshipped as the kumari. A group of priests sat below a tree whose roots sheltered a stone sculpture of a tiger's head. The priests were surrounded by a sea of young women in bright red and gold saris and jewelry. Mothers fussed with their shawls while their relatives all held up cell phones to take their pictures. This had happened in the city days before, now the villagers were getting a chance to do the festival ritual. It seemed like a sweet family moment.

Kenduli Village and the Jayadeva Temple

Our guide didn't announce this stop, it was a nice surprise to complete our countryside tour. The village of Kenduli is a 45 minute drive from Shantiniketan. On the day we visited the village had its market day in the square and our driver navigated gingerly through the stalls.

Our destination was an unassuming little shrine on the banks of the Ajay river. Curious children gathered around our guide while we slipped away to look at the cluster of small white buildings. Our guide told us this was the place where the poet Jayadeva lived while composing the masterpiece Gita Govinda which tells the story of Krishna's love for the milkmaid Radha.

Our guide told us the story of the place. As Jayadeva neared completion of the poem he hesitated to write the description of how Krishna had worshipped Radha. How could it be seemly for a god to worship his worshipper? Jayadeva's wife Padmavati advised him to take a bath in the river to clear his mind. A few minutes later he ran in dripping wet, grabbed the pen, finished the manuscript, and ran off. Then Padmavati saw Jayadeva slowly returning from the river. Confused, she told him she had just seen him finish the poem. Jayadeva picked up the manuscript and read "Krishna bows his head to the lotus feet of Sri Radha." Jayadeva realized Krishna himself had returned to complete the poem. He also realized that the god had honored not him, the poet, but his faithful wife. It's such a Bengali story.

One of the buildings drew us in with paintings of Jayadeva and Padmavati flanking the doorway. We peered through the gate at a small statue of Padmavati smeared with kumkum. Afterwards we walked down to the river and breathed in the peacefulness of the place. I tried to imagine Jayadeva walking back to his house.

On our way back to the car our guide pointed out a small building where local villagers met to conduct their own worship. The tiny sect had been started by a local man, Hariprad. He had bathed in the river and was chastised by Brahmin priests for putting on priestly airs. In response he became anti-Brahminical and founded his own line of worship. On his death his wife Sati Ma continued his lineage. This too is a such a Bengali story.

A Night with the Baul

Birbhum District is a countryside filled with poets. This is the homeland of the famous Baul singers, villagers who inherit a song tradition which incorporates Hindu, Tantric, and Islamic imagery to describe a spiritual journey, a combination of art and devotion.

That night our guide brought three Baul men to the hotel to perform for us. The staff brought out chairs for Alex and me while the musicians set up on the cool stone porch of one of the buildings on the grounds. Our guide let us know that Nitai Das Baul was a master singer and the two younger men who accompanied him were his disciple Sasthi Das Baul and his son Manas Das Baul.

All the Baul take the same last name. They are musicians from families of musicians who live in the West Bengal countryside, particularly in the villages of Birbhum Province. Their songs are famous throughout the world for their beauty and their deep emotional impact. Both women and men sing, some performing for commuters who pay in rice and coins, some travelling around the world to sing in concert halls and museums. The songs combine Vaisnavite and Shaivite imagery with Islamic ideas and Tantric understandings, a mixture of all the spiritual influences that have affected India in general and West Bengal in particular.

As the musicians settled in I asked our guide how to listen to them. He said "If you clap like this," patting his hands gently, "and say 'Wonderful music!' then you do not know. If you behave as the music moves you then we will know you hear."

I had a tough moment processing this. I care so much about being respectful and being appropriate. Projecting the right image. Fitting in. When I don't know the rules how is this possible? I was truly frantic for a moment. I prayed to Chandi: help me understand. She replied, the challenge is to be authentic.

When the music started I hummed the tonic and tapped the beat against my thigh. To enter into music I have to make music. When the son tuned his stringed dotara I scooted down next to our guide on the floor to get a closer look. Our guide flashed me a smile and softly translated lyrics for me, about crossing a river, a bird in a cage, the path of spirit embodied.

Alex sat motionless for an hour holding up his cell phone to film the songs. The hotel staff crept up to the veranda in the darkness to listen to the music. The moon shone through the palm trees. Flowers gently perfumed the still night air. When the master ran the notes up into the sky I felt them buzzing in my chest and closed my eyes. When I opened them our guide was smiling at me.

We are authentic when we feel it in the heart.

Modern Kolkata

It's a half day drive from Shantiniketan to Kolkata, moving from dirt roads to paved ones to the trunk line into the city. It's a journey from peace to chaos as well. We rejoined the traffic in town with all the noisy horns going off constantly. This time we passed through old Kolkata and headed back out to the newer parts of the city with high rise apartments and office complexes. It looked like any city I'd visited for my corporate jobs. I did a quick search and found that the company I'd retired from had an office in the area.

Our guide checked us into a modern hotel close to the airport. This turned out to be attached to a mall. A security guard let me out into a chaotic scene where little kids drove bumper cars around the shoppers in a perfect reproduction of the traffic outside. I was able to get cash from an ATM. We had luxurious showers and room service, decompressing from days of travel, re-acclimating to western conveniences.

The next day our driver picked us up to take us to the airport. He gravely invited us to come back to Kolkata. His skill as much as our guide's knowledge made everything we did possible.

We did see our guide again. When I said goodbye to him in the hotel he said "I will see you in Guwahati". I hadn't told him where we were staying and we didn't make any arrangements to meet, but a few days later he zoomed up to us in the lobby of our Guwahati hotel. He was guiding the American travel agent who employs him and they happened to be touring the hotel for future travelers when we walked through. The four of us had a lovely tea before we went on our separate ways. It was a satisfying closure to get to thank both of them for organizing our West Bengal experience.

What Kolkata Taught Me about Magic

I arrived in Kolkata thinking that I would have a spiritual experience. Instead I received a magical education I didn't know I needed.

As a Witch and magician I've traveled around the world to connect to the sources of the esoteric tradition. I've toured archaeological sites in Greece and Egypt. I've visited the great museums in London, Paris, New York and Chicago. But it wasn't until I took up Tantric practice that it occurred to me to travel to India. Even then I couldn't figure out how to focus a pilgrimage to a country so vast it's called a sub-continent. We haven't yet learned how to fit India into our historical narrative. What Alex and I found in Kolkata is the esoteric connection between east and west.

Until recently we've thought of magic as essentially western and we have treated eastern spirituality as fundamentally different from what we do. Now we are waking up from a fever dream of superiority. For centuries we have insisted that European civilization is the most advanced in the world: Greece gave the world science and philosophy and democracy, while Rome gave the world Christianity, the pinnacle of religions. That sense of superiority justified the brutal colonial exploitation Europe imposed on Africa and India and the forced conversion of colonized and enslaved peoples to Christianity. Now we are recognizing that the Greek philosophers who told us they studied in Egypt and studied with Indian teachers were telling the truth. European civilization has always learned from the more ancient civilizations of Africa and India.

In the wake of this insight the academic study of esotericism has recently lofted the idea that esotericism isn't divided into eastern and western, it's just esotericism. On the one hand this helps to break down the racist barriers that prevent us from learning from the venerable living traditions of India. On the other hand this attitude casts the wisdom traditions as part of a continuum that we are free to use in whatever way we like. It's a form of cultural colonialism.

Europeans didn't just take rice and tea and colorful cloth from India, they took ideas. Helena Blavatsky plundered the religious and spiritual traditions for raw material to shape her own metaphysical system. The German occultists of Ordo Templi Orientis repurposed kundalini yoga for their own magical system, recasting the creative power of Shakti as a potency inherent in semen and placing men firmly in charge. We have inherited the fruits of this methodology. Esotericists, Witches, magicians, Pagans, Goddess worshippers, use the material they handed us and ignore their original sources.

In Kolkata I gained a new perspective on the twentieth century occultists who visited India. As a white woman feminist I wish I could be proud of Annie Besant and her political career. Instead I was appalled to discover how condescending and racist her work turned out to be. Similarly, as a Thelemite who has learned so much from Aleister Crowley I thought that I would understand more about his work by visiting the home of Tantra. Instead I confronted just how little he actually knew. He didn't have anything like the conversations I had because he didn't approach the people of India as peers. When I read excerpts from Crowley's travel diaries in Tobias Churton's biography *Aleister Crowley in India* I learned to my intense dismay that he spent his time in country complaining about the servants and bragging about bullying his way into a temple. He spent his time in Kolkata dining with his British bureaucratic friends, writing bad poetry, and ultimately getting in trouble and fleeing the country. Crowley is not the Tantric connection to the esoteric world, it's Sir John Woodroffe and Atilal Bihari Ghose.

Academics too wander into India and come out playing with ideas. One description of the practices at Kamakhya begins with a proposal that the idea of Shakti can prop up the flaws in Foucault's philosophy. Another academic who spent many years embedding herself with a Baul family represented herself as studying their spirituality. She stayed in their homes, learned their music, even performed with them. When she finally did publish her study she didn't share anything about what they thought about their spiritual work or what she personally experienced as an adopted Baul. Instead she revealed the dirty secrets of their everyday lives - when they snuck out from work to take a cigarette break, the fights they had with their families, things that would humiliate any of us if known. Instead of respecting the privacy of friends who hosted and trusted her she treated everything she saw as fair game just as early ethnographers studied the private lives of "savages". This hostile disclosure is her failing and an indictment of the academic system that trained her and published her work.

People in the magical communities benefit from this scholastic approach too. Magicians pick up academic works on Tantra to mine them for practices and ideas instead of seeking out lineaged teachers to learn directly from them. It's not hard to spot the practitioner whose education is strictly academic, there are skills and standpoints that are only learned from knowledgeable tutoring. There's an essential attitude that's still missing in our approach to these wisdom lineages.

We've come quite far in western esotericism, but the legacy of the colonial era distorts our magical and academic studies. Traveling in West Bengal taught me that we still have a lot to learn. One of those things is humility. There is still a lot we don't know about what we've already incorporated into our magic and there's still a lot that we haven't yet absorbed. We can only understand these things by paying the price of respect, recognizing that the wisdom traditions of India predate our own.

We come to them not as teachers but as students. We need to respect the tradition, use its own language, practice on its own terms. This pays immediate and long term benefits. I am a better magician for learning Tantric practice.

Our failure to acknowledge the sources of our tradition has obscured their importance. When I was planning a magical pilgrimage, Kolkata should have been at the top of my list. We need to visit India just as we visit England and Greece and Egypt to connect to our magical roots. If we learn from Besant and Crowley we also need to learn from Ramakrishna, Vivekananda, Sarada Ma and Nivedita. If we want to understand our own magic we need to study the saints of Kolkata who deliberately invited us into Kolkata's religious and magical practice.

In West Bengal I also learned something less intellectual and more primal. I experienced the power of a sacred site where Goddess is worshipped. That power entered into my physical body and my energy body and my soul. I also learned that it is our responsibility to add to that power, to do our own devotionals and give back to sustain them. What I realized as I sat next to our guide listening to a Baul sing the secrets of magic is that we connect through our willingness to listen and take what we learn into our hearts.

Appendix A: Illustrations

Abanindranath Tagore, Bharat Mata. From Wikimedia, licensed under CC By SA 4.

Kolkata

Alex in the Oberoi Grand lobby

Indian Museum entrance

Indian Museum courtyard

Rabindra Setu bridge

College Street

College Street Coffee House

Paramount

Bengal Theosophical Society

Sri Aurobindo Hall

Sri Aurobindo Memorial

Countryside

Heritage Plantation

Attahas Temple

Five Skull Shrine at Attahas

Shantiniketan classroom

Ramkiner Baij statue of Gandhi

Garden Bungalow

Kumari Puja Kankalitala

Niti Das Baul

Appendix B:
A Quick Guide to the Saints and Teachers of Kolkata

Founding fathers: David Hare and Raja Rammohun Roy

David Hare's College Street story starts with Raja Rammohun Roy. In 1815 Roy invited a few acquaintances to his Calcutta house to establish the Atmiya Sabha, Society of Friends. Roy had translated the Vedas and Upanishads from Sanskrit into Bengali, Hindi and English. He had also studied Islamic and Christian thought. From these studies he crafted the monotheistic Hindu theology called Brahmo Samaj. Roy proposed to his friends that they found an educational institution based on Brahmo Samaj principles.

David Hare joined Roy's Society of Friends and enthusiastically supported the idea of a college. However he steered away from religious-based education. He proposed instead to focus on western secular culture and science. What earned him the statue on College Street was that he donated land for this purpose. In 1817 the Hindu College opened its doors with twenty students.

Hare's biographer Peary Chand Mittra describes two schools of thought about education in India at the time. Anglicists proposed replacing native culture altogether, creating students "Indian in blood and colour but English in tastes, in opinions, in morals and in intellect." Orientalists agreed that English education was essential but advocated teaching Sanskrit and Arabic literature as well.

In a sense both sides won. Today half a dozen colleges sit on the street itself, and the University of Calcutta alone has ten campuses spread across the city. Their students speak fluent English and have a solid grounding in Western philosophy and politics. Not long after the first college opened its doors the Young Bengal Society gained traction among the students, attacking traditional Hinduism and advocating cultural reforms such as abolishing the caste system and educating women.

Where there are students there is revolution. The Young Bengal Society faded into the Bengali Renaissance, a political and cultural movement led by Raja Rammohun Roy and supported by David Hare.

Roy fought colonial abuses, particularly press censorship. Importantly, he promoted the Bengali language, publishing works and writing songs in the Bengali tongue.

Renewed appreciation of Bengali culture inspired efforts toward political independence. Again and again self-rule movements sprang up on College Street and were squelched by the British. Finally in 1911 the empire shifted its capital from Kolkata to Delhi partly to escape the revolutionary efforts.

Social revolution: Annie Besant and Mahatma Gandhi

If you know your Theosophical history hers is a name to conjure by. Helena Blavatsky may have created Theosophical philosophy but Annie Besant popularized it.

Born in 1847 in London to Irish parents, Besant developed into a talented speaker and writer. She rallied for women's rights and birth control, worker's rights, and Irish self-rule. Scandalously, she preached atheism and Free Thought. Then she met Helena Blavatsky.

Blavatsky's books introduced Besant to a heady brew of western esotericism infused with Hindu and Buddhist thought. Blavatsky announced to the Western world that the eastern religions contained insights that Christianity lacked. However she did not come as a student but as a savior: she proclaimed that she had rescued esoteric truths from the eastern traditions that had been degraded in contemporary India.

Blavatsky's work so impressed Besant that she joined the Theosophical Society as an enthusiastic convert. In 1893 Besant represented Theosophy at the Parliament of the World's Religions. That same year she moved to India where she continued her social justice efforts, among other works founding a girls school in Varanasi which still teaches female students today. After Blavatsky's death the Theosophical Society split into American and International branches, and eventually Besant became president of the International branch.

Besant transferred her home to India and pledged her life as a gift of service to the motherland. She said "All that I have and am, I lay on the altar of the Mother". She co-founded the Indian Home Rule League and advocated self-rule for India just as she had for Ireland. The British government arrested her for this in 1917 but quickly released her, largely due to the pressure brought by the political party of the India National Congress. Besant rode a wave of popularity into the annual meeting of the congress. Five thousand delegates elected the seventy-year-old British woman as the party's first woman president.

It went to her head. Her acceptance speech reads to my twenty-first century eyes as pompous and condescending. Where Blavatsky positioned herself as a European savior of Hindu wisdom, Besant positioned herself as a European savior of Indian politics. It didn't play well. She advocated constitutional reform through transferring self-rule to Indian provinces which would continue to answer to the British Parliament. The majority of the delegates leaned away from her solution, holding out for a strategy that would deliver complete independence.

The man who stepped up to deliver that plan was Mohandas Karamchand Gandhi. He was born in Gujarat to a deeply religious mother and a moderately successful father. He was expected to follow his father into administration and become a barrister. The family sent him to England to complete his education. There he encountered Theosophical thought. In his autobiography he credited Blavatsky's *Key to Theosophy* with inspiring him to read other books on Hinduism. He was introduced to Annie Besant when he attended her lecture "Why I Became a Theosophist" in London. It is clear that Gandhi admired Besant in particular; when he established a law practice in South Africa he mounted her photo in his office.

Gandhi's work in South Africa included defending Indian migrants like himself against violent racist policies. It was here that he developed his strategy of satyagraha, non-violent resistance. Gandhi offered satyagraha to the Indian National Congress as a strategy to achieve self-rule and overthrow the yoke of the British Raj.

This put Besant and Gandhi in direct conflict. She didn't believe that his movement could remain non-violent. However Gandhi's leadership suited the tenor of the party. Biographers generally note that Besant's influence waned as Gandhi's rose.

Gandhi's satyagraha movement was pivotal in achieving India's full independence from the British government. This independence came at a price as Britain partitioned Bengal, assigning Hindu-majority

West Bengal to India and Muslim-majority East Bengal to Pakistan. Gandhi spent Independence Day in Kolkata in 1947 working to calm anti-Muslim riots. He was killed for this a few months later by a Hindu nationalist.

Besant left the Indian National Party and was never again as politically important. She remained president of the Theosophical Society and continued her social justice work, founding schools and holding women's conferences. She died in 1933.

Besant was present on the world stage when India emerged as a power. She was in the room when Vivekananda addressed the Parliament of the World's Religions. She championed Indian independence. As a feminist I am inclined to be proud of the first woman president of a political party, an early proponent of birth control, someone who worked for the freedom of subject peoples. But as a white woman who interrogates her own racism I am unable to wholeheartedly lean into admiration. Besant seemed to hold whiteness in general and herself in particular as superior to the Indian people for whom she worked. She was British, above and apart.

Theosophical history claims an influence on Gandhi, but it's an open question how important Theosophical thought was to his development. While his Theosophical schoolmates in England encouraged Gandhi to read Hindu literature, he grew up in a devout Hindu family, and the stories and values were familiar to him. By the time Besant was elected president of the Indian National Congress he had left the Theosophical Society and had developed his own spiritual understanding. History notes his political impact but India called him Mahatma, great soul, for his religious devotion.

Gandhi was a native son and succeeded where Besant fell short. His influence helped India achieve her independence, and his memory is loved.

Tantric scholars: Sir John Woodroffe and Atilal Behari Ghose (Arthur Avalon)

John Woodroffe was born in India to Irish Catholic parents. He received his Bachelor of Civil Law at Oxford and joined his father at the Calcutta

Bar in 1889. His mother died just a few years later, and in his grief he was advised by a Bengali Tantric to "seek out the Mother of the Universe" and study Tantra. Woodroffe kept his interest in Tantric religion quiet to avoid alienating his staunchly Catholic father and risk being disinherited.

John Woodroffe married the Theosophist Ellen Grimson in 1902. She shared his interest in Indian religion and they began to study Sanskrit together. When Woodroffe's father retired and left India in 1904 the Woodroffes were free to pursue their studies.

John's wife was his first collaborator. The name Ellen Avalon appeared as co-author on an early version of *Hymns to the Goddess*, a translation of prayers scattered throughout Hindu and Tantric literature. Ellen Grimson Woodroffe was a concert pianist and gave performances at evening gatherings which included both British and Indian guests. The Woodroffes supported the Indian Society for Oriental Art which promoted the New Bengal school of art, including the works of Abanindranath and Gagenendranath Tagore. The Woodroffe and Tagore families formed part of the vibrant cultural scene in early twentieth-century Calcutta.

John and Ellen moved in Theosophical circles as well. When Annie Besant was elected president of the Indian Nation Congress in 1917 the Woodroffes showed her around town. Like Annie, John Woodroffe openly supported Indian self-rule, an unusually radical position for a high-ranking member of the judiciary. He published these views under his own name in the collection of essays *Is India Civilized?*, a passionate defense of Indian culture.

It was in the courts of Calcutta that John Woodroffe met Atilal Behari Ghose. While Woodroffe served on the high court and was ultimately appointed chief justice, Ghose practiced at the Court of Small Causes. Ghose came from a Shakta Indian family and received a middle class Bengali English education.

Woodroffe's biographer Kathleen Taylor tracked down Ghose's grandson, a fascinating story in itself, and gained permission to look through his grandfather's papers. Reading the Ghose family correspondence, interviewing the descendants of Ghose and Woodroffe, and collecting oral history held in the Kolkata judicial community, Taylor pieced together evidence for a circle of European Tantric practitioners in early twentieth century Kolkata. At least three members of the Indian Society for Oriental Art studied Tantra. They met at the houses Ghose maintained in Kolkata and Ranchi.

Ghoses' grandchildren believe that Woodroffe and Ghose were drawn together by their interest in Tantra. John and Ellen were initiated together by the Tantric saint Sivacandra Vidyarnava. Ghose was himself a disciple of Sivacandra Vidyarnava. Eventually Ghose developed into the spiritual guide for the European Tantrics in Calcutta.

Several photographs capture Ghose with Woodroffe and other men, including one taken at the temple of Konarak with its famous erotic sculptures, where Ghose and Woodroffe were rumored to practice rituals. In the photograph Woodroffe wore the dhoti of a Bramacharya or student. That photograph, along with his support for Annie Besant's radical views about Indian independence, eventually caused Woodroffes' rejection by Calcutta's polite British society.

When John left the judiciary the Woodroffes moved to England. John taught Indian law at Oxford, Ellen converted to Catholicism and ceased to pursue her Tantric studies. At the end of his life John re-converted to Catholicism as well.

The Serpent Power and *Shakti and Shakta* introduced the western world to the concept of the subtle body with its cakras, and the female kundalini serpent that rises through them. *Tantrik Texts* translated numerous works from Sanskrit to English. Woodroffe claimed authorship of these works in his lifetime, it was no secret that he was the man behind the pseudonym. In that case, why write as "Arthur Avalon" at all?

Taylor makes the case that the pseudonym was not intended to protect Woodroffe. It protected Ghose. The collaboration allowed Ghose as a Tantric insider to present the philosophy and practice of Tantra while borrowing Woodroffe's prestige as a colonial judge.

This is a credible argument which corrects for the automatic assumption of white superiority. Why would we think an Englishman could write with such authority about Tantric practice? Ghose grew up in a Shakta family, Woodroffe grew up in a Catholic one and returned to that religion in his age. Woodroffe could read and translate the texts and he adopted the practices for a time, but the depth of knowledge and comprehension in the Arthur Avalon works is clearly rooted in culture and commitment. Arthur Avalon is not one man, but two: Sir John Woodroffe, the public face, and Atilal Bihari Ghose, his secret teacher and friend.

The Bengal Art Movement: Tagore Family

The independence effort began as an art movement. Kolkata's western educated upper class families connected their new lifestyles with a Shakta Hindu spiritual core. This blossomed in a form of art that combined classical Indian painting traditions with folk art and a humanist sensibility. The images of the New Bengal school offered an image of Bharat, India, as a proudly independent cultural force.

Many families and artists contributed to the art movement. First among these was the Tagore family. As Brahmans of the zamindar or merchant class they mingled with the upper class British families in Kolkata. They hosted gatherings in their home which drew the prominent figures of the cultural renaissance, including the Woodroffes, Vivekananda and Sister Nivedita. They promoted the Indian Society for Oriental Art and established the university Shantiniketan. As a family they provided the structural underpinning for India's new self-image.

Debendranath Tagore

The family patriarch was born in 1817, the year the Hindu College was founded, and was educated on College Street. He learned both English and Sanskrit, Western and Hindu philosophy. He was a social champion, speaking out against the practice of widows immolating themselves on their husband's funeral pyres. He joined Raja Rammohun Roy to found the Brahmo Samaj which presented Vedic religious ideas in a framework inspired by Unitarian services; the Vedas were read out loud just as the Bible was and the Upanishads were sung as hymns for audiences of all castes and religions. The movement attracted many poets, intellectuals and artists in Calcutta's cultural scene. The Brahmo Samaj and eventually developed a democratic constitution and advocated India's independence from colonial rule. Debendranath interest lay more in the religions side of the movement and he established an ashram at Shantiniketan to promote religious devotion. He died in 1905.

Rabindranath Tagore

Rabindranath Tagore is the most famous member of the family. He was educated in England but spent much of his adult life managing the family's estates in East Bengal, what is now Bangladesh, where he wrote hundreds of poems and songs inspired by the beauty of the countryside. Two of those songs became the national anthems of West Bengal and Bangladesh. He translated his own work Gitanjali (Song Offerings) into English and it won the Nobel Prize for literature in 1913. By then he was living full time at Shantiniketan, established by his father Debendranath as an ashram. Rabindranath turned it into an art school combining eastern and western ideas about education and firmly grounded in a love for the natural world. His own art works are collected in the four-volume set Rabindra Chitravali; they express the fluid lines of the trees, animals and people of the villages which captured his heart. The great cantilever bridge in Kolkata was renamed from Howrah Bridge to Rabindra Setu in 1965 to honor Kolkata's most famous citizen.

Gagenendranath Tagore

Rabindranath's uncle Gagenendranath assumed responsibility for his side of the family at just fourteen when his father died and left him to direct the zamindar estate. Like many in his family he was drawn to art and developed his own self-taught style. He used his wealth to promote the Indian Society of Oriental Art and to sponsor his own family's artistic efforts. He was an actor as well as an artist and appeared in Rabindranath's play Falguni which he also produced.

His commitment to Bengali art extended to furniture and folk crafts. Just as the Arts and Crafts movement in England rejected Victorian excesses to favor simple home crafts, Gagenendranath swept out the Victorian furniture in the family's home in Kolkata and worked to promote local handicrafts.

His paintings absorbed French and German influences along with Bengalis motifs to depict the natural world, and later in life, the supernatural world as well. His works were exhibited in Paris, London, Berlin, and America, and drew praise as one of the founders of modern Bengali art.

One image in particular endears him to me. As we rode back to the hotel after watching the procession of pandal images down to the river, our guide pulled up an image on his cell phone, a watercolor Gagenendranath had painted in 1914. It showed the same procession in that year lit with torches along dark Kolkata streets. It's such a romantic image capturing an enduring cultural moment and creating a sense of connection to history among Kolkatans.

Abanindranath Tagore

Gagenendranath's brother was also an artist. Abanindranath Tagore's humanist style earned him the reputation as the founder of modern Bengal art and the Bengal Art School.

He's known and loved for one painting in particular. In 1905 the British colonial administration divided Bengal into East and West. Bengalis viewed this partition as an attempt to defuse the growing nationalist movement. It was one of the sparks that created the idea of a unified India. In response that same year the artist Abanindranath Tagore created an image of India that evoked the Bengali love of the Mother: Bharat Mata, Mother India.

The painting shows a beautiful woman in a realistic style combined with religious imagery. She wears a saffron colored robe and has four arms in which she holds a mala or religious rosary and a book of sacred scripture, both traditional images, and a sheaf of rice and length of white cloth, new images pointing to India's wealth. A halo surrounds her head reminiscent of the halos surrounding European images of Mary and the saints, while lotuses bloom at her feet, traditional images of Hindu and Buddhist spirituality.

Sister Nivedita recognized the potential of this image. She promoted the image and encouraged its printing and distribution in political posters and banners. In just a few years the image spread across India. It is held today in the collection of the Rabindra Bharati Society and is occasionally exhibited.

Sunayana Devi

Just as Abinendranath Tagore is hailed as the founder of modern Bengal Art, Sunayana Devi is considered to be the first woman modern artist in India. As a toddler she was inspired by her brothers Gagenendranath and Abanindranath to pick up a brush and play with color. She was married at 11 to the grandson of Raja Rammohun Roy and did not receive a formal education. Fortunately her husband encouraged her artistic explorations and she developed her own distinctive style. She was inspired by Bengali folk art and was the first modern artist to champion rural folk art.

Her subjects included classical stories and scenes from domestic life. In her images women hold children, birds, flutes, sit in contemplation, look dreamily at the moon. Her watercolor washes drew international attention. In 1922 the Society of Oriental Art in Kolkata exhibited works of Klee and Kandinsky together with Bengali artists including Sunayana Devi. In 1927 her art was exhibited in London by the Women's International Art Club.

The Tagore family produced so many notable artists that this is not an exhaustive list. Their work powered the artistic flowering of the Bengali Renaissance both culturally and politically and remains a source of pride and self-definition for Bengalis and for India.

Dakshineswar: Rani Rashmoni and Ramakrishna

Rani Rashmoni

Rani Rashmoni's story is a fairy tale, the poor village girl who marries a propertied man with a huge fortune. Her father, a farmer, taught her to read and her husband, a zamindar or landowner, continued her education. Babu Rajachandra Das gradually trained his wife to manage his zamindari, and when he died she took control of his estate, working with her daughter's husbands to control a sizeable fortune.

She had been pious as a village girl and she was pious as a wealthy widow. Stories are still told about the times she stood up to the East India Company. Here's one: when poor fishermen complained to her that they were being overly taxed, she had a chain draped across the river from her properties, halting the shipping trade until the tax was rescinded. She built roads and docks, contributed to the first college on College Street, funded famine relief, protected women, supported a library.

Her lasting monument is Dakshineswar. Her biographers report that she had planned a pilgrimage to Varanasi. Kali appeared to her in a dream and commanded her to use the money instead to build a temple. When she completed the monumental structure she found that no Brahman priest would install the image of Kali and tend it. Since she was born into a farming caste she could not cook food for a Brahman priest. She sent messages to all the scholars she could locate. How could she resolve this dilemma? Only one returned to her with a solution. Ramkumar Chattopadhyay advised her to deed the property to a Brahman priest. Rani Rashmoni turned the property over to her family guru and persuaded Ramkumar himself to install the statue and tend to it.

Ramakrishna

Ramkumar had inherited the care of his family on his father's death. He was particularly concerned for the welfare of his younger brother Ramakrishna. How was the boy going to make a living? He would abandon his schooling at a moment's notice to play at being Krishna with his friends. So when Ramkumar took the position of priest of Kali at Dakshineswar he sent for his brother to join him, intending to train him to work as a priest.

Ramakrishna spent his days decorating the image of Kali and singing to her. His fortunes rose when he provided an elegant solution to a dilemma. The temple complex includes a Radha-kanta, a shrine housing statues of Radha and Krishna. Each night the image of Krishna was carried into the retiring chamber to join the image of Radha. One day the priest carrying Krishna slipped and broke one of the statue's legs. Scripture prohibited worshipping a broken image so the temple priests proposed to return the statue to the river and replace it with a new one. However Rani Rashmoni was particularly attached to this particular image (which she had commissioned) and objected to the plan.

Ramakrishna offered this observation: if your son-in-law breaks his leg, do you get a new son-in-law? He took the idol and repaired it so that the break was no longer visible. Both the new statue and the repaired statue are still kept in the temple today.

Ramakrishna spent hours at the feet of Kali's statue begging her to reveal herself to him. His religious fervor blossomed into intense devotion. Eventually she granted him the visions he craved: he saw her alive in the statue. Then he saw her everywhere, standing on the temple roof gazing down at the river, chatting with him as he gathered flowers in the gardens. The other priests became alarmed when he treated the statue as alive, pressing food to her mouth and taking her hand. They sent for Rani Rashmoni's son-in-law Mathuranath Biswas to handle the situation. Instead of reigning him in, Mathur and Rani Rashmoni recognized the priest was god-touched. They relieved him of his priestly duties and provided him with the home where he lived the rest of his life.

In 1861 a boat docked and a woman with disheveled hair stepped onto the grounds. Ramakrishna saw her arrival and sent for her. When she saw him she immediately greeted him as a mother: "My son! I have been searching for you for so long and now I have found you."

The woman was a Brahman Vaisnavite Tantrika, a renunciate nun called Yogeshwari. She confirmed for him that he was not insane but instead experiencing mahabhava, religious ecstasy. She compared him to other famous saints who had lived in this state. Ramakrishna accepted her as a teacher and she taught him Tantric rituals. Ramakrishna had the five skull site constructed so he could perform the Tantric Pancha Munda meditation there.

A Vedantic monk named Totapuri offered to train Ramakrishna in the discipline that leads to samadhi, the state of ultimate spiritual realization. Ramakrishna shaved his head and took the vows of renunciation. After receiving the mantras he released attachment to everything except the image of the Mother. When he mentally sliced this image it dissolved and he fell into samadhi. He sat motionless and not eating for three days. Finally Totapuri roused him from that state and brought him back down to earth. Totapuri stayed at Dakshineswar for several months to ensure that Ramakrishna roused himself enough from samadhi to stay alive. When he finally left Ramakrishna fell into trance again. He only remained alive physically because another monk on the grounds tended to him and pressed food into his mouth. Only when his body became ill did Ramakrishna return to full consciousness.

Ramakrishna had received Tantric and Vedantic initiation. His interest then broadened to include other faiths. A Sufi mystic named Govinda Ray came to live at Dakshineswar. Ramakrishna recognized the Sufi's spiritual state as similar to the state of samadhi. He asked to be instructed in Islamic practice and dedicated himself to it for a short but intense period. He had a vision of a divine being with a beard which then dissolved into the realization of Brahman without attributes, and came to the realization that devotion to Islam would lead to the same enlightenment as devotion to Advaita Vedanta.

Some years later Ramakrishna had a similar encounter with Christianity. One of his devotees read the Bible aloud to him which familiarized him with the stories and teachings. One day he happened to see an image of Madonna and Child and was swept away by their spiritual force. He spent days immersed in visions of devotees offering candles and incense to statues of the Madonna and Jesus. After a few days of this he was walking in the gardens of Dakshineswar when he saw a foreign man walking toward him serenely. He said "Here is Yogi Jesus!" The man embraced him and then merged into him.

Ramakrishna approached the idea of teaching with the same extravagant passion that marked all his endeavors. He sent spiritual calls to followers to come to him and collected a circle of devotees who dedicated themselves to him. Ramakrishna himself never wrote. His teachings were preserved through the notes his followers took and later published. This period of Ramakrishna's life lasted only a few years. He died in 1886 at the age of 50 of throat cancer.

Ramakrishna's lineage: Sarada Ma and Gauri Ma

I first heard the story of Sarada Ma's life from our guide. In 1872 an inconvenient woman turned up at Dakshineswar. She turned out to be Ramakrishna's abandoned wife. When Ramakrishna was 23 his family tried to anchor the trance-prone mystic to everyday life by marrying him to a five-year-old village girl. In the intervening years Ramakrishna had taken up the life of a priest, conducted Tantric practice, and had taken the vow of a sannyasin to be a celibate monk. When she turned 18 Sarada Devi traveled on her own to Dakshineswar to join her husband. The problem was that celibate monks aren't supposed to be husbands. Ramakrishna explained to her that he would not consummate the marriage and asked her not to pull him away from his intense devotional focus.

Ramakrishna provided Sarada Ma with a tiny room some distance from his own. The room was so small she would hit her head on the lintel when she moved too quickly. There she settled into a life of devotional service. She would wake before dawn to wash in the river and spend some time in meditation. As a Brahman wife in her time period she observed purdah, keeping a screen in front of her door and staying indoors during the day to stay out of the public eye. She commented that the manager of Dakshineswar said the priests knew she lived there but they had never seen her. When women visited Ramakrishna they lodged with her, all of them crammed into the same small space.

Sarada Ma cooked for Ramakrishna every day. Her husband's digestion was sensitive and only her food suited him. She saw him only when she took him his meals, and if one of his women followers took the food to him she didn't see him at all. Her tiny room also served as her pantry and kitchen. She not only cooked for Ramakrishna but also his mother and later for increasing numbers of his followers, each of whom had different dietary requirements. Biographer Swami Tapasyananda records Ramakrishna's comment "Well, what does a 'wife' signify in the case of one like me?" Then he added, "But for her, who would have prepared my food in just the way that suits my health?"

Sarada Ma's biographers say that Ramakrishna cared for her well-being and blame her penury on the manager who took over Dakshineswar after the deaths of Rani Rashmoni and Mathur. Others are less inclined to let Ramakrishna off the hook, commenting that he didn't give her the life she deserved.

Ramakrishna was not a husband to her but instead became her spiritual guide. He trained her in yogic and devotional practices. One night Ramakrishna prepared a Shodashi Puja. He set up a platform for the image of the Mother and set out offerings. Then he sent for Sarada

Ma. He placed her on the platform and worshipped her as the avatar of the Divine Mother herself. Thereafter he regarded her as the living image of the Mother.

Ramakrishna's death made Sarada Ma a widow. At that time a widow of the Brahminic caste was expected to stop wearing jewelry and wear only plain clothing. Sarada Ma reported that when she went to put off her bangles Ramakrishna appeared to her and told her to continue to wear them – she could not be a widow, he was still alive, just in another state. She compromised by wearing a small amount of adornment for the rest of her life, although even this scandalized her family village.

In the first years after her husband's death Sarada Ma went on pilgrimages. She spent some time in the company of some of Ramakrishna's followers, including Yogen. Ramakrishna appeared in a dream to Yogen and told him to seek initiation from Sarada Ma. Then Ramakrishna appeared in a dream to Sarada Ma and told her he had not initiated Yogen and asked that she provide initiation to him. When Yogen came to her with his story she fulfilled Ramakrishna's request and initiated Yogen. This marked the beginning of her own spiritual ministry.

When the management at Dakshineswar cut off her stipend Sarada Ma ended up living in poverty alone. Eventually word reached Ramakrishna's followers and they obtained a house for her in Kolkata where they supported her for the rest of her life. It was that house that we visited on the day we went to College Street, the mission which still feeds people every day, and allows devotees to meditate upstairs in her bedroom.

When Ramakrishna died his disciple Vivekananda inherited leadership of his devotees. However Ramakrishna had not initiated Vivekananda. The Ramakrishna Mission notes that Sarada Ma became the lineage holder of the Ramakrishna order on Ramakrishna's death. Our guide made a point of noting that the Ramakrishna empowerments passed through the female line, through Sarada Ma and Gauri Ma, the only two people he initiated.

Gauri Ma wandered on her own for some years before meeting Ramakrishna. She was the only woman who received the vows of sannyas from Ramakrishna. She bonded with Sarada Ma as a spiritual mother and stayed with her after Ramakrishna's death. Her biographers record the story that she wanted to return to spiritual wandering, but Ramakrishna directed her to start a school for women. Today the Saradeswari Ashram she founded maintains a free Hindu school for girls and a free medical clinic.

East Meets West: Vivekananda, Nivedita and Yogananda

Vivekananda

Vivekananda was born Narendranath Dutta. In his youth he was a product of college street. He wasn't a ruling caste Brahmin but he wasn't Shudra or servant class either, he was born into the Kayastha caste. In the villages the Kayastha caste becomes clerks, in the city they fill the ranks of government administrators.

Vivekananda's mother was a devout Hindu. He studied yoga and meditation as a child, but his western education at Presidency College and Calcutta University brought his faith into question. He joined Raja Rammohun Roy's Brahmo Samaj group of religious reformers and spent time with the Tagore family, involved in all the political and artistic revolutions in early twentieth century Kolkata.

By then Ramakrishna's extraordinary practices were famous on College Street. In 1881 Vivekananda visited Ramakrishna at Dakshineswar. At first glance this westernized young man was an unlikely candidate to answer Ramakrishna's spiritual call. Vivekananda credited Ramakrishna with his conversion.

Here's how he told the story: Vivekananda was poor and worried about providing for his family. Ramakrishna was demonstrably devoted to Kali the mother. Vivekananda asked Ramakrishna to intercede with Kali to provide for him. Ramakrishna refused. *It's Tuesday, Kali's day*, Ramakrishna said, *go to the temple and pray for yourself.*

When Vivekananda entered the temple he experienced the statue as alive, conscious, and filled with love. With awestruck sincerity he asked only that he would be able to know her. When he returned he reported this to Ramakrishna. His teacher laughed, *you didn't ask her for money? Go back again!* When Vivekananda returned to the temple he was again struck with the mother's love and asked only for knowledge. This pattern repeated one more time before Vivekananda finally gave up. He said Ramakrishna had charmed his mind so that he would only think of dedicating himself to her. In the end Ramakrishna relented and asked Kali to provide a simple living for his disciple's family.

Ramakrishna had more than a dozen male devotees when he died. He charged Vivekananda with keeping the group together after his death. While Sarada Ma went on pilgrimage and Gauri Ma went with her, Vivekananda gathered the men together to form a new monastic order. Under Vivekananda's guidance they dedicated themselves to a life of renunciation.

After living together for a period of time the monks scattered to engage in wandering pilgrimage. Vivekananda spread Ramakrishna's message as he went. As he traveled throughout India he was struck by the material condition of the people. He met wealthy men and learned scholars who suggested to him that he take his teachings to the west. His travels ultimately took him to the southernmost tip of India. He swam out to a rock to meditate. He reported that the vision came to him to travel to America to appeal for western material wealth in exchange for the spiritual wealth of Vedanta. There's a shrine on that rock today.

The 1893 Parliament of the World's Religions offered an opportunity to put his vision into action. He learned about the Parliament from a disciple who rounded up funds for him to attend. Vivekananda wrote to Sarada Ma with the plan; she gave him her blessing to undertake what came to be known as the mission to the west.

Vivekananda arrived in Chicago with no friends and little money. He also discovered that registration for the Parliament had closed. Heading back to the railway station he was dismayed to find it was not possible to sleep there as in India. He spent one miserable night shivering in a boxcar. He learned that it was cheaper to live in Boston than Chicago so took a train to Boston. On the train he met a wealthy woman who invited him to stay on her estate. He wrote to his supporters at home for additional funds, noting "I am now living as a guest of an old lady in a village near Boston, who shows me off to her friends as a curio from India." Despite her genial disdain she made an important connection for him: she introduced him to a friend who convinced the Parliament organizers to accept him as a delegate.

When Vivekananda showed up to the Parliament he was expected to demonstrate that Hindu religion was unsophisticated idol-worshipping. Instead he offered sophisticated commentary on the world's religions in fluent English. When he started his opening address "Brothers and Sisters of America" the crowd leapt to its feet and responded with thunderous applause for many minutes.

Vivekananda went on,

> It fills my heart with joy unspeakable to rise in response to the warm and cordial welcome which you have given us. I thank you in the name of the most ancient order of monks in the world, I thank you in the name of the mother of religions, and I thank you in the name of millions and millions of Hindu people of all classes and sects.
>
> My thanks, also, to some of the speakers on this platform who, referring to the delegates from the Orient, have told you that these men from far-off nations may well claim the honor of bearing to different lands the idea of toleration. I am proud to belong to a religion which has taught the world both tolerance and universal acceptance. We believe not only in universal toleration, but we accept all religions as true.

The message of spiritual unity that Ramakrishna had preached reached its most influential audience. By all accounts Vivekananda was the star of the Parliament. A newspaper reported "At the Parliament of Religions they used to keep Vivekananda until the end of the programme to make people stay until the end of the session." The poor monk from Kolkata single-handedly shifted the Hindu-religion-as-Pagan-superstition narrative to Hindu religion source-of-Eastern-wisdom.

The Parliament launched Vivekananda's speaking career. He toured America and England preaching Ramakrishna's doctrine of religious universality, educating eager westerners about the Hindu philosophy of Vedanta. When he returned to India and set foot in his native country he was hailed as a celebrity by a cheering throng. He engaged in a whirlwind tour of India lecturing on the principles of Vedanta. Ramakrishna had shaped his spirituality but College Street had shaped his politics, and he also spoke to the future of India and independence from British rule.

As Ramakrishna had promised Kali provided for her devotee. Early in 1898 Vivekananda was able to purchase a sizeable property just across the Ganges from Dakshineswar. He intended to house a monastery for the Ramakrishna Order and a temple for Ramakrishna. To kick the project off he installed an urn containing Ramakrishna's ashes and invited Sarada Ma to consecrate the site.

Vivekananda spent the next few years life touring, teaching students, and giving sannyas vows to his own disciples. In 1901 he returned to Belur Math and retired from active life. He continued to teach but increasingly devoted himself to meditation. In 1902 he died peacefully in his sleep at the age of just 39.

The Ramakrishna Order continued after his death to build out his vision, finally completing the temple in 1938. Today the mission maintains hospices and hospitals, schools, and disaster relief efforts all over India.

Nivedita

There is one more woman in this story who is honored in Kolkata and virtually unknown in the west. In 1895 when Vivekananda made one of his visits to England he gave a lecture in a London drawing room. His audience included Margaret Elizabeth Noble. His words struck her as a revelation. She had a lot in common with Annie Besant - she was also an Irishwoman, also a writer, and also had a fiery political conscience. Unlike Annie though she didn't take what she learned and shape it into something else, she converted completely to Vedanta.

Three years after she met Vivekananda she travelled to Kolkata. Almost as soon as she arrived Swami Vivekananda gave her the sannyas vows. He named her Nivedita, the dedicated one. She learned to speak Bengali and threw herself into the work of the Ramakrishna Mission. She arrived in January; by November she had founded a school for girls, going door to door to encourage parents to educate their female children as well as their boys. She met Sarada Ma who called her "Khooki" or little girl. Nivedita remained devoted to Sarada Ma throughout her life.

Nivedita was already known for her personal work when bubonic plague swept Calcutta in March 1899. While the British government offered very little assistance the Ramakrishna Mission responded in force. Sister Nivedita organized cleaning efforts. She gave speeches on the need for cleanliness. She didn't just lecture and organize, she pitched in to clean the streets herself, and nursed victims in their own homes. Doctors called her an angel of mercy.

Following in the footsteps of Vivekananda she toured England and America collecting funds for the school for girls. She did get to meet Annie Besant and they became friends. Nivedita knew the Tagore family and helped to shape the Bengal School of Art. She wrote several influential books, including a biography of Swami Vivekananda, *The Master as I Saw Him.*

As she traveled through India and witnessed the effect of British rule she became increasingly political, which eventually caused her separation from the Ramakrishna Mission, a decision they arrived at mutually for the mission's own protection. She came to the attention of the College Street revolutionary Sri Aurobindo when he read her book *Kali the Mother.* He tapped her to help organize his revolutionary cell. Eventually she helped him to escape to French-held Pondicherry to escape the British authorities.

Sister Nivedita contracted malaria and died in Darjeeling 1911 at the age of 44. Her memorial reads "Here reposes Sister Nivedita who gave her all to India."

Yogananda

Vivekananda opened the road from east to west, other teachers followed. Yogananda's family moved to Kolkata in 1906 when he was 12. Ramakrishna, Vivekananda, and Nivedita had all passed on, but Master Mahasaya remained to anchor their memory and teachings. M. Mahendranath Gupta was a householder who spent years recording Ramakrishna's lectures and issued them as *The Gospel of Ramakrishna.* He opened his home to people sincerely interested in the spiritual life in general and Ramakrishna in particular. Young Yogananda, then Mukunda Lal Ghose, spent many hours rapturously listening to him.

Mukunda loved to walk the gardens at Dakshineswar and felt deeply called to renunciation. As soon as he completed his lower school education he joined a monastery in Varanasi. On the streets of Varanasi Mukunda met his guru Sri Yukteswar Giri. Yukteswar was a disciple of the Ghose family guru Lahiri Mahasaya. Mukunda was immediately overjoyed. He was then deeply dismayed to be told to return to his family and finish his education! Yukteswar lived in Serampor just outside Kolkata and proposed to educate Mukunda there.

Mukunda spent most of his time with his guru learning the spiritual exercises of Kriya Yoga. He spent just enough time on College Street to receive his degree. As soon as he graduated Swami Sri Yukteswar Giri gave the vows of sannyas or renunciation to Mukunda and named him Swami Yogananda Giri.

In 1917, the year Annie Besant was elected president of the Indian National Congress, Yogananda founded his first school and began his teaching career. This would become the Yogoda Satasanga Society of India. Later he established an ashram in the Dakshineswar district not far from the Kali temple where Ramakrishna spent his life.

In 1920 Yogananda was invited to attend a religious conference in Boston as the delegate from India. He left with the blessing of his guru. Just as the Parliament of the World's Religions launched Vivekananda's career, the Boston conference launched Yogananda's touring life. He spent years lecturing across the country and attracting famous disciples. He translated the Yogoda Satasanga Society to the English name Self Realization Fellowship and developed this into a monastic order.

Yogananda settled in Encinitas California where a wealthy disciple built a retreat. There he dictated *Autobiography of a Yogi*, published in 1946 and a perennial bestseller; Steve Jobs arranged for everyone attending his memorial to receive a copy.

Yukteswar had insisted that Mukunda complete his education to be able to relate to westerners. Yogananda successfully translated the experience of the life of spiritual renunciation to an American context.

The Revolutionary Saint: Sri Aurobindo

Aurobindo Ghose was born in 1872 in Calcutta. His father expressly prevented him from learning anything about his native culture, and at seven he was packed off to England, where his education at Cambridge completed his Anglicization. On his return to India he entered into the life of a colonial clerk. Eventually however he did reconnect to his heritage, studying Sanskrit and practicing yoga.

In 1908 he moved to Kolkata specifically to connect with the revolutionary struggle. He joined the emerging All-India Party, published the party's newspaper, and was the first writer to advocate India's complete independence from Britain. He was arrested for sedition three times between 1907 and 1909, the last time spending a year in prison. On his release he learned the other party leaders had been arrested and the independence movement effectively disbanded. Under threat of being arrested again he slipped out of Bengal and escaped to French-controlled Pondicherry.

In Pondicherry he went into a spiritual retreat. In 1914 he began publish a newsletter which serialized his important writings, including *The Life Divine*, *The Synthesis of Yoga* and *Essays on the Gita*. In 1926 he founded an ashram for his followers which continues today. He died in 1950.

The Mother

Sri Aurobindo collaborated with a woman as his spiritual companion, the French woman Mirra Alfassa, known to him and to his followers as The Mother. She was a student of Max and Alma Theon and led her own spiritual group in Paris before travelling to Pondicherry to work with Sri Aurobindo. As soon as the ashram was founded Sri Aurobindo turned the community over to her as its material and spiritual guide. She wrote many works on her own account. She died in 1973.

Sri Aurobindo's Legacy

Sri Aurobindo and The Mother named their spiritual system Integral Yoga. In their view spiritual pursuit didn't require vowing to give up family life, anyone including married people and householders could practice, study, and contemplate.

Sri Aurobindo's life exemplifies the legacy of Kolkata. Educated as a westerner, he found his spiritual center in India's deep and ancient practices. He worked with Sister Nivedita and with The Mother, European women drawn to him to support his spiritual work. He spent time as a political revolutionary but his true revolution was in creating a form of spiritual practice. He wrote his works on spirituality in English as a native speaker. He integrated the best traditions of Europe and India, west and east. It's not a surprise that his work is widely read by Tantrics in Bengal. It is a living example of theurgy, the human connection to the divine.

Bibliography

Advaita Ashrama. *The Life of Swami Vivekananda by His Eastern and Western Disciples*, 1912.

"Annie Besant (1847-1933)". *Theosophical Society Adyar*, www.ts-adyar. org/content/annie-besant-1847-1933. Accessed Nov. 9 2020.

Art Institute of Chicago. "Swami Vivekananda and His 1893 Speech". Web site: https://www.artic.edu/about-us/mission-and-history/swami-vivekananda. Accessed Nov. 9, 2020.

"Art Tour: Shantiniketan". *The Heritage Lab*, August 9 2018, www. theheritagelab.in/shantiniketan-art-tour/. Accessed March 5 2023.

Avalon, Arthur. *Tantric Texts*, 1913.

— *The Serpent Power*, 1918.

— *Shakti and Shakta*, 1918.

Balakhana. "Heritage Home Stay", *Balakhana*, www.balakhana.com/. Accessed March 5 2023.

Blavatsky, Helena. *The Secret Doctrine*, 1888.

Besant, Annie. *An Autobiography*, 1885.

Bergunder, Michael. "Experiments with Theosophical Truth: Gandhi, Esotericism, and Global Religious History". *Journal of the American Academy of Religion*, June 2014, Vol. 82, No. 2 (June 2014), pp. 398-426 Oxford University Press, www.jstor.org/stable/24488158. Accessed Nov. 9 2020.

Chetanananda. *They Lived with God: Life Stories of Some Devotees of Sri Ramakrishna*. Vedanta Society of St. Louis, 1989.

Churton, Tobias. *Aleister Crowley in India: The Secret Influence of Eastern Mysticism on Magic and the Occult*. Inner Traditions, 2019.

Crowley, Aleister. *Liber XV, the Gnostic Mass*, sabazius.oto-usa.org/gnostic-mass/. Accessed March 5 2023.

Deshvidesh. "Alasinga Perumal – He inspired Swami Vivekananda to visit America". April 21, 2005, //www.deshvidesh.com/alasinga-perumal/. Accessed Nov. 9 2020.

Dey, Monidipa Bose. "Sister Nivedita, Calcutta's Angel of Mercy". *Live History India*, April 7, 2020, https://www.livehistoryindia. com/history-daily/2020/04/07/sister-nivedita-calcuttas-an- gel-of-mercy. Accessed Nov. 9 2020.

The Garden Bungalow, www.thegardenbungalow.com. Accessed March 5 2023.

Goldberg, Philip. *The Life of Yogananda: The Story of the Yogi Who Became the First Modern Guru.* Hay House, 2018.

Gupta, Mahendranath (M.). *The Gospel of Ramakrishna.* 1942. Swami Nikhilananda, translator, www.vedanta-nl.org/GOSPEL.pdf, Accessed Nov. 9 2020.

Hanson, J.W., editor. *The World's Congress of Religions: The Addresses and Papers Delivered Before the Parliament.* International Publishing Company, 1894.

Harding, Elizabeth U. *Kali: the Black Goddess of Dakshineswar.* Nicholas-Hays, Inc, 1993.

Ivanov, Alex. *Gandhi.* CreateSpace Independent Publishing Platform, 2018.

Johnson, Paul K. *The Masters Revealed: Madame Blavatsky and the Myth of the Great White Lodge.* State University of New York Press, 1994.

Khan, Matluba. "Patha Bhavana, Shantiniketan – More than 100 years of outdoor learning practice". *PHD-The Other Half,* June 17, 2015, matlubaanalysingandwriting.blogspot.com/2015/06/patha-bhava- na-shantiniketan-more-than.html. Accessed March 5 2023.

Kung, Hans. "A Global Ethic. The Declaration of the Parliament of the World's Religions". SCM Press, 1993, www.parliamentofreli- gions.org/_includes/FCKcontent/File/TowardsAGlobalEthic.pdf. Accessed Nov. 9 2020.

Marshall, Katherine. "The Parliament of the World's Religions: 1893 and 1993". *Georgetown University Berkeley Center for Religion, Peace and World Affairs*, Sept. 3 2015, berkleycenter.georgetown.edu/essays/the-parliament-of-the-world-s-religions-1893-and-1993. Accessed Nov. 9 2020.

McDaniel, June. *Offering Flowers, Feeding Skulls: Popular Goddess Worship in West Bengal.* Oxford University Press, 2004.

Menon, Ajitha. "Bengal's Tribal Women Lead Change, Ensure Food-Security and Fight Social Ills". *The Better India*, May 23, 2012, www.thebetterindia.com/5222/bengals-tribal-women-lead-change-ensure-food-security-and-fight-social-ills/. Accessed March 5 2023.

Michaud, Derek. "World Parliament of Religions (1893)". Boston Collaborative Encyclopedia of Western Theology, Wesley Wildman, editor, 1994, people.bu.edu/wwildman/bce/worldparliamentofreligions1893.htm. Accessed Nov. 18 2020.

Mittra, Peary Chand. *A Biographical Sketch of David Hare.* Calcutta: W. Newman and Company, 1877.

"Painting that had the idea of Bharat Mata". *Get Bengal,* January 7 2021, www.getbengal.com/details/painting-that-had-the-idea-of-bharat-mata. Accessed March 5 2023.

Prabhananda. *Nivedita of India.* Ramakrishna Mission, 2002.

Shah, Aditi. "Kolkata's Rani Rashmoni". *Live India History.org,* October 4 2018, www.livehistoryindia.com/herstory/2018/10/04/kolkatas-rani-rashmoni. Accessed Nov. 9 2020.

Sadhu Rangarajan. "Sister Nivedita, Dedicated Daughter of Mother India." *Arise Bharat,* arisebharat.com/2011/03/21/sister-nivedita-a-beacon-for-freedom-fighters/. Accessed March 5 2023.

"Genesis and Brief History". *Shri Shri Saradeswari Ashram,* saradeswariashram.org/about. Accessed 10/29/2020.

Sri Raj Rajeshwari Temple, Konnagar, Houghly, West Bengal, India, www.maabhagwatitripurasundari.org/. Accessed March 5 2023.

"Sunayani Devi". *Indian Culture*, indianculture.gov.in/node/2686647. Accessed March 5 2023.

"Sunayani Devi – forgotten first modern woman artist of Bengal School of Art". *Get Bengal*, February 9 2020, www.getbengal.com/details/sunayani-devi-forgotten-first-modern-woman-artist-of-bengal-school-of-art. Accessed March 5 2023.

Swami Tapasyananda. *Sri Sarada Devi, the Holy Mother, Her Life and Teachings*. Sri Ramakrishna Math, 2020.

Tagore, Rabindranath. *Rabindra Chitravali: Paintings of Rabindranath Tagore*. Edited by R. Siva Kumar. Pratikshan, 2011.

Tagore, Saumyendranath (1960). *Raja Rammohun Roy*. Sahitya Akademi, 1960.

Taylor, Kathleen. *Sir John Woodroffe, Tantra and Bengal, 'An Indian Soul in a European Body?'* London: Routledge Curzon, 2012.

Tejasananda. *A Short Life of Sri Ramakrishna*. Advaita Ashrama, 2019.

Williams, Brandy (1993). "Wiccan Devotionals". Presented to the Parliament of the World's Religions, 1993, brandywilliamsauthor.com/wiccan-devotionals/.

— *Ecstatic Ritual, Practical Sex Magic*. Prism Press, 1990. Immanion Press, 2008.

— *For the Love of the Gods, The History and Modern Practice of Theurgy, Our Pagan Inheritance*. Llewellyn, 2016. Mnemosyne Press, 2022.

Woodroffe, Sir John (1919). *Is India Civilized? Essays on Indian Culture*. Madras: Ganesh and Co. Publishers.

Tejasananda (2017). *A Short Life of Swami Vivekananda*. Kolkata: Advaita Ashrama.

Yogananda (1946). *Autobiography of a Yogi*. Web site: https://www.ananda.org/free-inspiration/books/autobiography-of-a-yogi/.

BOOK TWO:
DURGA PUJA IN KOLKATA

Introduction

Can you name the largest Goddess festival in the world? It isn't a Pagan festival in America or the Day of the Virgin of Guadalupe. It's Durga Puja in Kolkata. Every autumn a city of 14 million people throws an elaborate five-day party in the streets.

I have searched the world for the Goddess, in academic texts, in temple ruins in Egypt and Greece, in library-quiet museums filled with glass cabinets where her statues are held like hostages away from worship. We are told that she is history, past, gone.

In Kolkata the Goddess lives out loud. Durga Puja is anything but quiet. Drummers pound out beloved rhythms and loudspeakers broadcast songs. Her temples are not stone but bamboo, her statues are not stone but clay, a literal epiphany. Goddess emerges through the deliberate evocation of her worshippers. While she resides in the clay she is showered with flowers, plied with food and incense, entertained with dance, offered hymns and chants and songs. In Kolkata at Durga Puja the Goddess is most definitely present.

My husband Alex and I visited Kolkata at Durga Puja in 2019. We were very fortunate to go just before the COVID-19 pandemic shut down travel. When we came home I started researching the background of what we had experienced. I found that there is very little written in English about this festival in Bengal. For that reason alone I thought it would be worth recording our experience and what I've learned about it since.

This travelogue is meant to encourage readers to learn more about India and Durga. Most of all I want to share the joy of traveling to places in the world where the Goddess is central. She isn't a memory of the past or spouse of a god, she is the ultimate power which creates and sustains the universe. Her yearly festival is the most important religious and cultural celebration in West Bengal. This is inspiring for Goddess worshippers, Pagans and Witches, and Tantric practitioners.

In creating this chapter I have had several guides. The first was our contact in West Bengal, a lifelong resident of Kolkata who comes from a Shakta family. His knowledge and connections gave us entry into experiences we could not have navigated on our own. He gave us an insider's look at the history and religious significance of the festival. He spent hours in conversation with us helping us to understand what we were seeing. He hosted us as fellow practitioners, not as researchers, and for that reason I keep his name and his family private.

In post-trip research four authors have provided critical information that has informed my understanding of Durga Puja. June McDaniel documented some of her field work in West Bengal in her book *Offering Flowers, Feeding Skulls: Popular Goddess Worship in West Bengal.* As I travelled I often tripped over the traces of ideas she had followed up.

Hilary Peters Rodrigues chose to study Durga Puja for his doctoral dissertation. He found a Bengali family in Varanasi who allowed him to document their family rituals. They connected him with priests who could translate the chants and texts which he documents in *Ritual Worship of the Great Goddess, The Liturgy of the Durga Puja with Interpretations.* Although Rodrigues worked with a Bengali family in Varanasi his book provided context and detail for the celebrations I observed in Kolkata. His work is especially helpful because of his essential sympathy for the rites. His descriptions of the meaning of the rituals match the comments of my guide in Kolkata, my teacher's lessons, and my own experience.

Tapati Guha-Thakurta's ten-year survey of the festival *In the Name of the Goddess, the Durga Pujas of Contemporary Kolkata* provides the vital connection to the event as it is experienced by the people who make it today. She studies Pujo (as it is called in Kolkata) not only as a religious event but as a public cultural one, as an academic and as a resident of Kolkata who grew up with the festival.

Finally, my encounter with Durga is continually deepened by the work of Laura Amazzone. Her work *Goddess Durga and Sacred Female Power* opens a portal into the liberating power of the Mother Goddess. I find new meaning whenever I re-read it.

In Transit: Prathama, Dwitiya, Tritiya

Her face is everywhere. From the moment we drove into town until the day we returned to the airport her numinous eyes looked out at us from posters, shrines, advertisements. Durga is the one who comes when you call and during her festival she is luminously present. Her gaze enveloped me, drawing me in, calling me home to my heart. The call rang out on every street, "Jai Ma!" Victory to the Mother!

Alex and I arrived on the last frantic days of preparation for the grand yearly celebration of Durga Puja. Navaratri is celebrated all over India but West Bengal takes the holiday to the next level. People flood into Kolkata from all over India to celebrate the largest Goddess festival in the world. The whole city strings up lights and sets up statues on every street corner. Women dress up in brand new saris, vendors serve holiday sweets, crowds of people gape at the elaborate displays. It's like Christmas, if Christmas was about a lion-riding Goddess slaying a buffalo demon.

Navaratri and Durga Puja

Alex and I developed a relationship with a travel agent in America who works with a Kolkata guide. As we jointly planned our itinerary the difference between Navaratri and Durga Puja in Kolkata kept tripping me up. I didn't actually get it until I experienced it.

Navaratri is a fall harvest festival celebrated over nine nights (literally nava, nine and ratri, nights). Our travel agent explained that in Kolkata the celebration of Durga Puja begins on the fifth day of Navaratri. I thought that meant that Durga Puja was just another name for Navaratri, that people were celebrating quietly for the beginning of the holy days and then took the last few days off work to spend with their families. I didn't realize that Kolkata's Pujo has its own distinct rituals and its own story arc about the Goddess.

Navaratri is about the goddess Durga. The tale is told in several texts, notably the Devi Mahatmya or Chandi Path. In this story powerful demons have chased the gods from their homes. They call piteously on Durga to rescue them - she is the only force in the universe who can vanquish the demons. She engages in fierce battles and ultimately triumphs.

Her victory restores order for the gods and for humanity. Although Durga vanquishes many different demons West Bengal focuses on one story in particular, Durga's triumph over the buffalo demon Mahishasur.

Navaratri is both a religious and a cultural occasion. Devotees read chapters in the Chandi Path daily. Each day is associated with a form of the goddess called the NavaDurga or nine Durgas. Each day also has a different color and people wear the color on that day. Dance floors spring up in cities in India where people try out garba dance moves and party with their friends. It is a colorful and exuberant celebration of Goddess energy, Shakti.

Devi Returning

There is another story about the Goddess that is told across India. In this tale Devi decided to take human form. She was born to the king of the Himalayas, Himavan, and the daughter of Mount Meru, Menavati. When Parvati was old enough to marry she undertook a severe practice, chanting without eating or sleeping, for the boon of marrying Shiva. She succeeded. When she married Shiva she left Himavan and Menavati's home and moved to Shiva's home on Mount Kailash. There she became mother to the gods Ganesh and Kartikeya.

Parvati's story layers on top of Durga's story at Navaratri. In India brides often move into their husband's homes, leaving their families and friends to live with virtual strangers. The dislocation is keenly felt. At Navaratri daughters journey back to their paternal homes and bring their children along. In West Bengal Durga is understood to be coming home, bringing her sons Ganesh and Kartikeya with her. Bengalis add the goddesses Lakshmi and Saraswati to the family group as Durga's daughters.

In the weeks and days before navaratri preparations are made to welcome the returning daughter and the returning goddess. Temporary shrines called pandals are set up all around the city to house clay statues of Durga and her children. The Goddess leaves Mount Kailash on Mahalaya, a day which is fixed by priests consulting the lunar calendar, and usually falls six days before Shashti. A recording featuring the beloved singer Birendra Krishna Bhadra has been played on All India Radio continually since 1932 to kick off the holiday season.[1]

Navaratri proper begins on the new moon day, Prathama. Bengalis move statues into the pandals and home shrines on the fifth day, Panchami. On Shashti, the sixth day, she is invoked into the statues in private homes, neighborhood pandals, and major temples. This is the beginning of Pujo. Devi stays through Saptami, Ashtami and Navami and then leaves on Dashami for Mount Kailash while the statues are dissolved in the river. These five days are Kolkata's Durga Puja.

In one sense Devi comes home at Durga Puja. In another sense she has never left. Rodrigues details the rituals which coax her latent presence into active manifestation, in the wood apple tree, in a pot filled with water, in a bundle of plants, in the clay statues, in young girls, and finally in all women. Each manifestation sets up the possibility of darshan. The individual worshiper has an encounter in which deity and person mutually recognize each other.[2]

Alex and I made our own transit to India on the first three days of Navratri. By the time our Kolkata itinerary commenced I was already well into my observance of Navaratri. At night in the hotel I chanted the Chandi Path, plunging into the story of Durga's battles and triumphs. By day on the streets I watched the community evoke Durga tangibly for everyone to see and feel. These two experiences, the private religious and public cultural one, proceeded for me as intertwining tracks.

Preparing for Devi: Chaturthi

On the fourth day of Navaratri, Chaturthi, we plunged into the preparations for the Durga Puja festivities. Our first stop grounded me to the Shakti of India's earth and water.

Flowers for Devi: The Malik Ghat Flower Market

While our driver parked the car our guide led us between buildings down to the river. We stepped out into a postcard scene: a river, a bridge, steps

---

1   "Mahishasura Mardini", Birendra Krishna Bhadra.
2   Rodrigues, *Ritual Worship*, p. 12.

leading down to the water crowded with people taking a bath, a red brick building, women in bright saris sitting on the packed mud stringing flowers. I took in a deep breath and thought, *I'm in India!*

Our guide swept his arm at the vista before us. "The Ganges," he said.

This confused me instantly. The Ganges is the great sacred river of India flowing from the Himalayas down to the Ganges Delta. The river herself is a goddess whose water purifies and consecrates; devout Hindus make pilgrimages to bathe in her waters and tiny vials of Ganges water are sold in puja kits. However the maps called this particular river the Hooghly and it runs into the Bay of Bengal. I learned later that the official name of the river is a colonial relic of the Portuguese incursion. The Ganges shifted in the mid-1700s and turned the arm flowing through Kolkata into a distributary. Even though the water is now channelized to a great extent Kolkata residents still treat this branch as the Ganges - they bathe in it, cremate bodies beside it, and return clay statues to the waters.

The women sitting on the packed earth ground stringing flowers had spilled over from the Malik Flower Market, one of the oldest and largest in India. It's named for the Malik Ghat. A ghat gives access to the river and almost always includes mud or stone steps down to the water. The market and ghat sit beneath the colonial Howrah Bridge (renamed Rabindranath Setu Bridge), the fourth largest cantilever bridge in the world.

Our guide led us to a set of steel stairs descending beneath the bridge. I took in the scene and faltered. Alex and I had prepared for our trip by going to the gym five days a week for a solid year. We made a particular effort to climb the stairs up to the second floor walking track. This turned out to be a completely inadequate preparation. The decorous gym stairs were level, evenly spaced, and had a handrail to the right. I had failed to account for the fact that India's traffic patterns were set by the British who drive on the left hand side of the road; it turns out they walk on the left side too. It didn't matter much that the handrail was on the opposite side than I was used to because I couldn't get to it anyway, the edges of the bridge were lined with bags of bright yellow and orange flower garlands. Picking up my skirt I stepped gingerly down the stairs and managed to make it to the ground level without falling.

What spread before us is one of the largest flower markets in Asia. Devi loves flowers, every shrine and statue is decorated with garlands, and this is where Kolkata goes to get them. Thousands of vendors line the walkway beneath the bridge, working in shifts from early in the morning to well after dinner.[3]

Our guide plunged into the river of people pushing between the flower stalls lining both sides of the walkway. All three of us avidly snapped pictures of the beautiful displays. Women and men sat on the ground amidst huge open bags of colorful blossoms. Porters heaved massive bags of blooms onto their shoulders and trotted away. Beside every woman stringing a garland stood a porter holding the finished strings ready to hurry them off to their customers.

All throughout Durga Puja we would see those garlands everywhere, draped on statues, decorating the pillars of the pandals, hanging from the stalls around the temples. Surrounded by all these colors I couldn't help but wish I could cart an armful home to decorate my own altars.

Making Devi: Potter's Lane

Potter's Lane is where the goddess takes shape.

We piled back into the car and raced off to Kumortuli. Our guide called it Potter's Lane, a literal translation, Kumor – potter, tuli – place. The word lane implies a street but it's really a district incorporating multiple blocks. Brick and concrete houses rise two, three and four stories, all roofed over with bamboo scaffolds and polythene sheets. Larger streets allowed carts to pass but most of the narrow lanes between houses did not permit any wheeled traffic, just pedestrians, making an oasis of calm in a city where cars honk incessantly. The area was so quiet I didn't register its scale until our guide pointed to a house and said, "Hundreds of people live on every block." I looked down the streets counting up blocks and lost my breath for a moment as I registered the psychic weight of so many people around me.

The artisans in this district make the statues that are displayed in private and public shrines all around the city. As we strolled past the hundreds of little workshops a picture of the process slowly came into

---

3   De, "Howrah Mullick Ghat Phool Bazar".

95

focus. First straw is pressed into a wire framework and shaped into the poses of the deities. Clay is slathered onto the straw. When the clay dries the statues are painted, sometimes airbrushed but mostly by hand. Hair, clothing, tinsel and gilt finish the images. Once again the three of us took many pictures. I was trying to document as much of the process as I could.

The last touch is to paint in the eyes of the statues. I saw one artisan do this with great concentration. For the potters this brings the statues to life. This is exactly what happened in antiquity in the great Egyptian and Mesopotamian temples – once the statues of the gods were finished priests would touch their eyes and mouths with special tools to open them to enable them to see, eat, and receive offerings.

Once the statues are complete they have to navigate out from the workshops. In the narrowest of lanes they were lifted up over heads to make their way to the larger walkways. Medium-sized tableaus were lashed onto bamboo poles to be carried on shoulders. The wider alleyways were large enough to accommodate hand-pulled carts. All of these were taken out to the nearest street to be loaded onto trucks and carried to pandals all over the city. As each statue left the workshop a cry would ring out, "Jai Ma!" and everyone on the street would answer, "Jai Ma!"

On the day we toured the district all the big pieces had long ago been finished and installed. A few workshops were hustling to send out the last of the displays ordered by the smaller neighborhood clubs. Most potters had already pivoted to cranking out the statues of Lakshmi for the celebration of Divali that falls just a few weeks after Durga Puja.

Our guide gave us a story that rarely shows up on the tourist web sites: every potter has to obtain a little clay from a sex worker in the red light district near Kumortuli. This clay is taken from the sex worker's doorstep to be mixed into the Durga statues. Our guide said this honors the understanding that everyone is sacred and that prostitutes do important work. He believed that other parts of India don't keep this practice, just Bengal, which has held onto the religion of the mother. Guha-Thakurta notes that the sex workers sell the bags of soil to the potters for a few rupees one month before the pujas.[4]

---

4   Guha-Thakurta, *In the Name of the Goddess*, p. 151.

A neighborhood shrine

In Kumortuli we saw our first shrine to Kali. Tucked in among the potters shops was a little altar. A priest sat cross-legged below a shelf crowded with deity statues. Because it was a shrine I did not take a photograph so I don't have an record to check my memory of the statues. While Alex paused to pay his respects to the goddess I worked to identify the other images on a shelf behind the priest while our guide corrected my identifications. I came away with the certain knowledge that there is a great deal of detail in the localized deities that doesn't make it into the books.

There was a metal object in front of the shrine that I couldn't immediately identify. It gradually dawned on me that this was a sacrifice yoke. West Bengal is Tantric country and Kali eats goats. Actually she receives the goat sacrifice on behalf of the petitioner while the priests eat the goat meat. The presence of this sacrifice area in a public lane signaled the widespread acceptance of the practice.

The artisan's pandal

We finished our tour of Kumortuli at a neighborhood pandal. Our guide told us that art students had constructed this display. A bamboo scaffold wrapped with bright yarn formed a tunnel into a courtyard. The front wall of the pandal itself was an elaborately sculpted art installation.

The courtyard stood directly adjacent to a tree. I was arrested by a bundle of branches strung from the tree trunk through a circular hole in the pandal's front wall. Once inside I saw that the bundle of branches dropped down behind the image of Durga in the tableau. As a yogini I know that trees are important, they sometimes house the spirits called yakshis and yakshas, and village women wrap yarn around trees to honor the spirits. Later I thought that this linkage of tree and statue might also draw on the tradition of the plant bundles called navapatrika which embody the goddess. On an energetic level it seemed clear that the tree was powering the statue.

While most neighborhood pandals stick to the traditional tableau imagery some clubs experiment with new imagery each year. The young artists had produced a distinctive Durga. She was delicate, finely detailed, smiling. Her usual attendants Lakshmi, Saraswati and Kartikeya were joined by Krishna playing on his flute. The image of Mahishasur at her feet was not ferocious or distressed but calm, gesturing upward toward her.

The artistry, the intimate scale, and the connection to the tree charmed me. I predicted to our guide that this would be my favorite pandal. He advised me that this was my first pandal and to wait to make that decision until I had seen more of them. Going back through my photographs my judgement stands: the Durga of the potters spoke to me more than the statues of the aristocratic families or the massive neighborhood displays. It was fresh, young, and heartfelt. And they knew to connect her to the tree.

The potters of potters lane

The tour of Kumortuli left me with a lot of questions. Who were the potters? What is their quality of life? Are there any women potters? Torsa Ghosal, Geir Heierstad and Tapati Guha-Thakurta helped me build an understanding of the history and the lives of the residents.

Kumortuli, the potter's district, lies beside the Hooghly or Ganges river. This facilitates transport of the specific clay used in the statues as well as the water of the river. The district was created during the colonial period when the British East India Company designated geographical districts for specific castes. They marked out a swamp near the river as the live-work neighborhood for the potters caste. Today it's a heritage site and the last caste-based neighborhood in Kolkata.[5]

Before the commercial production of housewares the potters made ordinary clay vessels like the cups still used in streetside tea stalls. The business of the district shifted when wealthy merchant-landowners turned the autumn harvest festival into a competitive entertainment. Then the workshops started turning out clay statues of Durga and her family for the Durga Puja celebrations.

Guha-Thakurta reports that a little over 500 families live in the district. Their cramped quarters and uncertain livelihood has been a concern for decades. The potters formerly depended on money lenders to

---

5   Ghosal, "How Immigrant Sculptors Shaped an Artists' Hub".

fund the workshops but recent unionization of the trade has made bank loans accessible. Even so income remains variable and loan repayment uncertain.[6]

In the early 2000s an urban renewal project proposed to replace the leaky-roof shanties of the district. This involved moving the potters to temporary quarters, demolishing their homes, and building new multi-story structures with apartments above and modern studios below. In the mid-2000s the first phase of the project relocated 170 families into temporary quarters.[7] When the project was suspended by a new government the temporary quarters became semi-permanent. The dislocated families report a sense of loss of connection to the district and in particular to the soil, rain and sun of their open-air workshops.[8]

Being a potter, shaping the body of a deity, is about more than making a living or creating art. Heierstad reports that potters identify their ability to make the statues as hereditary, it's in the blood, and call themselves murtikars, makers of murtis or sacred images.[9]

Sacred statues

The centerpiece of the Durga Puja festival is the statue that sits at the heart of every pandal. The unfired clay statues are called pratima, images which are worthy to manifest the deity. When Durga's presence is called into them they become murti, a physical object carrying the energy of deity. Scholars struggle to find an English term for these images which become a goddess: figure, idol, effigy, statue complex, icon.

For Durga Puja in particular these displays function like a Christmas creche with instantly recognizable images. The earliest form of this image remains popular. Durga is central, surrounded by smaller figures of her children Ganesh, Saraswati, Lakshmi and Kartikeya. She has ten arms with their particular tools. At her feet her lion Simha attacks the demon Mahishasur while she spears the demon's heart.[10]

---

6   Guha-Thakurta, *In the Name of the Goddess*, p. 157.
7   Guha-Thakurta, *In the Name of the Goddess*, p. 159.
8   Mukhopadhyay, "Contesting Spaces of Urban Renewal Project".
9   Heierstad, *Caste, Entrepreneurship and the Illusions of Tradition,* location 265.
10   Guha-Thakurta, *In the Name of the Goddess*, p. 161-163.

The potters use clay shipped along the river from the village Uluberia. They prefer this clay for its workability and for the way it dries without cracking, although efforts have been made to substitute clay from other locations.[11] Recently potters have branched out from clay to using lime plaster and fiberglass.

The gold and silver foil decorations and ornaments for the statues are created in shops surrounding the district. Jute fiber used to create the lion's mane and the hair of the goddess has traditionally been supplied by Muslim women from the Howrah neighborhood, although this traditional craft is being replaced by nylon doll hair.[12]

Durga's changing face

The artistic representation of Durga has shifted in the last century. In the traditional form the eyes of the goddess are elongated, she is painted yellow, and Mahishasur is painted green. When potters made statues for the aristocratic families they tended to portray Durga's features as a white woman, a memsaheb style that appealed to colonial tastes. Gradually the shapes of the statues shifted. Artistic developments in the 1900s introduced realistic human and animal forms, tableaus broken up into individual statues, and ornate decorations of silver foil.

An influx of refugee potters brought a new style into the district. In the 1940s the British government separated Muslim-majority East Bengal from Hindu-majority West Bengal. Hindu potters from East Bengal fled to Kolkata and took up residence in Kumortuli. The immigrants brought a new sensibility, fashioning their Durga as a round-faced Bengali mother.[13]

Ghosal notes that the first potter to get an education at the Government Art College was looked on with suspicion as having an unfair competitive advantage. Our guide identified the pandal we toured in the district as created by art students so this may be changing. Today established artists create elaborate statues for the theme pandals. In the

---

11 Ganguly, "Komortuli artists make idols with soil from Diamond Harbor instead of Uluberia".
12 Guha-Thakurta, *In the Name of the Goddess*, p. 157-158.
13 Ghosal, "How Immigrant Sculptors Shaped an Artists' Hub Called Kumartuli".

workshops of Kumortuli the statue faces are made separately from molds that are kept from year to year as a trademark of the workshop.[14]

Guha-Thakurta comments that every change in the face of the goddess echoes the political and cultural concerns of the time.[15]

Women potters

All the artisans I saw were men and boys. The profession is caste-based and hereditary and sons usually inherit the workshops. However there are women in the profession. Some inherit workshops from their fathers and husbands, others grew up with the trade.

China Pal and Mala Pal felt a strong calling to make the images and took up the profession despite their fathers' opposition. (The potters share the surname Pal). Mala Pal inherited her father's workshop when none of his sons wanted to follow him into the trade. Kakoli Pal turned to making murtis after her husband died to support herself and her children.[16] Other women specialize in making clothing and tinsel for the statues, and at least one woman learned the trade from her mother.[17] The women report that they faced down social opposition from the men around them to follow their profession.

Guha-Thakurta reports that the women potters Kanchi Pal Datta, Bharati Pal and Sandhya Pal were vocal participants in the protests against the relocations, raising concerns about displacing women's families and drawing attention to the invisible and unacknowledged work of women in the family workshops.[18]

Offerings to Devi: Panchami

Music for Devi: Drummers

Durga Puja has a drumbeat.

---

14 Guha-Thakurta, *In the Name of the Goddess*, p. 151.
15 Guha-Thakurta, *In the Name of the Goddess, p* 165.
16 "The Women Artisans of Kumartuli".
17 Sengupta, "The female sculptors of Kumartuli".
18 Guha-Thakurta, *In the Name of the Goddess*, p.159.

On Panchami our guide took us to the loudest street corner in Kolkata. We parked nearby and walked toward the Sealdah Railway Station drawn by the thumping sound. Troupes of men bearing large two-sided drums set up shop along the street and worked through their repertoire of beats. Commuters streaming in and out of the station paused to listen to the sounds while Alex, our guide and I filmed the drummers.

Our guide explained that these performances were a form of advertising. Sealdah Station is the largest in Kolkata. It's fronted by a major street so there's plenty of room and everyone knows where it is. This makes an excellent location for drummers to demonstrate their skill for prospective employers for the home and neighborhood celebrations. In 2019 there were at least 4000 celebrations around Kolkata and music is essential. Live music gets the crowd dancing.

What I noticed at the time was that the drummers, like the potters, were entirely men, and a few had brought young boys with them. The drums were decorated with plumes and I wondered what they signified. I wanted to know where they came from and what their lives were like. Since the trip I've been able to assemble a bit more information about them.

Dhakis, the drummers

Viplob Majumder's documentary *Divine Drums* is not translated into English, but Shoma A. Chatterji provides a translation of some of the comments in *Filming Reality: The Independent Documentary Movement in India*. News sources writing in English on the web also post articles about the drummers during Durga Puja.

The drums are called dhaks and the drummers are called dhakis. They come from no particular caste but it's a hereditary profession, sons play with their fathers and uncles and grow up as drummers. They come from several country districts including Birbhum Province (which was studied by McDaniel and which we toured later in our trip).[19]

Dhakis flow into the city from country districts at Durga Puja and often stay until Kali Puja three weeks later. In this time frame they

19 "Durga Puja: Meet dhakis".

earn almost all the money they will make from their drumming all year. Consequently many have other occupations as construction workers, brick layers and rickshaw pullers. They're strong men. They have to be, the drums are enormous.[20]

Traditionally the drummers have all been men. However all it takes to cross a gender barrier is one man willing to break ranks. For the drummers that man is Gokul Chandra Das, a famous drummer from Machlandapur village. He started with one daughter and daughter-in-law, built up to five women, then twenty-five, and grew to seventy players pre-pandemic. They toured other parts of India before braving the pandals of Kolkata where they were warmly received. They've even traveled to London to perform.[21]

Chatterji reports that the drummers say their way of life is fading.[22] Brass bands and DJs playing recorded music are replacing them, and when dhakis are hired the fees for appearances are meager. Sons don't want to follow their fathers into a low-paid profession. It's not surprising to see women moving into drumming - as with the potters, where sons do not pick up the family business a space is opened for the daughters to do so. Gender-restricted trades with diminishing numbers find their pool of candidates double when the restriction is lifted.

One objection raised to women playing the drum was that the traditional dhak would be too heavy for them to carry. Gokul Chandra Das solved this problem by having drums constructed from fiberglass. This is one of the several innovations that are modernizing the drums themselves.

Dhaks, the drums

Until the new fiberglass drums were commissioned Dhak drums have been constructed from wood in a barrel shape. They're double sided with cow or goat skins stretched across each side to form the drum heads. They hang on a strap which can be slung over one shoulder for one-handed play or around the neck to play with both hands. They can also be placed on the ground and played from above. Smaller versions are

---

20   Chatterji, "The Distant Drummers of Durga Pooja".
21   Goswami, "These women dhakis or drummers".
22   Chatterji, *Filming Reality,* p. 90-91.

played with bare hands, the larger ones are played with a thin wooden striker in each hand.

Chatterji records the comments of several dhakis about their drums. Dinabandhu Das noted that he plays 12 different percussion instruments. He makes the drums along with his son and learned the trade from his father. He hollows out the trunk of mango, neem, and other trees to make the drums. Each wood makes a different sound.[23]

We saw other drum types than the large dhak. A troupe of young men carried drums on their necks with both wood and metal rims. They resembled western style marching drums and were played the same way. Other percussive instruments included rattles, hand-held metal cymbals held by straps, and wood-and-skin tambourines also held by straps.

Dhak drums are often decorated, wrapped with colorful cloth or ridged with ribbons. Some of the drums sport a traditional plume of white feathers and black cow tails which drew my attention at first sight. The tails and drum head skins cause some controversy. Conservative Hindus are vegetarian and object to killing animals. Since each dhak drum represents at least one dead cow or goat there is a protest against their use. I note that the Hindu and Tantric temples of West Bengal sacrifice goats and other animals, and culturally West Bengal consumes meat, so this is a social clash that affects more than just drummers.

The use of feathers on the other hand is specific to the drummers. The white plumes arching over the drums are constructed from stork, heron and egret feathers. It takes three to four birds to collect enough feathers for one drum and each year hundreds of birds are killed for the purpose. These birds are protected by the Indian Wildlife Act so there's a suspicion that the law is being broken. Dhakis protest that they obtain the feathers from a scheduled tribe who have permission to catch the birds. However the feathers are taken to the city and sold in batches so it's impossible to tell whether they were procured legally or not. Forest rangers try to stop poaching but it's difficult to police the entire countryside. Wildlife enthusiasts protest the destruction of wild birds and the threat to the viability of their protected populations. In the past decade there's been a campaign to require pandal organizers not to hire dhakis

23 Chatterji, *Filming Reality,* p. 90-91.

who have the plumes. Police spring spot checks at neighborhood pandals and issue fines to organizers who haven't enforced this.[24]

Videos posted online in the last decade turn up examples of traditional feather-and-cow-tail plumes along with drums decorated with plumes of crinkled tinsel and drums without plumes altogether.

The press accounts of this discussion don't talk about the power of the animals. There's an energy to sacrifice, an energy in skin and tail and feather that is not present in crinkled tinsel. The plumes give off the aura of the countryside and the natural world. I haven't seen a discussion of this but I imagine that this is part of what the drummers will be losing in giving up traditional plumes.

Rituals and dances

Many commentators say the drummers are essential to Durga Puja ritual. The rhythmic patterns are as distinctive as Brazilian samba drums or Voudon drum beats that call specific Orishas. Chatterji reports that dhakis have rhythms for six different moments in Durga Puja, including the moment the statue is lifted onto its platform, the moment Durga is welcomed, and during puja when she is worshipped by day and by night. Chatterji quotes a drummer saying "I cannot give it up as it is a compulsory ritual of worship, is sacred and is our own tribute to the Mother Goddess." Drummers perform for many hours at a time and report falling into a trance while they drum.[25]

The drummers play for an evening ritual in which incense is presented to Durga. The incense is called dhuno, the resin of the sal tree, and is compared to frankincense. The sal tree grows in West Bengal and provides many substances for commercial and subsistence use; management of the sal forests is under review to ensure the sustainability of the practices.[26]

The dhuno resin is burned in a clay pot called a dhunuchi. Dancers wave the burning dhunuchi pots in front of the murtis or clay tableaus. The dance is called the Dhunuchi Naach (or nauch or nautch). An article

---

24 "Dhak minus feather frills" and "Dhak feathers for Durga Puja at the cost of birds".
25 Chatterji, *Filming Reality*, p. 90-91.
26 Shahabuddin, "Ecological sustainability of forest management practices".

in The Statesman notes that it was formerly danced mostly by men but that women increasingly perform it.[27] However the videos I found online almost all feature groups of women performing this dance. The dancers perform to the beat of the dhakis, the drummers circle outside and inside the rings and lines of dhunuchi dancers.

The music is called essential not just because it is needed for ritual but because it is woven into the culture. Bengalis writing about the dhakis say that the drum beats instantly conjure a nostalgia for the sights and scents and emotions of the Durga Puja celebration. They report that the rhythms are maddening and call them to dance.

I celebrate Navaratri as a Tantric practitioner, not Hindu or ethnic Indian, so I experience nostalgia for the drumming differently. For me hearing the beats reminds me of the power I felt in the land, the water, and the people of West Bengal. I'm glad I had the opportunity to feel the drumming in person and build the beat into my experience of Durga Puja.

Food of Devi: Kolay Market

In the Devi Mahatmaya the Goddess promises that when she is needed she will return as Shakumbari, the one who nourishes with vegetables. From Sealdah Railway Station it's just a short walk to Kolay Market, one of the biggest wholesale vegetable markets in the city and the region.

We paused outside the building to watch a group of men heave an enormous bundle onto a truck. It was an impressive coordination of effort. Much of the produce that flows into Kolay Market and back out again is transported by hand.

Our guide led us confidently into the dark interior of the building. Baskets hung in the rafters of the market. On the floor they spilled over with the bright colors of vegetables: purple potatoes, red peppers, yellow onions, green herbs. Along the narrow aisles sellers sat with their wares, buyers looked them over and made purchases, and porters heaved bags onto their shoulders to trot out the door. Many of the photos I took here are blurred as I continually hopped out of the way of the porters who

---

27 "Durga Puja: What is Dhunuchi Naach?" and Jha, *Dhunuchi Dance by Bharti jha*.

zipped past us at a tremendous clip. It occurred to me that this was a hazardous place for a tourist to be.

The market is open 24/7. The sellers are women and men, Hindu and Moslem, casual and commercial. Farmers come in on the railway several days a week to set up in the stalls, while in the interior of the market huge quantities are bought and sold. [28] Our guide told us that many of the contracts are still concluded with a handshake in a trusted network of connection.

The word for a ritual food offering is naivedyam, an essential part of every puja. Fresh and cooked vegetables are presented formally and then distributed to the worshippers. The body of Shakumbari herself is made up of vegetables which she gives to the starving people. Kolay Market may seem like a commonplace commercial center, but here too the Goddess is manifestly visible.

Devi in the Temple: Shashti - Durga Puja Day One

Shashti is the first day of Durga Puja proper. In private rituals priests perform rites to welcome Durga into the physical objects which carry her presence. Our guide chose this day to take us to one of the major temples in India.

Kalighat Temple

The parking lot was jammed at festival time. Our driver let us off at the temple gate and swung away to park the car. For me there was a distinct click as we entered the temple grounds, a place where the energy started. I felt the emotional impact of the Mother slam my heart. My eyes filled with tears. I thought, *this is what we came for.* The experience definitively answered the question, why travel if you can see a photo or a film? Because only through physical presence can you feel the power of the land herself.

I had anxiously prepared for our visits to the temples of India. What was appropriate to wear? I settled on patterned cotton maxi dresses that

---

28 "The wholesale markets of Kolkata" and Mukherjee, "An Appraisal Of Wholesale Marketing In Kolkata"

covered me completely but remained clearly western. Alex wore cotton pants and tunics. As we entered the crowd streaming in and out of the temple grounds it was clear that Alex's garb was closer to what the men wore. I on the other hand fell far short of the women's finery. I gaped at the brilliant saris adorning every woman from oldest grandmother to smallest child. Later I learned that every woman wears a new sari at Durga Puja, and the wealthiest women change saris several times a day during the festival.

The temple is surrounded by a kind of sacred market, lanes crowded with little stalls selling items to offer to the goddess and souvenirs to take home. I had read that this is where visitors leave their shoes to enter the temple with bare feet. I'd fretted about this, how would that work?

Our guide threaded the throng and led us directly to a little shop that was already prepared for our arrival. The proprietress perched in the window and waved us in. Our guide parked us on a bench at the back of the shop so we could take off our shoes and sit while we waited. He went off to fetch a priest while we watched the shopkeeper hand down marigold garlands to her customers.

When our guide returned we stepped onto the temple grounds in bare feet. I'd worried about this too. Would the ground be dirty, or hot? It turned out the temple grounds were kept clean and were mostly tiled so they were cool and smooth. As we walked I started chanting a Kali mantra. Alex and our guide chanted too.

The priest led our guide, Alex and me past the long lines waiting to see the goddess and slotted us into the premium line. People kept pushing past us and trying to go with us while the priests shoved us and asked us for more money. When we reached the inner temple we gave our flowers to one of the priests. He put my hand on an aarti lamp. Alex and I tried to see the statue's eyes but didn't have the time to connect, we had only a few seconds before we were pulled out of line to make room for the next pilgrim. Later we learned that there was a place in the temple where it is possible to stand and look at the statue in a more leisurely way. That would probably have been crowded too but I would have liked to try for Alex's sake. At seventy and hard of hearing, being shoved and shouted at while he tried to make a connection was deeply unsettling to him.

The priest quickly left us. Our guide spent a few minutes touring us around the temple grounds. The first stop was a Shiva lingam shrine. Our guide said a Shiva lingam is necessary in a Kali temple, but the actual Bhairava who is paired with this Kali is in another location. Later I learned that the Bhairava for Kalighat is Nakuleshwar whose small temple is near Kalighat and is much less well visited.[29]

Our guide also showed us a little Radha-Krishna shrine. Although there is tension between Vaisnavites and Shaktas, in West Bengal and Assam we saw Krishna's shrines sitting companionably in several of Shakti temples, and Krishna imagery was included in some of the pandals. After our tour of the grounds we did a little shopping and found a statue of Durga spearing the demon Mahishasur which is installed on our house altar.

On our way out of the temple grounds we passed a tree hung with ribbons. Tree is one the very oldest forms of the Goddess. I would have liked to stop there to spend some time with them but our guide quick-marched us back to the car. He and our driver were both eager to get out of the festival crowds.

A Kali in every neighborhood

At a less crowded neighborhood the driver let us off on the street and parked the car. On our way to the next temple our guide stopped at a tea stall. He ordered a chai for each of us and we sipped it standing in the street. The tea came in little cups called bhar which are made by the city's potters from Ganges clay. We threw them into a large trash can where they broke into pieces. Later they would be tipped into the river to return the clay to its source. Kolkatans are proud of this tradition which has elsewhere been replaced by the use of plastic which can't be thrown back into the river.

Our destination was another Kali temple. I suspect our guide had planned the day's itinerary knowing that Kali Ghat's commercial atmosphere would hamper our devotional. This little street temple lacked the crowds of the Shakti pith and was frequented mostly by people in the

---

29 Avishek, "Nakuleshwar Bhairav Temple, Kolkata – The eternal guard of Kalighat".

neighborhood. Like many temples in West Bengal it had an iron yoke where goats could be sacrificed. The head of the goat is offered to the goddess, the body of the goat is eaten. Our guide told us that this temple is where Ramakrishna would send Vivekananda to get goat meat from the sacrifices. Later I learned that Ramakrishna's meat eating scandalizes his contemporary vegetarian followers.

We left our shoes and all our belongings in the car as we stepped into the street. Our guide bought flowers and gave them to the priest. He turned to us quickly and said "Do you have diksha names?" We told him. The priest offered us his blessing.

Only one woman stood in front of the statue of the goddess. Alex stepped up to stand next to her. There in the peace of the shrine he was able to spend as much time as he wanted, looking into the eyes of Devi, touching his forehead to the railing. I was deeply grateful to our guide for arranging this stop where Alex could have the experience he had longed for. Later he told me she said to him, *not yet*. It was not time for him to make his sacrifice. She was leaving his life in place for now, but one day he knows she will come for him.

Kali the Mother

West Bengal has been called the land of Kali. While the rest of India celebrates Diwali a few weeks after Durga Puja, West Bengal celebrates Kali Puja. We visited four major temples and numerous smaller shrines to Kali in our fortnight in the province.

Alex came to Kolkata to experience Kali and I came to experience Durga. There's no contradiction in this, Kali and Durga are aspects of the Goddess. Hindu goddesses don't slot into neat functional categories like the Pagan goddesses of the west where, for example, austere Athena is distinct from earthy Demeter. In the stories about Durga's battles with the demons she brings other goddesses out from herself. They spring forth in sets, seven mothers, nine Durgas, ten Mahavidyas. In one of the stories Durga brings forth Kali. In another story Shiva's wife Parvati becomes enraged and turns into Kali, dancing to destroy the world until Shiva throws himself under her feet to stop her. Kali and Durga both hold the power to destroy and create.

Kalighat is a Shakti pith or goddess seat. Among the millions of temples in India only fifty-one earn the designation (although there are several variations of the list). Each Shakti pith is the temple of a local goddess, Kamakhya, Varahi, Lalita, Ambika, Durga. They are brought into relationship through the story of Sati, Shiva's first wife whose body was cut into pieces and scattered across India. Each Shakti Pith identifies the piece of Sati's body it enshrines; Kali Ghat has her right big toe. The temples vibrate with the power of the earth and the energy of centuries of devotion.

Devi in the Palaces: Saptami - Durga Puja Day Two

Devi's Plants: Navapatrika

Devi manifests in plants.

We were up early on Saptami. Our driver let us off among busloads of people heading to the river. Women in saris and men in dhotis carted armloads of plants, pots and puja materials down to the river. It was a good spot for this ritual as the river bank sloped from the street down to the water's edge. Groups would come to do their ritual and then leave again to be replaced by others. Half a dozen families were on the river at any given time.

The three of us set about taking still pictures and film. Alex and I have more shots of this ritual than any other place we went, we spent at least two hours watching and filming. It struck us as an extraordinary opportunity to witness and document something that we had heard nothing about. We were far from the only photographers though, every little group was surrounded by people with cell phones and large cameras madly clicking away, some family, some not. No one seemed to mind.

It was very festive. The ritual took a while so people settled in to spend time. Some families brought dhakis with them pounding out the beats. Women made a ululation which echoed up and down the river. Families jumped into the river while the rite was going on, women and men and children immersing themselves in the water, diving and splashing.

Meanwhile the serious puja commenced. A priest set up a puja tray. Family members held the navapatrika, nava – nine, patrika – plants. These plants had already been lashed together before they arrived at the river. The large waving leaves of the banana plant topped the bundle. Sometimes the men of the family held the bundle. My favorite family had half a dozen women surrounding their priest.

The priest said prayers, made mudras or hand gestures, and offered ritual items to the navapatrika, including flowers, rice, and incense. This made something of a mess but the priests brought plastic bags and neatly swept up these items at the end. Some families also brought a clay pot or kalash, some decorated, most not. These had also been prepared with leaves poking out of the mouth of the pot.

Next the priest and the family carried the navapatrika, and the pot if they had one, down to the river. Whoever was carrying the navapatrika walked straight into the river to immerse the bundle in the water. The pot was carried into the water as well.

When everyone emerged from the water the navapatrika was wrapped in a new sari. Various web sites say that the sari should be white edged with red and we saw some of these, but we also saw cloth with bright red and yellow patterns. The newly wrapped bundle was brought back to the puja tray on the river bank for additional worship.

During the rite people anointed themselves as well. One of my film clips captured a priest dipping his hand in the water and making a complex series of gestures. The family of women I followed took a plate of some substance and wiped it on each other's faces.

At the end the family would pack up their materials and cart off the navapatrika and kalash, trailing their dhakis with them.

My five minutes of fame

After we'd been there for some time our guide approached me diffidently to point out a camera crew. They had observed the three of us shrewdly and detected that he was guiding us. They had asked to interview me. I consented.

The interviewer was a young man in white shirt and trousers. He smiled and said, "It's primitive isn't it?" I said immediately, "Oh no, it's wonderful! It's about the harvest and about honoring Ma." He brightened. He spent a few minutes asking me questions and getting my answers. He said "This is the kolabau, the banana bride. She is the bride of Lord Ganesh." As a Tantric and educated westerner I knew the navapatrika as a form of Durga and part of the Navaratri ritual, but I did not presume to correct his own cultural experience.

Satisfied, he set me up where he wanted to film me and told me to stand by for the camera. While we were waiting he said, "You're about to go live." I said, "Okay." He said, "Everything you do will be seen. Worldwide." It was a nice warning and a little intimidating. As it happens I have been a public Pagan for several decades and have been trained to look at the camera and speak clearly.

When we went live the interviewer gave an intro to the camera and then repeated his questions. I put my hands on my heart and talked earnestly about how wonderful it was to see women honoring Devi and how we all feel her in our heart. "Oh, there goes one now," he said as a navapatrika passed by heading up the street. I said, "Jai Ma!" He asked how I'd been treated in Kolkata and I said, truthfully, that everyone had been warm and welcoming. He asked me if I had anything to add and I said "West Bengal tourism!" which made him laugh. At the end he said "And the banana plant is the wife of?" I chirped, "Lord Ganesh!" He smiled and gave his sendoff to the camera.

After the interview he thanked me politely. Our guide reconnected with me. "The wife of Lord Ganesh?" I said. He winced. "I don't know where it comes from," he said.

I have spoken live on camera to small audiences. This is the only occasion in my life so far where I have been seen worldwide, as a snippet of local color during Durga Puja. Later I searched online to see if there was a recording but didn't find anything. Alex filmed the interview so I do have a record of it although our conversation is mostly drowned out by drums.

The navapatrika ritual

Our guide explained that the navapatrika is a form of Durga. When I asked him what the nine plants were he referred me to Madhu Khanna's written work. He didn't have the reference but Laura Amazzone has since kindly pointed me to the paper "The Ritual Capsule of Durga, An Ecological Perspective". Khanna not only identifies the plants but also nine aspects of Durga that each represents. The appendix "Navapatrika" includes several lists of plants and their associated devis.

How can a bundle of plants represent the goddess? The navapatrika strikes many as a very old recognition of Durga as the life of plants. It seems to come from the tribal villages in the forest in pre-Vedic times. The TV host who interviewed me called the ritual primitive and laughed apologetically. I surmise that it's a bit embarrassing to see plant worship in the midst of a modern metropolis.

Whatever its origins, the navapatrika ritual has been incorporated into the fall Navaratri rituals. Rodrigues details the rituals of Bengali families living in Varanasi and describes the worship of the navapatrika on Saptami. The purohita bathes each of the nine plants in nine waters and invokes a different form of the goddess into each of the plants.[30] Rodrigues and the *New Age Purohit Darpan* manual both specify that when the navapatrika has been bathed it should be placed on the right side of Ganesh on the clay tableau. We saw several examples of this in the family homes and pandals.

The rite Rodrigues observed in Varanasi is performed in the family home. This is different from the ritual which I saw in Kolkata where the navapatrika was dunked directly in the Ganges. Writing about his own family puja, Dhruba Chaudhury says that the men of his family carry the navapatrika to the river early in the morning, bringing along several priests. It is possible that the indoor rite Rodrigues documented is also performed in Kolkata. I wonder if some Bengali families in Varanasi carry their navapatrikas down to the Ganges.

At least some of the neighborhood associations participate in this ritual. I found a video by Arjun Dey made October 9 2019, the same day I saw the ritual, though he filmed at different locations. He followed priests to a public pandal where they installed the navapatrika beside Ganesh in their tableau (time stamp 3:08 in the video).[31]

---

30 Rodrigues, Ritual Worship, p. 47-56
31 Dey, *Maha Saptamir.*

Kola Bou, the banana bride

It caught me by surprise when the TV interviewer called the navapatrika the wife of Ganesh since Ganesh is widely held to be Durga's son, not her husband. Why is the navapatrika identified as the wife of Ganesh? Rodrigues notes that his educated informant called this ignorant and my guide called it incorrect. Priests conducting the ritual know the navapatrika as a form of Durga.

However, Rodrigues says that most people he talked to were positive the navapatrika is the banana bride of Ganesh. They often are not aware that there are nine plants in the collection, they just see a banana tree wrapped with a sari that looks like a bride. There are also groups of women from neighborhood pandal clubs who conduct the ritual without a priest present. It would be interesting to interview one of these groups to learn whether they view the navapatrika as the kola bou.

The sari makes the navapatrika seem like a bride, but why the bride of Ganesh? Possibly because it's placed beside Ganesh in the tableau. Rodrigues says the idea makes sense to him as a connection through the spirits of the forest. Pre-Vedic village religion recognized the spirits of the wild areas as yakshas and yakshis. Ganesh emerged as a yaksha. So if the plant bundle is a bride, and is placed next to Ganesh, the navapatrika must be the kola bou, Ganesh's banana bride.[32]

A web search on "navapatrika" brings up a few references to the plants themselves, while a search on "kola bou" will bring up pages and videos describing the navapatrika immersions as part of the Durga Puja rites.

The palaces of Kolkata

Our guide told us that Kolkata is the city of palaces. On Saptami we toured the Bonedi Bari houses where Durga Puja has been celebrated for centuries. They were rightly called palaces, magnificent, opulent, and superbly decorated for the festival.

This tour was an extraordinary opportunity for westerners. Tour buses move between the neighborhood pandals but we wouldn't have been able to navigate the heritage houses on our own. They're hard even

---

32 Rodrigues, *Ritual Worship*, p. 147-148.

for native Kolkatans to find; Amitabha Gupta compiled a guide to more than forty heritage houses to help people locate them.[33] Our guide drew on his connections and his knowledge of the town to pick the oldest and grandest pujas for us to see.

The first home we visited lifted two stories above the street. The public streamed through massive open doors into an open-air courtyard wrapped with hallways, stone pillars and latticework. At the end of the courtyard massive stone steps led up to a marble floor. This is where the clay statue of Durga and her entourage had been set up. All the figures were buried in flower garlands; piles of food and flowers and coins spread on the floor around them.

The house was cool and welcoming. A fabric canopy shielded the courtyard, chairs were dotted around for people to rest, and an amplified chant filled the air. People held up their cell phones to take pictures and videos.

Alex and I wanted to get closer to the statue but we eyed the marble stairs dubiously. "They're wet," Alex said. He was walking with a cane and didn't want to risk a fall. I was slightly steadier on my feet and decided to brave it even without a handrail. I stepped very carefully on my way up and back. I was rewarded with a better view of the statues. The navapatrika, wrapped in an all-red sari, stood prominently on the platform looking very much like a person.

On our way out I spotted a kalash with a bilva tree branch at the base of one of the pillars. It had been smeared with a red design which wasn't clear but had probably started out as a sun symbol (swastika).

I didn't capture the name of the first house we visited. Fortunately the second house featured a plaque explaining that this was the Ramdulal Nibas where Durga Puja has been celebrated for more than 200 years. Here the statue was locked behind a metal grate so visitors couldn't walk up to it as we had at the first house. It featured a large Durga surrounded by smaller figures of Ganesh, Saraswati and Lakshmi, all of them virtually buried under mountains of flowers.

This house is where a bug finally caught up with me. Travel is inherently dangerous, and travel in the tropics is particularly hazardous for pampered westerners. I have friends who have come home from Egypt

---

33 Gupta, "Durga Puja of 'Bonedi' Families at Kolkata".

and India with illnesses they couldn't shake for years. Alex and I did our best to stay healthy. We took anti-malaria pills, drank bottled water, ate at the hotel or at restaurants vetted by our guide, and never consumed anything but cooked food. All of us, Alex, me, our guide and our driver religiously sanitized our hands every time we got in and out of the car. Even so we were moving in very crowded spaces and my number eventually came up. I wanted to go on with my day but when the nausea hit I was worried I was going to be sick in one of those beautiful courtyards. I decided it would be prudent to retreat to the hotel.

The hotel was a palace in itself. The Oberoi Grand is a five-star hotel with marble floors, a massive lobby chandelier, and the most attentive staff I have ever experienced. As I walked through the doors the manager fell in step with me with immediate concern. He and our guide chatted every morning and he had seen us go out early to catch the navapatrika immersion. Since I was coming back alone mid-morning something was clearly amiss. I confessed my queasiness. He promised to send something immediately. Before the hour was out he had sent up a lime Perrier on a tray. Meanwhile our guide called the hotel pharmacist and had an electrolyte packet delivered as well.

Since I had to cut the day short I asked Alex to continue the tour. Our guide took him to another three houses. Alex reported that he had participated in a puja in one of the houses, the priest had sprinkled everyone there with water and waved incense over them.

That night we had a room service dinner. The hotel is used to travelers with stomach upsets and recommended a soothing gruel and plain bread for me. Whatever ailed me subsided by the next morning. I was fortunate. Dengue fever swept through the pandals that year, and six months later the COVID-19 pandemic took over the world. Modern medicine, meticulous attention to sanitation, and the caring concern of our in-country hosts brought me through a month of travel with only half a day of illness.

Landowners and Merchants

The houses we toured are today called heritage houses. They were built in an era when money flowed into the city. The colonial government exerted control through English speaking administrators as well as landowners and merchants whose interests aligned with the British.

Rodrigues thinks that the first Durga Puja in West Bengal was probably celebrated in the early 1600s as a protest against Mughal (Moslem) rule. It continued quietly for a century and a half. When the British overthrew the Mughal dynasties one wealthy landowning family threw a lavish public display in celebration and the party took off.[34]

In colonial times the zamindars, landowners, opened their houses to the public to share their Durga Puja celebrations in a display of civic pride and family status. The idea spread to the caste families of merchants and British East India Company bureaucrats. They vied with each other for the most lavish displays to attract customers and impress colonial officials. Today these are described as Bonedi Bari, aristocratic house pujas.[35]

The fortunes of the landowning and merchant families declined sharply with the withdrawal of the British East India Company after Indian independence. Many of the mansions are in disrepair and there are fewer displays in private homes. Post-independence the patronage of the festival has shifted to corporate sponsorship of pandals open to the public.[36]

Devi in the Home: Ashtami, Durga Puja Day Three

On Ashtami Durga is celebrated at home.

Sandhi Puja is held all over Kolkata. The timing is particular. In 2019 the eighth day Ashtami changed to the ninth day Navami in the middle of the morning. The days of Navaratri are calculated by a lunar calendar. The change between one day and another can happen at any time during the solar day. The ritual of Sandhi Puja is performed in a 48 minute period spanning the end of Ashtami and the beginning of Navami. For Bengali families this marks the time that Durga in her aspect as Chandi slays the buffalo demon Mahishasur.[37]

---

34   Rodrigues, *Ritual Worship*, p. 19-21.
35   Ghose, "Spaces of Recognition", p. 296-297.
36   Guha-Thakurta, *In the Name of the Goddess*, p. 32.
37   Rodrigues, *Ritual Worship*, p. 59

Alex and I were invited into a home for a private ritual. Thus far we had toured the pandals and the houses as a traveler, an outsider, but this home visit brought us into Durga Puja as active participants. We were humbled and grateful for the opportunity. We were also trusted to keep the ritual private, so we do.

However there are public accounts. Rodrigues details the elaborate Sandhi Puja performed in Varanasi by the purohita on behalf of the family. This ritual traditionally includes animal sacrifice, although in conservative Varanasi that custom is fading among Bengali families. The sacrificed goats are made into goat curry.

For the Kolkata version the Ramakrishna Mission posted the video "Sandhi Puja 2019 at Belur Math" documenting the ritual the priests performed publicly at that moment. Listening to the chanting on the video recreates for me the feeling of that moment.

Kumari Puja

Kumari Puja is the ritual worship of Durga in a living human. A pre-pubescent girl is dressed as the young goddess Kumari and worshipped with flowers and offerings. Rodrigues reports that Ashtami is also the traditional day to perform Kumari Puja. However, because this day is so filled with rituals, it often moves to Navami, day nine. He notes that one of the families he studied actually performed the ritual on three successive days to include a large number of girls.[38]

I've seen Kumari Puja performed but not in Kolkata and not on Ashtami. When Durga Puja ended in Kolkata Alex and I toured Birbhum Province where we ran into Durga Puja festivities. In the countryside the rituals are sometimes delayed as villagers pour into the city to work during the festival, then come home to their own postponed holiday. We saw a kumari puja at Kankalitala Temple three days after Dashami. Several priests faced a row of little girls decked out in red-and-gold finery while their mothers fussed at their dresses and their fathers held up their cell phones to record the event.

Alex and I also saw a Kumari Puja at the Hindu Temple and Cultural Center in Bothell, Washington in 2018 when we visited at Navami. A

---

38 Rodrigues, *Ritual Worship*, p. 219.

row of little girls was lined up on the floor in front of a statue of Durga while women placed foil-wrapped packets in front of them. There the activity seemed to have shifted from the priests, who were quite busy with Navami activities, to the women of the community.

The travel blogger Mariellen Ward witnessed a private kumari puja in Kolkata on Ashtami in 2019. She was invited by fellow travel blogger Ayandrali Dutta to participate in the Dutta family rituals which they have been performing for more than 165 years. Ward filmed one of the women of the house describing the ritual in English while the little kumari fidgeted, the film is embedded in her post. Ward reports that the women of the family performed the ritual and describes it as woman-centered.[39]

Kumari Puja is associated with Navaratri and Durga Puja but it can be performed at any time of the year. Ira Trivedi also reported participating in a Kumari Puja when she visited Kamakhya Temple outside the festival seasons. She describes the ritual in a bit more detail. She was invited by a "loin-clothed man" to participate in a puja which would guarantee her marriage and the birth of a "rajkumar", a princely son. The man produced a ten-year-old girl in a school uniform. Trivedi was instructed to wash the girl's feet with water poured from a bowl representing the yoni of the goddess. She made a border around the girl's feet with red dye representing blood, and poured flowers and rice and water over her feet while chanting mantras. She says "After a quick ten minutes, my man gives the girl ☒50 and she goes scampering away to school."[40]

Rodrigues notes that throughout the Durga Puja rituals the priests invoke Durga into.

- themselves;
- objects including a pot, mirror, and sword;
- the navapatrika;
- the clay statues of Durga;
- a little girl.

The Kumari Puja brings the worshipper face to face with the goddess in a living human form.

---

39 Ward, "About Durga Puja in Kolkata: A complete guide".
40 Trivedi, *India in Love*, p. 14.

Devi on the Street: Navami - Durga Puja Day Four

On Durga Puja Devi lives in the streets.

There are two distinct types of pandals: neighborhood displays which house traditional images and provide pujas for local families, and massive theme pandals with corporate sponsorship making artistic and political statements.

We viewed a number of pandals throughout the festival. We'd pass a pandal on our way somewhere and our driver would drop us off so we could walk through it while he drove around the block. The crowds come out at night and traffic becomes impossible to navigate so we did almost all our visits during the day.

Some of the pandals we passed barely had room for the statues. Others were multi-room complexes where a series of halls led to the room which held the statues. Usually that's where the pandal ended, but one that we toured included a ramp that let us walk behind the statues to admire them in three dimensions. There were paintings on the walls, art objects hanging from the ceilings, and music piped through speakers. Each pandal cast a different ambiance. It was like walking into an enchanted world.

Durga is the focus but the pandals incorporate many other images and religious themes. One pandal had images of the matrikas, little mothers, on the walls. Another featured stories from the life of Krishna. In another a glowing golden Durga stood serenely atop a sturdy Mahishasur which did not menace her but instead supported her. I responded to this as a powerful image, a re-imagining of Mahishasur's role in the story.

Neighborhood pandals

The public celebration of Durga Puja developed out of the landowner and merchant house displays. In the eighteenth century a group of Brahmin elders were prevented from attending one of the Bonedi Bari Pujas. They formed the first Barowari Puja specifically meant to include people who had not been welcomed at the house pujas. In the twentieth century the nationalist movement developed a new identity for the neighborhood puja, the Sarbojanin Pujo open to everyone.[41]

These neighborhood pandals serve the local families where rituals are conducted by priests. Alex and I saw navapatrikas in pandals and heard a Sandhi Puja ritual broadcast outside our guide's house. The priests of these associations seemed to be conducting the same rituals that Rodrigues describes in the aristocratic homes.

Durga Puja is the major festival of the year much as Christmas is the major festival in America. Kolkata residents and emigrants reminisce about their hometown memories: helping to build the pandals, eating the special holiday foods, spending a whole day catching up with relatives and friends, shopping for gifts, wearing new clothes.[42]

Guha-Thakurta describes her childhood experience of Durga Puja. She grew up in a new neighborhood of Kolkata, New Alipore, where a Sarbojanin Puja was held in a local park. Her grandmother and her friends treated this as their own personal puja, cutting up fruits and vegetables and preparing the ritual food (bhog) to be handed out to visitors. She watched her uncle perform in puja theater and dance with his friends. Meanwhile she spent time with her cousins showing off their new-clothing finery.[43]

Durga Puja also resembles Christmas in its increasing commercialization and emphasis on consumption. The custom of having new clothes for the festival has evolved into having a new sari for each of the five days, and in wealthy families, new saris every morning and evening of the five days. Families trade presents and Durga's face smiles from posters advertising Durga Puja sales.[44]

This lavish spending on display and gifting comes under some criticism as people long for the simpler family experiences of the past. However Guha-Thakurta points out that Durga Puja has focused on the ostentatious display of wealth dating back to the original zamindar and

---

41 Guha-Thakurta, *In the Name of the Goddess*, p. 91-93.
42 Ward, "About Durga Puja in Kolkata"; Chaudhuri, "Outlook Traveller asks eminent personalities from Bengal about their favourite Pujo memories"; Sinjana, "Kolkata's Durga Puja – A Complete Guide" and "Durga Puja in Kolkata - 5 Reasons why it is Unique".
43 Guha-Thakurta, *In the Name of the Goddess*, p. 99.
44 Guha-Thakurta, *In the Name of the Goddess*, p. 45.

merchant families. [45] Another way in which Durga Puja and Christmas resemble each other is that each sparks nostalgia for the perfect holiday which exists primarily in our desire for it.

Theme pandals

Durga Puja is a religious and cultural festival, but it is also one of the world's largest open air art festivals. The whole city turns out to go pandal hopping - as many as 10 million people crowd the streets every night. [46]

In the 2000s theme pandals emerged. They are sponsored by corporations who donate the thousands of rupees necessary to construct the elaborate buildings. While there is concern that these have stepped on the homely neighborhood pandals, Guha-Thakurta argues that they layer on top of the smaller neighborhood pandals and add to the public extravaganza. [47]

Another layer of the pandal experience is the contest. Puja committees register on contest sites and compete for prizes sponsored by businesses and corporations. Each contest has numerous categories – best Bonedi Bari pandal, best neighborhood pandal, most visited pandal. The planning committees for the large corporate sponsored theme pandals train their members to give interviews to the press and even create theme saris for their teams of volunteers.[48]

Corporate sponsorship of theme pandals is all about attracting crowds. These gigantic displays arch over streets and blaze with electric lights while blasting music into the street. The massive statues at their heart are created on site and can take months to complete.[49]

Corporate sponsored pandals can be huge and semi-permanent, erecting replicas of temples, palaces, opera houses, caves, villages. They can create fanciful shapes like the sphinx or Hogwarts. In addition to faithful replicas of existing buildings, artists materialize their visions of houses and temples and other worlds. They are built not only of bamboo

45 Guha-Thakurta, *In the Name of the Goddess*, p. 91.
46 Guha-Thakurta, *In the Name of the Goddess*, p. 66.
47 Guha-Thakurta, *In the Name of the Goddess*, p. 32.
48 Guha-Thakurta, *In the Name of the Goddess*, p. 39.
49 Guha-Thakurta, *In the Name of the Goddess*, p. 102.

and clay but plaster, plywood and terra cotta. They compete to attract the greatest number of the visitors who flood the streets.

Guha-Thakurta reports that in the early 2000s a counter-esthetic emerged valuing smallness and natural materials. Pandal designers squeezed into tiny spaces decorating the surrounding house fronts as part of the display. Small areas allowed artists to explore individual styles. Artists working in these spaces sometimes created the statues first and then designed the pandal around it. The emphasis on natural materials also aligned with new fire and environmental regulations. [50]

Some pandals make decidedly political statements. Alex and I saw one of the most controversial. The Beliaghata 33 Pally Durga Puja wanted to portray Hinduism, Christianity and Islam in harmony. The pandal included hundreds of small models of churches and mosques and synagogues hung from the ceiling, while hands projecting from the walls held symbols of the three religions. The spark for controversy was the sound piped into the pandal which was meant to represent all three religions. Some thought they heard the azaan, the Moslem call to prayer, in the soundscape and were offended to hear this in a pandal dedicated to Durga. They made complaints but the civil authorities declined to intervene.[51]

In 2020 the Barisha Club pandal was reported to have a portrayal of Durga as a refugee woman, with Lakshmi and Saraswati as her small daughters and Ganesh and Kartikeya as her sons. [52] This drew attention to the pandemic transportation shutdown which stranded many migrant workers who were forced to walk hundreds of miles to return to their homes.[53]

Images can be playful and political. One idol maker modeled his Mahishasur to resemble a controversial cricket team coach, others shaped the face of Osama Bin Laden onto the demon.[54] In 1944, two

---

50 Guha-Thakurta, *In the Name of the Goddess*, p. 203.
51 "Kolkata: 'Secular' Durga Puja pandal leads to social media outrage".
52 "A Durga puja pandal showcases women migrant workers in place of the goddess".
53 Biswas, "Coronavirus: India's pandemic lockdown turns into a human tragedy".
54 Guha-Thakurta, *In the Name of the Goddess*, p. 86.

years before independence, a village pandal featured a British general being mauled by Durga's lion.[55]

The neighborhood puja with a traditional statue is created as a collective effort of potters, pandal makers, food preparers, and local family entertainers. In contrast the theme pandals facilitated the development of individual puja artists, some with art college degrees, others working in the neighborhood traditions who developed a broader reputation. In the 2000s these tended to be men, although women artists with established reputations have been able to break into this field.[56]

Holiday lights

One evening our guide kept us out after dark so we could experience some of the colorful lights that festoon the city. They decorate shop fronts, hang over the streets, and light up the brilliantly painted pandals. It's clearly a festive and special time of year.

In our younger days we would have spent at least one night pandal-hopping along with the rest of the city. As older folk we were happy to tour the pandals by day and return to our hotel at night. This allowed our driver to get home before the holiday traffic made driving impossible. It also allowed him to take his kids out to the pandals to build their own Durga Puja experiences.

Devi Departing: Dashami - Durga Puja Day Five

The day after Navaratri is the tenth of the lunar period. In Bengal's celebration it is the fifth day of Durga Puja. This is the end of both Navaratri and Durga Puja, the day in which the goddess leaves.

On Dashami many of the statues are hauled with great cheer down to the river where they are thrown into the water. In a city of 14 million people there are thousands of neighborhood shrines so this process goes on all day and into the night. It's the end of the story, the goddess has vanquished the demons which plague humanity and dissolves in the triumph of her victory.

---

55 Guha-Thakurta, *In the Name of the Goddess*, p. 97.
56 Guha-Thakurta, *In the Name of the Goddess*, p. 207-208.

Immersion

On Dashami our guide picked us up early. He was on edge all day trying to make the timings work.

Our first stop was at one of the Bonedi Bari houses. He said it was the first house in Kolkata that held a Durga Puja in the 1750s. The Chaudhury family makes that claim but I am not certain that this was the house we visited. Our guide explained that this is also the first house that sends its tableau to the river. When we arrived at the house and found the idol was still present he relaxed.

The statue had been taken to the courtyard across the street from the house. The lane was filled with people who crowded around to watch the festivities. Dhakis drummed while a man, presumably either the priest or the family head, removed tools from the hands of Durga and replaced them with foil versions. He also replaced her headpiece and fixed a paper arch behind the statue. When he was done the dhakis stopped drumming. A woman of the house then stepped up to smear food on Durga's mouth. Every statue of Durga we saw that day had food on her lips.

A group of men dressed in white sleeveless shirts took over the process. Our guide explained that they came from families who had been providing this service to the aristocrats since before independence and that they still held to the custom. They tied the tableau to two large bamboo poles and carefully lifted it onto their shoulders.

Our guide moved us down the street to an open area where we could see the procession and take pictures. At the moment the statue set off a bunch of balloons were released into the air. The balloons have replaced the custom of releasing birds at that moment.

We saw the paper arch of the image coming around the corner. The procession was now accompanied by a marching brass band. The porters moved down the street at a smart clip, hand-carrying the statue to the river. Our guide told us that this is the way the statues were moved before powered transport and the traditional family still did it the traditional way.

Next we drove down to the river ourselves. Many of the roads were closed by police to make way for the processions and the surrounding roads were clogged with people. The driving was so difficult even our unflappable guide commented "dangerous!" Our driver made some deft moves and got us within blocks of the water.

Our guide found us a position on the road overlooking one of the ghats where the statues are returned to the river. Here they came, the statues from the pandals, loaded onto trucks for transport to the river. The trucks would stop and men would offload the statues to carry them down by hand. Some of them would stop and turn the statue around and around, then continue to process down to the water.

One particularly large statue showed up with its own brass band. There were so many people around us it was difficult to move and it looked like the procession might mow us down. Then the band planted itself right in front of us. They were so close Alex couldn't lift his hands to take pictures but I appreciated the protection.

Our guide found us there trapped behind the band. He shared my concern that Alex would get pushed over in the crowd. He moved us down the street to a stone platform looking upriver at one of the ghats where the idols are dropped into the river. As we waited a crowd gathered around us, singing and lifting up their cell phone cameras. We watched a statue being loaded onto a boat which maneuvered to the center of the river. Another boat hovered nearby with a large balloon. Finally the statue was pushed into the river, the balloon was released to the sky, and the people around us sang softly.

We'd heard the triumphant shout "Jai!" as the statues left the potter's district to be delivered to their pandals. This "Jai" was a quiet one; there's a sadness to the end of the festival, the moment the daughter leaves the family home again, the moment the Devi withdraws from all her visible physical manifestations. The girl returns to being a girl, the pot becomes a pot, the clay returns to the river.

Our guide returned from his own photo shooting and moved us back to the car. He offered to take us to another ghat to see more immersions, but we had run out of energy and we didn't see the need to put our driver to the effort.

With the thousands of pandals in the city the process of pushing all those statues into the water would take all day and all night. As we drove back to the hotel our guide pulled up an image on his cell phone. It was a water color painted in 1915 by Gagenendranath Tagore, a member of the artistic Tagore family. The image shows a torchlight procession escorting a Durga idol along dark streets.[57] Seeing this hundred-year-old image cherished by a contemporary native of Kolkata deeply affected me. It linked the present to the past in a grand procession like the thousands of statues flowing from the neighborhoods and homes back to the river.

Family Ritual

Rodrigues explains that in the rituals of the wealthy houses the family priest conducts the final rituals on Dashami. He asks Devi to withdraw from the objects where she has been dwelling: the statue, the pot, the mirror. However he asks her to remain in the house, the earth, and the water. She is always there, ready to emerge again when she is called.

The women of the house conduct one more ceremony, smearing the mouths of the statues with food, as we had seen on the street. Rodrigues explains that the women are feeding the daughter before she leaves. She is returning to Mount Kailash to share the austerities of her husband, and they are feeding her to withstand the rigors of the coming year and to encourage her to return again next year.[58]

Rodrigues asked his host family why they observe Durga Puja at such expense year after year. His host replied that he could not imagine life without it. It's the time of year when his daughters return, the house is filled with children and grandchildren, everyone is happy. It is, he said, the focal point of his life. Rodrigues comments, "although she is perceived as a returning daughter, the Devi also presides as the arch matriarch, the symbol and embodiment of womanhood, under whose nurturing and protective wing the family's female lineage may gather. The Devi brings them together..."[59]

---

57 See the Wikimedia image "Pratima Visarjan by Gagenendranath Tagore", upload.wikimedia.org/wikipedia/commons/7/7e/Pratima_Visarjan_by_ Gaganendranath_Tagore.png.
58 Rodrigues, *Ritual Worship*, p. 64.
59 Rodrigues, *Ritual Worship*, p. 66.

Changes to Durga Puja

Confronting pollution

Traditionally statues were made of clay and painted with natural colors, so they could be returned to the river just like clay tea cups from the chai stalls. Today the statues contain plaster of paris and are decorated with toxic paint and plastics. Throwing these materials into the river results in significant pollution.[60]

Efforts to end the immersion ceremony have been unsuccessful, however there are moves to mitigate the environmental impact. For several years cranes have been placed at a few of the ghats where the idols are dropped in the river to fish them back out again. Among the things I did not see that I learned about later I would have liked to see the idols recovered.

In 2020 the municipal authorities set up ponds near two of the pandals. The statues were taken to the ponds where they were melted with sprays of water. The ponds were lined with plastic to contain the chemicals and plastic which were later cleaned up by the municipality.[61]

Challenging the caste system

Our guide made us aware that some tribal people do not celebrate Durga Puja. For them the story encapsulates the Aryan conquest and the literal demonization of their people. There is a tribe called Asur and the people of the tribe bear that surname; this tribe is designated as a Particularly Vulnerable Tribal Group and faces discrimination.[62] Some tribal people hold a festival to honor their benevolent king Mahishasur, others hide until Durga Puja is over. [63]

Some Bengali writers declare that they do not participate in Durga Puja celebrations in solidarity with the tribal people. For them Durga Puja reinforces the caste system, with male Brahmin priests in charge

---

60 Basu, "Idol immersions after Durga Puja leave rivers polluted yet again".
61 Basu, "Rare green immersion stands out after Durga Puja".
62 Sundaram, "Reclaiming Mahisasura, Durga Puja, and Bengali Identity Politics".
63 Pandy, "Meet the Asurs — a marginal tribe that describes Durga as a goddess who enticed Mahishasur".

of neighborhood celebrations, and the zamindar families continuing to display their wealth in the Bonedi Bari festivities.[64]

There is a challenge to gender distinctions as well. In 2021 one pandal club announced their theme as "Mother goddess will be worshipped by mothers". Their senior priest had died and they decided to replace him with four women to serve as the officiants. Women have become potters and organizers, they said, why not priestesses?[65]

Pandemic effects

Just a few months after Durga Puja in 2019 the COVID-19 pandemic spread across the world. The 2020 version of Durga Puja was severely curtailed as civil authorities limited crowd sizes and people opted to stay home. The pandemic eased up in 2021 but uncertainty dampened planning.[66] Durga Puja organizers planned to cut back on grand displays, feeling this was not the year to throw an elaborate display.

This has severely impacted the artisans who create the Durga Puja experience. The potters of Kumortuli reported that 2020 and 2021 brought a small fraction of the orders they had received in 2019. Some clubs have shifted to buying fiberglass displays to be for several years in a row to cut costs. The artisans who create the hair for the statues and the workers who cart the clay to the potters lost their orders too. Fewer drummers were commissioned to come to the city.[67]

Up until 2019 pandals were shaped like a funnel channeling visitors from the entrance to the inner sanctum housing the image of Durga. In 2020 and 2021 the civil authorities instructed the pandal committees to make the image visible from a distance to cut down on crowding. To encourage smaller crowds club organizers arranged for digital displays

---

64   Jyoti, "Taking a stand for tribal rights: Why I am not celebrating Durga Pujo".
65   "This famous Kolkata Durga Puja has appointed four female priests for the first time".
66   "Durga Puja celebrations set to be low-ley affair in Bengal for second year in row".
67   Ray, "With six weeks to go for Durga Puja, the Kumartuli potters are hoping for a miracle".

on their own social media accounts. Digitaldurga.com offered a virtual pandal-hopping experience for people staying home.[68]

In 2020 and 2021 puja committees chose to redirect some of their funds to support children orphaned by COVID-19 and artists who have seen a drop in festival demand.[69] Public funds have been redirected to distribute masks and hand sanitizer.[70] The pandemic has been incorporated into the changing imagery; one theme pandal featured a Durga wearing a gold face mask, replacing her traditional tools with medical supplies like syringes.[71]

Continuing Durga Puja

Durga Puja fades slowly in the days after Dashami. If space permits the pandals remain in place to be re-used for the Kali Puja eighteen days later, then the bamboo poles are stacked away until the next year's festival. In the 2000s the creation of public pandals became a year-round event, with planning for the next year starting as soon as the idols marched down to the river.

Guha-Thakurta says "The resonance of the Pujas wraps the city thickly, and then slowly wears thin, but never seems to entirely leave it."[72]

Postscript: Bringing Durga Puja Home

Durga Puja is both a religious and a cultural celebration. It is pointedly public. The Bonedi Bari or household celebrations have always integrated caste workers in the production of the festival and have integrated Moslem artists.[73] Writer Oindri Ghosh says, "The best thing about it is the fact that it is not a festival for the Bengali Hindus alone. All are

---

68 "Kolkata gears up for Durga Puja, all involved to be vaccinated in 3 months".

69 "Durga puja committees cut costs to support orphans, poor".

70 "Durga Puja organisers need to spend 75% of ₹50,000 grant on COVID-19 equipment".

71 "Coming up in Kolkata: 20 gm gold mask for goddess Durga to keep Covid at bay".

72 Guha-Thakurta, *In the Name of the Goddess*, p. 30-31.

73 Guha-Thakurta, *In the Name of the Goddess*, p. 96.

welcome," noting that Muslim, Christian, Parsi and Sikh residents participate in pandal building, and everyone loves to go pandal-hopping.[74]

As an American and ethnically White I came to Kolkata as an outsider. I am deeply grateful to have been welcomed to Kolkata at festival time. This warm welcome allowed me to experience my journey to Kolkata as a return of the daughter to the mother. Visiting the Goddess in temple ruins and museums around the world was like sipping Shakti through a straw. In Kolkata I was tossed into the Shakti pool, surrounded by her, immersed in her.

I didn't grow up with Durga Puja but I celebrate it now, adding it to the Pagan religious festivals I keep and the secular holidays of the American calendar. At Navaratri I put the Mahishasuramardini statue on my puja altar and center offerings there while I read the Chandi Path. In that tangible sense I went to Kolkata and brought Durga home.

As I write I am celebrating Navaratri 2021. Alex and I continue to find videos documenting Durga Puja in Kolkata. In one documentary a dhak drum maker demonstrates the craft and his explanations are translated in English in subtitles.[75] The Ahritola 1st Lane neighborhood pandal club documented their navapatrika blessing, walking down to the river and returning to the pandal.[76] Mindia Films made an English language film describing the festival. Footage includes dhak drumming, pandal hopping, and a neighborhood association taking the navapatrika down to the local pond, with a cameo appearance by Devdutt Pattanaik describing the navapatrika as an ancient form of plant worship, and also as the kola bou, Ganesh's wife.[77]

It is clear that research is never-ending. Also more people are making videos available, and a number of the films that have been helpful to my understanding were made or uploaded in 2019. The move to digital displays sparked by the pandemic makes the festival more accessible to worldwide audiences. I've enjoyed 3-D views of pandals on thepuja. app which lets viewers see 34 different pandals. The view of Sreebhumi Sporting Club's massive Burj Khalifa pandal begins with a drone view

74 Ghosh, "Durga Puja: Cultural or Religious Festival?"
75 Kaahon, "Joy Dhak, An Ecstasy with Dhak, Process of Making Dhak".
76 Saha, "Durga Puja 2019 Kola Bou Snan".
77 Mindia, "Durga Pujo feat. Devdutt Pattanaik".

overhead! I've been able to catch some of the livestreams from Belur Math where the Ramakrishna Mission is conducting the traditional rituals, including the sandhi and kumari pujas.[78] My own experience continues to evolve as my appreciation for Bengali culture deepens.

During Durga Puja I encountered Goddess in all the forms Rodrigues lists – the tree, the pots, the navapatrika plants, the young girls, and the stunning number and variety of statues. Each successive encounter deepened my relationship with her and my ability to encounter her presence within myself. At Durga Puja she lives in every woman, even a White woman, even an outsider. She lives in me.

---

78 Belur Math, "Durga Puja 2021, Sandhi Puja" and "Durga Puja 2021 : Mahashtami Puja & Kumari Puja".

Appendix A: Illustrations

Malik Ghat Flower Market

River at the Chottelal Ki Ghat.

Women stringing flower garlands at the Chottelal Ki Ghat.

Flower sellers drape garlands on the stair handrails.

Malik Ghat flower stalls.

Porters waiting for garlands.

Kumortuli – Potters District

Narrow alleys, open-air studios below, housing above.

Kumortuli houses.

Straw is shaped into the poses of the statues.

A young artisan applies layers of mud to build up the statue.

*One artisan presses straw onto a shaped frame
while another applies clay over the straw to shape the statues.*

A row of Lakshmis drying in the street.

Partially painted statues including Saraswati, Ganesh and Lakshmi.

An artisan paints small statues by hand.

Artisans apply details to the statues.

A fully painted and decorated display ready for transport.

Securing a statue onto bamboo poles to be carried out on shoulders.

Pulling a cart loaded with a statue out to the street.

Drummers

Dhak drum with feather and cow tail plume, two without.

Troupe of young men playing smaller drums in marching band fashion.

Kolay Market

Porters lifting enormous bundle cooperatively.

Porters lifting a bundle onto a truck.

Vendors line the lanes while baskets hang overhead.

Porters run rapidly down the narrow aisles of the market.

Vendors sell peppers and vegetables.

Baskets of purple yams.

Navapatrika Immersion

Bundles going into the water and coming out to the road.

Family navapatrika puja with dhak drummers.

Bonedi Bari Puja

Crowding into the entrance.

House courtyard.

The statue of the house.

Kalash with Bilva tree.

Pandals

Kumortuli pandal. A tree is linked into the pandal.

Kumortuli pandal: the cable of branches flows behind the image of Durga.

Neighborhood pandal.

Neighborhood pandal.

You could walk behind this statue.

Detail of Mahishasur holding up Durga.

Pandal entrance hung with bells.

Bell pandal: traditional murti.

Beliaghata 33 Pally pandal entrance.

Beliaghata 33 Pally pandal models of churches, temples and mosques.

Beliaghata 33 Pally pandal symbols of Hinduism, Christianity and Islam.

Beliaghata 33 Pally pandal statues of Durga and family.

Statue with offerings and priest.

Pandal entrance.

Pandal corridor.

Pandal statue.

Pandal in the shape of a ship.

Ship statue open to the street.

Belur Math statue.

Immersion

Priest prepares statue for immersion in crowded family courtyard.

Woman of the family takes photo of porters.

Statue hand-carried down street.

Statue transported in truck.

Statue carried down to river.

Statue in boat ready to be tipped into river.

Street Decorations

Her face is everywhere, even on advertisements.

Holiday lights

Appendix B: Timeline

Because I did not grow up Indian it took me a while to realize that the religious festival of Navaratri relates to the solar-lunar calendar. The solar month is divided into two lunar fortnights, new moon to full moon, then back to the new moon. Navaratri counts the first nine days from the new moon. In that sense every month has a Navaratri. People do celebrate Navaratri festivals at other times of the year. I read Chandi during the spring, summer and winter Navaratri periods in addition to the main fall celebration. Our guide in Varanasi said his family celebrates nine Navaratris in the year.

The holiday of Durga Puja in Kolkata is celebrated on the last five days of the fall Navaratri. Here is the mapping of Navaratri and Durga Puja in 2019.

Date in 2019	Navaratri Day	Durga Puja
September 29	Prathama	
September 30	Dwitiya	
October 1	Tritiya	
October 2	Chaturthi	
October 3	Panchami	
October 4	Shashti	Day One
October 5	Saptami	Day Two
October 6	Ashtami	Day Three
October 7	Navami	Day Four
October 8	Dashami	Day Five

The days of the fortnight continue from Dashami to Ekadashi, Dvadasi, Travodasi, Chaturdasi, and either Amavasya and the new moon or Purnima and the full moon.

Appendix C: Navapatrika

My Bengali guide referred me to Madhu Khanna for a list of the plants in the navapatrika bundle. Laura Amazzone referred me to Madhu Khanna's article "The Ritual Capsule of Durga Puja". Khanna lists the plants along with their Linnean taxonomy and the aspect of Durga each embodies.[79]

Number	Plant	Taxonomy	Goddess
1	Banana	Musa paradisiaca	Brahmani
2	Kachu, Kacchavi	Colocasia antiaquorum	Kalika
3	Turmeric, haridra	Curuma longa	Durga
4	Jayanti	Clerodendrum phlomidis	Kartiki
5	Bilva, bel (bael)	Aegle marmelos	Shakti
6	Pomegranate, dadima	Punica granatum	Raktadantika
7	Asoka	Saraca indica	Shokarahita
8	Arum, mankacu	Alocasia indica	Camunda
9	Unhusked rice, dhan	Oryza sativa	Lakshmi

In *The Ritual Worship of the Goddess* Hilary Rodrigues lists the plants used by the families he studied in Varanasi along with notes about how their color links to the goddesses. The order of the plants differs from Khanna's but the plants themselves and goddesses are the same, with the exception of the bilva which Rodrigues assigns to Shiva and Khanna assigns to Shakti as the power of Devi.

Number	Plant	Goddess
1	Kadali/Rambha (plantain)	Brahmani
2	Mana (a broad-leaved plant)	Camunda
3	Kacvi (or Kacci) (a black-stalked plant)	Kalika (dark complexioned)
4	Haridra (turmeric)	Durga (golden complexioned)

---

79 Madhu Khanna, "The Ritual Capsule of Durga Puja", p. 476-478.

5	Jayanti (a kind of creeper, or barley)	Kartiki
6	Sriphala (a bilva branch containing two fruits resembling breasts)	Shiva
7	Dadimah/mi (pomegranate)	Raktadantika
8	Asoka (a large shady tree; in the month of Caitra it blossoms with small red flowers)	Sokarahita
9	Dhanya (rice paddy plant)	Lakshmi

Rodrigues notes "They are bound with the Aparajita (Clitora ternata) creeper." [80]

Later in the book Rodrigues details the ritual the purohita performs on Saptami which bathes the navapatrika in a variety of liquids. While being bathed in five products of the cow (urine, dung, milk, curd, ghee) the navapatrika is addressed the names of five goddesses - Candika, Gauri, Trinetrayai (She who Possesses the Third Eye), Bhairavi, and Bhuvanesvari. During a bath of nine waters the plants are addressed individually and as a goddess; three of the plants are not addressed by goddess name but by descriptions.[81]

Number	Plant	Goddess
1	Plantain (Kadali)	Candanayika
2	Kacci	Durga
3	Turmeric (haridra)	Hara (Shiva), Rudra
4	Jayanti	Jaya
5	Sriphala	(descriptions)
6	Pomegranate (dadima)	(descriptions)
7	Ashoka tree	Durga
8	Mana	(descriptions)
9	Rice (dhanya)	Lakshmi

80 Rodrigues, *Ritual Worship*, p. 129-130.
81 Rodrigues, *Ritual Worship*, p. 142-145.

The manual *New Age Purohit Darpan: Durga Puja* issued by the Association of Grandparents of Indian Immigrants records a list of plants but lists the goddesses they are associated with separately, so it's not clear which goddess is intended to be associated with which plant. The authors use the term "wood apple tree" interchangeably with "navapatrika", and the bathing ritual addresses the navapatrika as a whole.

Plant list
Banana (kalagaach)
Colocassia (kochu)
Turmeric (halud)
Jayani
Wood apple (bel gach)
Pomegranate (daalim gaach)
Arum (mankochu)
Rice plant (dhan)
Ashok tree

Goddess list
Brahmani
Kalika
Durga
Rudrani
Jayani
Kartiki
Shivani (wife of Shiva)
Raktadantika
Ahoka-Sokrahita
Chamunda-Lakshmi

This manual is intended for use by Indian emigrants outside of India. The authors recognize that many of these plants are not widely available outside the region. They note:

> With the spread of Bengali culture around the globe, sticking to the above plants in building the traditional Nabapatrika does not seem to be justified. Instead we choose any nine branches of trees growing in the area, preferably

fruit bearing. This is a compromise between the thought planted by our ancestors and the modification adjusted to the current environment of our lives.[82]

---

82 Mukherjee et. al., *New Age Purohit Darpan*, Durga Puja, p. 5-6.

Glossary

Bisarjan
Immersing clay statues of deity in a river.

Bhog
Food given as a blessing or prasad.

Bonedi Bari or Banedi Bari
Houses of the wealthy landowners and merchants who celebrate the traditional Durga Puja.

Dhak
Traditional drum. The drummers are called dhakis.

Dhunuch
Resin of the sal tree burned as incense.

Dhunuchi
Clay pot for burning dhunuch.

Ghat
A stone or clay slope or steps leading from a river's edge down to the water.

Kola Bau
Banana bride, another term for the navapatrika.

Kumor
A potter of the trade caste. In Kolkata many kumors live in Kumortuli, the potter's district. They share the surname Pal.

Kumari Puja
Ritual where a young girl is worshipped as Durga.

Murti
A statue which houses a divine presence. During Durga Puja the clay statues representing Durga and other deities become murtis.

Navapatrika
Nine plants bundled together to represent Durga.

Navaratri
Nine nights of the lunar calendar beginning on the new moon. They are:

- Prathama, day one
- Dwitiya, day two
- Tritiya, day three4
- Chaturthi, day four
- Panchami, day five
- Shashti, day six
- Saptami, day seven
- Ashtami, day eight
- Navami, day nine

Dashami is day ten, the day after the nine nights, when the festival concludes.

Pandal
A temporary structure of bamboo and other materials which house the statues of Durga and her entourage.

Patachitra
Folk art images painted on cloth.

Pratima
Word describing a statue of a deity, a sacred likeness which can become a manifestation of the deity.

Pujo
Kolkata natives call the festival Durga Pujo in addition to Durga Puja.

Purohita
Family priest versed in Vedic and Tantric ritual practices.

Sarbojanin Pujo
Public puja. The word breaks into Sarbo, for and jan, people, meaning for the people.

Yajamana
Family head who commissions the purohita to perform the Durga Puja rituals.

Zamindar
Wealthy landowner.

Bibliography

"A Durga puja pandal showcases women migrant workers in place of the goddess". *Indian Express online*, October 20, 2020, indianexpress.com/article/lifestyle/life-style/durga-puja-pandal-to-showcase-women-migrant-workers-in-place-of-goddess-6757447. Accessed August 29 2021.

Amazzone, Laura (2010). *Goddess Durga and Sacred Female Power*. Hamilton Books.

Avishek (2018), "Nakuleshwar Bhairav Temple, Kolkata – The eternal guard of Kalighat". *Discovering Kolkata*, Nov. 5 2018, discoveringkolkata.wordpress.com/2018/11/05/nakuleshwar-bhairav-the-eternal-guard-of-kalighat/. Accessed September 27 2021.

Basu, Jayanta (2020). "Rare green immersion stands out after Durga Puja". *The Third Pole*, November 3 2020, www.thethirdpole.net/en/pollution/rare-green-immersion-stands-out-after-durga-puja/. Accessed September 3 2021.

Basu, Soma (2013). "Idol immersions after Durga Puja leave rivers polluted yet again", *Down to Earth*, October 18 2013, www.downtoearth.org.in/news/idol-immersions-after-durga-puja-leave-rivers-polluted-yet-again-42509. Accessed September 3 2021.

Belur Math (2021). "Durga Puja 2021, Sandhi Puja, 13 Oct 2021, 7:44 pm, Belur Math". *Belur Math*, October 13 2021, youtu.be/_ANOxx7S4p4. Accessed October 13 2021.

— "Durga Puja 2021 : Mahashtami Puja & Kumari Puja, 13 Oct 2021, 5 : 40 am". *Belur Math*, October 13 2021, youtu.be/XYHevT4YqKs. Accessed October 13 2021.

Biswas, Soutik (2020). "Coronavirus: India's pandemic lockdown turns into a human tragedy". BBC News, March 30 2020, www.bbc.com/news/world-asia-india-52086274. Accessed Aug. 29 2021.

Chatterji, Shoma A. (2016). *Filming Reality: The Independent Documentary Movement in India*. Sage Publications India Pvt. Ltd.

Chatterji, Shoma A. (2019). "The Distant Drummers of Durga Pooja". *The Citizen*, October 6, www.thecitizen.in/index.php/en/NewsDetail/index/16/17665/The-Distant-Drummers-of-Durga-Pooja. Accessed 7/21/2021.

Chaudhury, Dhruba (2016). "Oldest Durga Puja in Howrah and Kolkata District." Dhruba Chaudhury, August 30 2016, www.scribd.com/document/322571468/Oldest-Durga-Puja-in-Howrah-and-Kolkata-district. Accessed July 21 2021.

Chaudhuri, Sharmistha (2017). "Outlook Traveller asks eminent personalities from Bengal about their favourite Pujo memories". *Outlook Traveller*, September 29 2017, www.outlookindia.com/outlooktraveller/travelnews/story/61582/durga-puja-oh-special-memories. Accessed August 31 2021.

Dey, Arjun (2019). "Maha Saptamir - KOLA BOU SNAAN - BODHON 2 BISHORJON - Durga Puja Kolkata 2019", youtu.be/nUndOhM54AU. Accessed August 4 2021.

De, Ellora (2020). "Howrah Mullick Ghat Phool Bazar: One of Asia's largest flower hubs". *Business Economics*, February 14 2020, businesseconomics.in/howrah-mullick-ghat-phool-bazar-one-asias-largest-flower-hubs. Accessed August 5 2020.

"Dhak feathers for Durga Puja at the cost of birds". *IndiaDivine.org*, September 15, 2006, www.indiadivine.org/content/topic/2110500-Dhak-feathers-for-durga-puja-at-the-cost-of-birds. Accessed July 28 2021.

Divine Drums. Directed by Viplab Majumder, 2010, vimeo.com/177442584. Accessed July 30 2021.

"Durga Puja celebrations set to be low-ley affair in Bengal for second year in row". India TV News Desk, July 05, 2021, www.indiatvnews.com/news/india/durga-puja-celebrations-guidelines-west-bengal-coronavirus-covid19-716961. Accessed September 5 2021.

"Durga puja committees cut costs to support orphans, poor", *Times of India*, September 6 2021, timesofindia.indiatimes.com/city/kolkata/kolkata-durga-puja-committees-cut-costs-to-support-orphans-poor/articleshow/85975279.cms. Accessed September 13 2021.

"Durga Puja: Meet dhakis - Bengal's traditional dhak drummers". *India Express Online*, October 3, 2019, youtu.be/A42CjHgw1c8. Accessed July 17 2021.

"Durga Puja organisers need to spend 75% of ₹50,000 grant on COVID-19 equipment", *Livemint.com*, October 16 2020, www.livemint.com/news/india/durga-puja-organisers-need-to-spend-75-of-rs-50-000-grant-on-covid-19-equipment-calcutta-hc-11602845452803.html. Accessed September 13 2021.

"Durga Puja: What is Dhunuchi Naach?" *The Statesman*, October 7, 2018, www.thestatesman.com/what-is/durga-puja-2018-dhunuchi-naach-significant-1502693696.html. Accessed July 29 2021.

Ganguly, Ruman (2018). "Kumortuli artists make idols with soil from Diamond Harbor instead of Uluberia". Times of India, July 27 2018, timesofindia.indiatimes.com/articleshow/65165151.cms.

Ghosal, Torsa (2018). "How Immigrant Sculptors Shaped an Artists' Hub Called Kumartuli". *Catapult Magazine*, July 12 2018, catapult.co/stories/how-immigrant-sculptors-shaped-an-artists-hub-called-kumartuli. Accessed July 21 2021.

Ghosh, Anjan (2000). "Spaces of Recognition: Puja and Power in Contemporary Calcutta". Journal of South African Studies, Vol. 26, No. 2, Special Issue: Popular culture and Democracy (Jun. 2000), pp. 289-299, www.jstor.org/stable/2637495. Accessed August 5 2021.

Ghosh, Oindrila (2020). "Durga Puja: Cultural or Religious Festival?" The Pangean, January 29, 2020, thepangean.com/Durga-Puja-Cultural-or-Religious-Festival. Accessed September 5 2021.

Ghosh, Sonali (2016). "Living with the Idols, Behind the Scenes With The Durga Makers". *News18.com*, https://www.news18.com/news/immersive/making-of-durga-puja-idols.html. Accessed August 5 2021.

Goswami, Shreya (2016). "These women dhakis or drummers are ushering in a new-age Durga Puja in Bengal". *India Today*, October 9, 2016, www.indiatoday.in/lifestyle/culture/story/women-drummers-dhakis-durga-puja-kolkata-gokul-chandra-das-lifest-345730-2016-10-09. Accessed July 25 2021.

Guha-Thakurta, Tapati (2015). *In the Name of the Goddess, the Durga Pujas of Contemporary Kolkata*. Primus Books.

Gupta, Amitabha (2013). "Durga Puja of 'Bonedi' Families at Kolkata". *Amitabha Gupta*, October 8 2013, amitabhagupta.wordpress.com/2013/10/08/durga-puja-of-bonedi-families-at-kolkata. Accessed August 6 2021.

Heierstad, Geir (2017). *Caste, Entrepreneurship and the Illusions of Tradition: Branding the Potters of Kolkata*. Anthem Press [Kindle version].

Javed, Zeeshan (2020). "Band parties fall silent in Kolkata in Covid season." *Times of India*, Sept. 6, 2020, timesofindia.indiatimes.com/city/kolkata/band-parties-fall-silent-in-covid-season/articleshow/77954266.cms. Accessed July 30 2021.

Jha, Bharti (2018). *Dhunuchi Dance by Bharti jha, Durga puja, Dhunuch nach*. Oct. 18 2020, youtu.be/eFOSFkvI5jI. Accessed July 25 2021.

Jyoti, Dhrubo (2016). "Taking a stand for tribal rights: Why I am not celebrating Durga Pujo". *Hindustan Times*, October 10 2016, www.hindustantimes.com/opinion/taking-a-stand-for-tribal-rights-why-i-am-not-celebrating-durga-pujo/story-RWvXVmwnIVlJd-KNcJWK7TK.html. Accessed September 3 2021.

Kaahon (2019). "Joy Dhak, An Ecstasy with Dhak, Process of Making Dhak". Oct 4 2019, www.youtube.com/watch?v=HcoyYuji3bc. Accessed October 7 2021.

Khanna, Madhu (2000). "The Ritual Capsule of Durga, An Ecological Perspective". *Hinduism and Ecology: The Intersection of Earth, Sky and Water*, edited by Christopher Key Chapple and Mary Evelyn Tucker. Harvard University Press, p. 469-498.

"Kolkata gears up for Durga Puja, all involved to be vaccinated in 3 months". Hindustan Times, July 15 2021, www.hindustantimes. com/cities/kolkata-news/kolkata-gears-up-for-durga-puja-all-involved-to-be-vaccinated-in-3-months-101626333922868.html. Accessed September 5 2021.

"Kolkata: 'Secular' Durga Puja pandal leads to social media outrage, triggers complaint". *Indian Express online*, October 6, 2019, indianexpress.com/article/cities/kolkata/kolkata-secular-durga-puja-pandal-leads-to-social-media-outrage-triggers-complaint-6056202/. Accessed August 29 2021.

McDaniel, June (2004). *Offering Flowers, Feeding Skulls: Popular Goddess Worship in West Bengal*. Oxford University Press.

Mindia (2020). "Durga Pujo feat. Devdutt Pattanaik". *Mind of India*, October 20 2020, www.youtube.com/watch?v=I6yj1kucSho. Accessed October 12 2021.

Mitra, Prithvijit (2009). "Dhak Minus Feather Frills". *The Times of India*, Sept. 14, 2009, timesofindia.indiatimes.com/city/kolkata/Dhak-minus-feather-frills/articleshow/5007307.cms. Accessed July 28 2021.

Mukherjee, Kanai L., Bibhas Bandyopadhyay and Aloka Chakravarty. *New Age Purohit Darpan: Durga Puja: Fourth Edition*. Association of Grandparents of Indian Immigrants. Accessed July 28 2021.

Mukherjee, Nabanita (2017). "An Appraisal Of Wholesale Marketing In Kolkata: A Case Of Kolay Market." *University of Burdwan*, April 2017, www.researchgate.net/publication/323545946_ AN_APPRAISAL_OF_WHOLESALE_MARKETING_ IN_KOLKATA_A_CASE_OF_KOLAY_MARKET_ INTRODUCTION. Accessed July 30 2021.

Mukhopadhyay, Rishika (2019). "Contesting Spaces of Urban Renewal Project: A study of Kumartuli's Artist Colony". *The Routledge Handbook of Henri Lefebvre, The City and Urban Society*, Michael E. Leary-Owhin and John P. McCarthy, editors. Routledge.

Pandy, Prashant and Premankur Biswas (2016). "Meet the Asurs — a marginal tribe that describes Durga as a goddess who enticed Mahishasur". *The Indian Express*, December 8 2016, indianexpress.com/article/india/india-news-india/meeting-the-asurs-a-marginal-tribe-in-eastern-india/. Accessed September 3 2021.

Rajaram, Prema (2021). "Coming up in Kolkata: 20 gm gold mask for goddess Durga to keep Covid at bay", India Today, August 9 2021, www.indiatoday.in/cities/kolkata/story/coming-up-in-kolkata-20-gram-gold-mask-for-goddess-durga-to-keep-covid-at-bay-1838487-2021-08-09. Accessed September 13 2021.

Ramakrishna Math and Ramakrishna Mission. "Sandhi Puja at Belur Math 2019", youtu.be/-4Oq1zO19rg. Accessed August 21 2021.

Rao, Rashmi Gopal (2016). "Mallik Ghat Flower Market". *Times Travel*, June 28 2016, timesofindia.indiatimes.com/travel/Kolkata/Mallik-Ghat-Flower-Market/ps52946781.cms. Accessed August 5 2021.

Ray, Shantanu Guha (2021). "With six weeks to go for Durga Puja, the Kumartuli potters are hoping for a miracle". Money Control, August 29 2021, www.moneycontrol.com/news/trends/features/durga-puja-is-just-six-weeks-away-kumartuli-potters-are-hoping-for-a-miracle-save-7337601.html. Accessed Sept. 5 2021.

Rodrigues, Hilary Peter (2003). *Ritual Worship of the Great Goddess, the Liturgy of the Durga Puja with Interpretations*. State University of New York Press.

Saha, Gopal Sankar (2019). "Durga Puja 2019 Kola Bou Snan". October 6 2019, www.youtube.com/watch?v=zN5usr1d6UI. Accessed October 7 2021.

Sengupta, Anuradha (2017). "The female sculptors of Kumartuli". *Gulf News*, March 29, 2017, gulfnews.com/lifestyle/the-female-sculptors-of-Kumartuli-1.2002364. Accessed July 17 2021.

Shahabuddin, Ghazala (2003). "Ecological sustainability of forest management practices: The case of the regenerating sal forests of south-western West Bengal, India." *Social Change* 33 (2-3): 142-172. June 2003, www.researchgate.net/publication/258185595_Ecological_sustainability_of_forest_management_practices_The_case_of_the_regenerating_sal_forests_of_south-western_West_Bengal_India. Accessed July 29 2021.

Sinjana (2018). "Durga Puja in Kolkata - 5 Reasons why it is Unique", backpacknxplore.com/durga-puja-bengal, September 2 2018. Accessed August 30 2021.

— (2019). "Kolkata's Durga Puja – A Complete Guide", www.backpacknxplore.com/kolkata-durga-puja-guide, September 13, 2019. Accessed August 30 2021.

Sundaram, Dheepa (2020). "Reclaiming Mahisasura, Durga Puja, and Bengali Identity Politics", *The Durga Puja Mystery Game*, blogs.helsinki.fi/durgapuja-the-videogame/reclaiming-mahisasura", November 23 2020. Accessed September 3 2021.

"The wholesale markets of Kolkata", www.ayashbasuphoto.com/kolkata-wholesale-markets. Accessed July 30 2021.

"The Women Artisans of Kumartuli, North Kolkata, Durga Puja 2019". *Indian Express Online*, Oct 4, 2019, www.youtube.com/watch?v=e6cNmVSDYcg. Accessed July 27 2021.

"This famous Kolkata Durga Puja has appointed four female priests for the first time", timesofindia.com, August 13 2021, timesofindia.indiatimes.com/travel/travel-news/this-famous-kolkata-durga-puja-has-appointed-four-female-priests-for-the-first-time/as85303267.cms. Accessed September 3 2021.

Trivedi, Ira (2014). *India in Love, Marriage and Sexuality in the 21st Century*. Aleph Book Company.

Ward, Mariellen (2020). "About Durga Puja in Kolkata: A complete guide". breathedreamgo.com, October 15, 2020, breathedreamgo.com/about-durga-puja-in-kolkata-a-complete-guide. Accessed Aug. 29 2021.

"What is so special about Durga Puja in Bengal: Eight amazing facts about the grand festival you should know". *India Today*, October 16 2015, www.indiatoday.in/education-today/gk-current-affairs/story/durga-puja-268437-2015-10-16. Accessed 8/5/2021.

"Why Soil from Brothels is Used to Make Goddess Durga's Idols". *News18.com*, October 7 2019, www.news18.com/news/india/durga-puja-2019-why-is-soil-from-brothels-used-to-make-the-goddess-idols-2331645.html. Accessed July 25 2021.

BOOK THREE:
A VISIT TO KAMAKHYA TEMPLE

Introduction

I was inspired to write this travelogue because of the dearth of information about Kamakhya written for the general traveler. Very few of the Tantric practitioners I know are aware of the importance of the temple. The local stories tell us that this is where Matsyendranath received his initiation, and this is the center from which Tantric practice spread, north to Nepal, south to Odisha. The temple here is two thousand years old. Ritual has been conducted at Kamakhya almost continuously for the past five hundred years. Goddess worshippers will find here the heart of the Mother Religion; Pagans will find a living temple complex of the type whose ruins we tour in Egypt and Greece.

It's fair to warn you that visiting Kamakhya Temple is not a risk-free pilgrimage. At the time we visited the U.S. State Department marked Assam as a high-risk destination and prohibited government employees from travelling there. This is still true at the time of writing. That means that there is limited help available if a U.S. citizen runs into trouble. On the other hand we stayed in a five-star hotel among business people conducting brisk trade in a tea-growing state. Millions of people visit the temple every year flowing in and out of the city peacefully. Much depends on the exact situation at the time of travel - the political environment in Assam is a fluidly changing situation.

We managed our travel risk by staying in a corporate level hotel (the Radisson Blu Guwahati). We also hired a local guide with a U.S. connection. Just a few months after our visit the entire country shut down during the COVID pandemic. Our guide was shepherding a European group at the time and was able to escort them safely out of the country. Both the hotel and the guide were definitely worth the extra expense.

Alex and I found the Assamese people to be friendly and welcoming. We shopped the Fancy Bazaar as the only white people on the street and we were treated just like every other person. Most of all we are enormously grateful that we were able to touch the ground at Nilachal

Hill. When I asked Alex what he wanted to do most in the world, he said to visit Kamakhya. So we did.

A Knowledgeable Guide

"They will need a car and driver at their disposal." Our guide spoke crisply into his mobile phone. It was our last day in West Bengal and he was reaching out to his colleague in Guwahati to organize the next phase of our pilgrimage. "Also a guide for Kamakhya Temple." Glancing at the book in my hands, he added, "He should be your most knowledgeable guide. They are well informed."

Three days later we were speeding toward Kamakhya Temple. I was syncing up as quickly as possible with our new guide. The temple is about seventeen kilometers from the city center, half an hour drive, so we didn't have a lot of time. "We want to start with the main shrine today," I said. "Also, can you show us how to get to the Mahavidya shrines?"

"Yes, which ones?"

"All of them. I'm not sure about the days." I showed him the book, Parimal Kumar Datta's *Kamakhyatantra and the Mysterious History of Kamakhya*. "This gives the days of the week for the shrines but it doesn't give them all."

His eyes lit up. "Today is Tuesday. After the main shrine we can visit Bagala," he said. "Wednesday is Chinnamasta." At Kamakhya the Mahavidyas are associated with astrological bodies. In astrology, both western and Jyotisha, these are also associated with the days of the week. "Chinnamasta is Rahu. At the Navagraha Temple Rahu and Ketu are on Saturday, but here they are on other days of the week." Navagraha means "nine planets". The Assamese spelling and pronunciation swaps in the "b" for the "v" used elsewhere.

I picked up the thread. "Thursday is Jupiter, Dhumavati."

"No, Tara is Jupiter," he corrected me. "Dhumabati is Ketu, also Thursday." I wondered immediately if Datta had reversed these as a deliberate blind, as Tantric practitioners often do. In any event both Dhumavati and Tara share Thursday as their active days.

"Friday, Bhubaneswari. Saturday, Kali. Sunday, Bhairabi," he said.

"We're flying out Sunday," I said. "What planet is Bhairavi?"

184

"No planet. She is the langal so she doesn't have a day of the week. You can visit her Wednesday with Chinnamasta." He smiled. "It's good you have enough time to see them all."

I asked him how long he had lived in Assam. "I am Guwahati born and bred," he said proudly. "My grandfather worked for the temple." He explained that he loves the temple and visits the Mahavidya shrines as often as he can. Our contact in Kolkata had done us a huge favor. Our contact in Assam was turning out to be a knowledgeable guide.

Tuesday

The Journey

Stepping onto the Hill

"Look," said, pointing ahead. "The blue mountains." I took in a breath. The Nilachal Hills emerge from the Guwahati cityscape in distinctive mounds covered with dark green forest. As the car wound up Kamakhya Mandir Road we passed a sign announcing "The Cradle of Tantra". I felt a little leap of excitement. In West Bengal the Tantric practitioners we spent time with hid their practice. They certainly didn't put out signs. We truly were in the heart of Tantric country.

Our driver pulled off to the side to let us all out, competing with taxis and buses for a temporary parking space. "He will park and come back for us," our guide said. As I stepped out of the car my eyes lit on a "welcome to Kamakhya Temple" sign.

Our guide led us up an ascending stairway lined with shops selling puja items and souvenirs. As we walked he gestured to the shrines we were passing. "Kali. Tara. Chinnamasta." He stopped at a vendor and pointed to a set of shelves at the back of the shop. "You can leave your shoes there."

"Should we buy something?" I asked him, kicking off my shoes.

"You can, but it isn't necessary." He nodded to the vendor and led us on.

The tiled walkway was clean and neither hot nor cold in October. Our guide had minimized our barefoot walking distance by picking the last vendor before the security gate. I later learned that security levels vary with the festival calendar and the terrorist threat level. Each gate into the temple has a metal detector. When the threat level goes up this may be augmented by male and female search lines, we encountered those later in Varanasi. Security forces monitor the main gate and patrol the grounds at night and guards also monitor a CCTV system. While we visited the threat level was very low and I barely noticed the guards near the entrance.

As we passed beneath the arch of the gate our guide touched the doorstep and then touched his forehead. I'd learned to do this at other temples and followed his lead.

We'd arrived at 7 am before the temple opened. The tile had been washed clean for the morning visitors. It was pretty slick, and as I walked I slipped, causing a gasp from our guide and other visitors. I managed to catch myself to everyone's relief. After that I moved more slowly and kept my footing.

Our guide pointed out the lavatories as we passed, right behind the information desk. I popped in to use them and learned there are separate sections for men and women, no gender neutral or family sections. The stalls are squat toilets with ceramic feet indicating where to stand. Yay for yoga class! There are wash fountains for both hands and feet. I used my little bottle of hand sanitizer.

Our guide parked us in a line while he went off to get tickets. The line self-organized with couples trading off keeping their place and sitting on a nearby ledge. The sign on the building announced "Waiting Hall for Devotees". We were waiting to get into the waiting hall! At 7 a.m. it was already full. The ticket office was in the same building. The cost of the "premium" ticket was 501 rupees or a few dollars. This enabled us to skip ahead of the free line. I'd read quite a few web sites describing this process, some of which said that the tickets had been discontinued, so I was guiltily relieved that the system was still in place.

We could tell the temple had opened when lines in other parts of the temple started to move. It was 7:30 a.m. At 8 a.m. we were led up the stairs into the waiting hall, so we'd waited outside for an hour. Our guide walked along with us imparting urgent last-minute instructions. "When you enter there will be water," he said. "There are three waters, one just inside, and two in the cave. The virtue is in the water." He stopped to talk to the guard at the door while we went inside.

My pre-trip research warned that it would take hours to get into the temple and I was fully prepared to spend the whole time standing. I found to my delight that the hall was filled with rows of plastic chairs and we spent most of the wait sitting. We ended up in the first line of chairs facing a white wall. The hall filled with the buzz of bored people, mostly in family clumps, Mothers and fathers and older relatives and kids, talking and playing videos on their mobile phones.

"I'm going to practice," I told Alex.

He smiled and nodded. "So am I."

I closed my eyes and dropped into another world.

In the Womb of the Mother

The first thing everyone learns about Kamakhya is that the temple is the yoni of the goddess. A spring constantly flows in a cleft in the floor of a cave. Every July the spring turns red for three days, the menstruation of the goddess. The water from the spring flows down the hill to the Brahmaputra River.

Kamakhya Temple is a Shakti pith, a place of goddess power. We had visited other Shakti piths in West Bengal. At two smaller Kali temples in the country I could feel the presence of Devi in the inner sanctum. At Kalighat the energy of the temple surrounded me as soon as I set foot on the grounds and my eyes filled with tears.

Nothing prepared me for the level of power I felt at Kamakhya.

As soon as I closed my eyes I was caught in a tide of power, tugged deep below the surface of the temple's massive energy field. I felt dizzy and my heartbeat accelerated. I thought, I'm still in the waiting hall! How much stronger will it be inside the cave? I need to prepare myself to encounter the Mother.

I grounded myself in place, imagined myself in my inner open-air temple, and brought up the visualization of the Devi and her attendants as I usually did. Only this time they weren't visualizations and I wasn't imaging that I was in a temple. I was *in* a temple. I could see the dirt floor, the rock walls, the sky. The goddess herself stood before me, smiling, enveloping me with her energy. I chanted her mantra.

When I finished 108 chants I ended the visualization and opened my eyes. I was shocked to see a white wall in front of me. The sounds of the waiting hall flooded back in. I looked at Alex who was coming out of his practice. "Are you praying to her?" I asked.

"I am," he said serenely. He was the reason we were there. When I asked him what he wanted to do most in the world he said he wanted to go to India, and specifically to Kamakhya, to the most sacred site of the Mother, to meet the goddess he had been praying to all his life. His happiness was a physical force and I felt blessed to share the experience with him.

I closed my eyes again. This time when I entered my internal space it was filled with a golden light. The light centered in my heart and spread to my entire self. I heard a chant echoing through the universe: "Ma! Ma!" reverberating as if it was chanted by millions of voices for thousands of years.

When I opened my eyes again our guide was standing in front of me. I startled. "Is there something wrong?"

"I am checking on you," he said apologetically. "Even in the premium line there is a wait. You must be patient."

I smiled at him. "It is a great blessing to be able to do practice here," I said.

He smiled back. "Just pray to Ma," he touched his chest, "here in your heart."

I touched my heart. "That's exactly what I am doing!"

When he left I took the opportunity to snap a picture of my ticket.

At 10:20 a.m. the guards opened the door on the other side of the hall. They shepherded us all down another flight of stairs and across the walkway. We all filed into a hallway. We could see through the glass walls that there were two other hallways in this new waiting room. Each hallway had a long metal bench. We organized ourselves into two lines, one sitting on the bench and one standing. In the hallway next to us I could see two pigeons marked with red huddled together beneath the bench. The man sitting above them heard them chittering. He gently picked them up and walked to the open end of the hall to set them free.

This was where the premium line joined up with the free line. Our hallway had filled up with people from the waiting hall, the other two hallways took in people from the free line. The farthest hallway opened and let out the occupants, then the one next to us. When the farthest one opened again some of the people in my line became agitated and waved at the guards: it was our turn! I didn't mind, I thought the people in the free line had paid with their much longer wait.

Finally our hallway opened and we shuffled into the temple proper. I saw a basin of water in the corner where a few people had stopped. I remembered what our guide had said about the water just inside the door and tried to join them, but the priest shepherding our line stopped me and kept me in place.

Photography is not permitted in the inner temple. The line snaked through a stone room called the chalanta (or calanta). I looked for the small statues of Kamakhya and her consort Kameswara that I knew should be there. I spotted a platform which I thought must be the location of the statues. All I could see was a mound of flowers which completely covered whatever was beneath. A priest sat near the platform chanting; I didn't see anyone interact with him.

Above this platform hung a small picture of Kamakhya. I did my best to commit it to memory. She stood on Shiva who lay on a lion. She had five sets of arms: green, gold, red, blue, white. Later we bought a similar picture of Kamakhya that had a sixth set of flesh-colored arms in front of her, so I expect that I didn't notice those arms in the temple image. The image we bought also depicts her with six heads matching the colors of the arms.

The main chamber is called the garbagriha, meaning "womb house". The calanta was separated from the inner cave by stone pillars. I knew from my reading that this is some of the most ancient stone work in the temple. I touched the pillar as I passed, feeling that I was touching one of the most ancient temples on the planet. We wound down a set of stone stairs. I was very grateful for the handrail! Accounts of the temple warned that the steps could be slippery with flowers, but they were bare and clean.

Since no photographs are permitted in the temple I hadn't seen an actual image of the cave and the yoni cleft. There are other images online from other temples, but none of Kamakhya. I had thought when I visited I would be able to see it live. However all I could see was red saris stretched over the area, and mounds of red flowers covering the yoni. A priest sat beside the spring. I knelt, he dabbed kumkum on my forehead and poured water into my hands. Since I had been trained not to drink any local water I poured it on my head. I gave rupees as offering.

I turned to make my way back up the stairs, but to my surprise the priest on the stairs pointed back into the temple. A man next to me said kindly, "It would be a shame to wait all this time and not take both of the waters." I remembered that our guide had said something about more than one water. So I turned back and registered a second priest sitting on the far side of the chamber. I knelt, he poured water into my hands, and also put kumkum on my forehead. I poured the water on my head.

Back up the stairs the line funneled through another chamber. This turned into a kind of gauntlet with priests standing next to shrines. They explained what the shrines were and asked for donations to give blessings. In my stunned bliss I didn't remember any of the names they gave me.

Then we were out the gate, blinking in the sunshine. It was 11:15. We'd spent about twenty minutes in the garbagriha, and about four hours waiting.

The Temple Grounds

Our guide picked us up immediately. "How are you?" he said. "Do you want to sit for a minute?" We must have looked as dazed as we felt. "Let's walk around," I said. I need to move to process.

Photography is permitted around the temple grounds. Our guide took a photo of us standing outside the main tower, the shikhara, in the Assamese beehive shape.

A ring of carved stone pillars surrounded the shikhara, elaborately decorated with bas-relief sculptures of Devis, Devas and yoginis. People walked up to the walls and touched them, even putting their heads against the walls. When I touched my forehead to one of the walls it felt as if I was falling down into the darkness of the cave, into the beating heart of Ma. I thought, you really only need to go into the cave once, after that you can feel it just standing on the grounds.

As we walked around the temple our guide pointed out the corridor filled with people standing in the free line. He said they had started lining up at 4 a.m. and waited for seven to eight hours.

Our guide showed us a bas-relief which he said replicated the little statues of Kamakhya and Kameswara in the calanta. I've seen photos of these sculptures coated with kumkum. Now they're behind bars and glass and it's hard to get a good picture of them.

We peered into one of the gates leading out of the temple. Our guide said if people don't have enough time to wait to get into the main temple he will take them here so they can have some touch of the place.

Then he walked us into the sacrificial area. I saw a priest working on a bucket of sacrificed pigeons. Our guide told us that visitors can buy a pigeon or goat and either release them or "go for the sacrifice". That explained the lost pigeons in the glass hall. After that I noticed a lot of pigeons and goats wandering around the temple grounds dabbed with red. The sacrificial hall had a yoke that could take a buffalo.

Our guide was matter-of-fact as he walked us in and out of the sacrificial hall. It helped me to stay non-reactive as I processed the new experience. I decided that I felt pretty much the same way that I feel on chicken slaughter day at a local farm - a little squeamish, but accepting the necessity. On the farm the slaughter is humane, and after all, before I committed to being vegetarian I would eat the chicken. At Kamakhya the slaughter is also humane, and the priests get shares of all the meat in rotation. But if I walked my friends through the place I'd prepare them for encountering blood on the ground.

With the new cleanliness initiative at the temple cleaning up the ground litter I'm not sure what the goats live on. I saw one sneak up on a basket of flowers an unwary visitor had left unattended and steal a mouthful. I dubbed him "the goat that lived."

Maa Bagala Temple

The drive up the hill from Kamakhya Temple to the Bagala shrine to didn't take long. The road was lined with vendors offering bright yellow cloths for sale. After our driver dropped us off, our guide bought a collection of puja supplies, then led us down the walkway. It split into two sections, one longer and gentler, one shorter and steeper. We took the long one down and the short one back.

Our first stop was a red-smeared image of Ganesh cut into the rock. Our guide said it was customary to begin by honoring Ganesh. This felt normal to us as we start every puja with a Ganesh chant. Our guide said his mantra silently, and Alex and I said ours silently too.

Our next stop was a large courtyard. This was the designated fire area, with shelves for lamps and two braziers for homa rituals. Our guide stepped us through how to make an offering. He had bought three lamp kits, plastic baskets filled with a clay diya lamp, a wick, a triangular bag of vegetable oil, a tiny pack of matches, and a box with exactly three sticks of incense. He set the clay lamps on a shelf and laid the wick to hang partly outside the lamp for lighting. He lit an incense stick and used this to poke a hole in the plastic oil bag so he could pour the oil into the diya. Then we lit the lamp wicks and waved the incense sticks in the air three times.

A priest came along behind us scraping the spent lamps, oil bags, matchbooks and incense packets into a trash can, part of the new cleanliness initiative.

Next we joined the line to enter the inner sanctum of the shrine. Bells hung over the walkway. Our guide reached up to ring one. Alex asked him when it was appropriate to ring them. "Whenever you feel it," he answered. Alex rang a bell.

The hallway skirted a rock wall carved with other images of Ganesh, all splashed with orange paint. I counted five and later read that there are eight images on the grounds. The line filed up to a tiled basin up against the rock wall. When my turn came I knelt by the basin and dipped my hand in as the others had done, and was surprised to find water. The priest dabbed my forehead and I dropped money in his tray. As we were leaving I explained to our guide that I felt awkward taking water because others were drinking it, but we are warned as westerners to drink only bottled water. He showed us how to dab the water right underneath the lower lip.

Back in the courtyard we saw a homa ritual in progress. A priest threw red chilies on the fire. Our guide explained that Bagala loves fiery things. People offer red cloths to other Devis but yellow cloths to Bagala. She protects against misfortune and in particular against enemies who make magic against you. People wear pink coral rings for her aid in balancing out an afflicted ketu. The shrine was so active because Bagala is associated with Mars and Tuesday is Mars day. The priests haul water up the hill to fill the basin on that day and staff the shrine for visitors.

The sense of power in the shrine was nearly as strong as Kamakhya Temple but different in quality. Kamakhya is Ma, the Mother, the source, fierce and loving. Bagala felt fierce too but in a more focused way. Our guide and the people visiting the shrine came to her for specific reasons, teasing out one strand of the fabric of Devi to grasp a narrower and more concentrated energy.

The Place

My first day on the hill left me with a lot of questions. I'd been to other Shakti piths and other temples of all sizes. Whether they were tiny shrines tucked into a street corner or huge monuments with extensive grounds, each of them was basically a building containing statues with human-shaped bodies and faces. Even when they were surrounded by smaller shrines the grounds were geographically limited.

The descriptions of Kamakhya as a Shakti pith surrounded by smaller shrines had seriously misled me. Sure, there's a temple and there are shrines, and there are numerous images of Devas and Devis with bodies and eyes, but in the inner sanctuaries the focus of devotion turned out to be rocks and springs. The entire hillside is alive with power. The pilgrimage destination isn't Kamakhya Temple, it's *Nilachal*.

With a good internet connection at the hotel I hit my online research sources each night. I stumbled on Shodganga, a treasure chest of doctoral theses mostly in English. Generations of Guwahati grad students have swarmed Nilachal documenting land use, architecture, social structure and ritual.

I felt an urgent need to understand the physical landscape. How high is the hill? Where do the springs come from? How big is the forest and how is it managed?

From Juthika Mahanta and Namita Devi I learned that Guwahati sits on the Shillong plain surrounded by hills. They have so many caves that the town takes its name from the Assamese word for cave, "guha". That's one of the features of Kamakhya as a sacred site, the dark chamber of the inner sanctum anciently called the Manobhava cave.

The Nilachal Hills are "inselbergs", meaning they rise up out of the plain like icebergs in an ocean. There are actually three hills in the Nilachal group, called locally the Shiva Pahar, Brahma Pahar and Vishnu Pahar. At their tallest they rise to 1000 feet. Kamakhya Temple sits on the Shiva Pahar at about 500 feet, the Bhubaneswari Temple sits higher up the road on the Brahma Pahar.

That's the rock. As for water, Guwahati is in a monsoon area. It gets wet and stays wet. Seasonal rains fill the ponds and springs, rivulets flow down the hills into the adjacent Brahmaputra River. There are also a few perennial springs. That's one of the features of the Kamakhya garbagriha too, a spring that wells up through the floor of the cave.

Guwahati is not only the city of caves, it might also be called the city of forests. The government of Assam manages nearly twenty reserved forested areas. Outside the reserves all other forested land is unclassed and unprotected. The Nilachal territory covers more than three square kilometers and falls into the unclassed category, although Kamakhya Temple and other organizations in the hills supervise some portions of the forest.

Dense evergreen forest covers the northern part of the hills, while the forest opens out to the south and west and turns into scrub. It is a diverse ecosystem, home to numerous plant and animal species. Paths up and down the hill cut through dense jungle.

Over the past twenty years the human occupied area has doubled, eating away nearly half the wild forest. There are numerous impacts. In particular, the change from closed forest to scrub land attracts leopards from the surrounding wildlife refuges. They are drawn by food sources, particularly backyard chickens, and the goats released by the temple. So the goat that lived isn't out of the woods yet.

The landscape frames the sacred site. How long have people been drawn to the spring in the cave? We know that humans have lived in the area for a very long time. There are Paleolithic sites that might be as old as 125,000 years. A number of tribal people still live in Assam and neighboring Meghalaya. These are woman-centered people, described as both matrilineal and matriarchal (which attracts intensely hostile reporting from male-centered culture). They worship very strong Mother goddesses with offerings that include animal sacrifice.

The sacred cave, the sacred spring, the sacred tree, these are the first places humans touched power, the first images of divine care. The spring gives us nourishing water, the tree breathes with us, the cave envelopes us in the fertile darkness of the Mother's womb. It is no wonder that I felt the chant "Ma" reverberating in the land around me; it is a prayer humans have been chanting for tens of thousands of years.

Wednesday

The Journey

We guided ourselves on our second day in Kamakhya. Our driver let us off at the drop-off point with instructions to call him when we were ready to go somewhere else. We connected to each other through WhatsApp before he drove off to park.

First stop, find a vendor to take our shoes. We picked one close to the main temple gate. Alex and I each bought a garland of red flowers from him. I was pleased we were able to manage the transaction on our own.

Chinnamasta Temple

Then we wandered around trying to find the Chinnamasta shrine. On the south side of Kamakhya Temple outside the main wall we found a line of goat vendors. We asked them for the Chinnamasta shrine and they pointed us back toward the main walkway. It occurred to me to check Google Maps. Alex had Google Fi and got no coverage, I had a Verizon phone and got excellent coverage. We were delighted to find that maps gave us walking directions from Kamakhya Temple to Chinnamasta Temple. We finally spotted the sign for the shrine half-hidden by foliage.

The temple was separated from the walkway by metal railing. Outside the building a small goat-sized sacrifice yoke was smeared with kumkum and adorned with red flowers.

The building itself sat below the level of the sidewalk. We walked down a few stairs to enter.

The chamber inside was lit only by the sunlight coming from the doorway. A plaque leaned against the far wall, possibly copper; whatever design it had was obscured by a coating of kumkum powder. People had left garland offerings there. The entrance to the garbagriha was just next to it. I peered inside.

Here is how Parimal Kumar Datta describes the shrine: "The Chinnamasta pitha is in the small Kunda. Devotees have to reach this pitha by going down through steps. It is about 15 feet below the ground level."

Here is what I actually saw: a rock wall sloped from the entrance down to the floor of the garbagriha. A series of steps had been hacked into the wall, unevenly spaced, so narrow that they could more properly be called a stone ladder rather than a stone stairway. There was a handrail, thank goodness, but it turns out that fifteen feet is quite a drop.

At that time I was in my early 60s, heavyset, and had arthritic knees. I looked down into the garbagriha and had a clear image of missing my footing and falling. I heard Her say "you don't have to come down here." I laid my garland at the plaque, sat against a wall, and started a quiet meditation.

While I was sitting Alex came up to me and said "I'm going to go down." I took a deep breath and said, "Whatever." To translate: Alex was 70 and walked with a cane. I was fearful that he would fall going down into the garbagriha and I wouldn't be going with him to assist him so I worried about the risk. On the other hand I didn't want to prevent him from doing something he felt called to do. I commended him to his fate, inshallah.

"She wants me to come down," he said.

I had a strong faith that if She wanted him She would get him down and back safely. He disappeared down the steps. As I continued to meditate other people entered the shrine, looked down the steps, and then stepped back. I got up and went to the entrance and saw Alex slowly pulling himself up with the handrail. I wanted to reach down and help him! I sent him a strong burst of energy to help bring him up. Our guides had been helping us up and down stairs, but this was one of those places where you really have to physically get yourself there and back on your own.

Alex reported that he found an elderly priest sitting next to a spring. Alex gave the priest his flower garland and the priest gave him water from the spring and dabbed kumkum on his forehead. Later he confessed that the descent was one of the most frightening things he had physically done. She kept telling him She would bring him back safely, and She did.

Although I didn't go down into the garbagriha I felt strongly connected to an energy there, distinct from the general energy of Kamakhya. Our language to describe these perceptions is not well developed and relies on metaphor. To me the energy felt blue, cool, and secret.

Since I was having such good luck with Google Maps I decided to try to find the Bhairabi Temple. I followed the instructions and ended up on a walkway looking down a stairway which Google Maps called "Ma Dhumavati Road". The map indicated a short distance from where I stood, but that distance was some ways down the hill. There was no sign so I wasn't sure this was the right place. I caught the eye of a man who was hanging out in the area, pointed down the stairs and said "Bhairabi?" He shook his head and said "No."

Alex wanted to spend some time in meditation near the Kamakhya garbagriha. He went off to find a spot. I found a perch near a Krishna shrine. When a family approached the shrine I moved away respectfully. Two older women motioned to me to stay. They touched their heads to the shrine and I did too. Then I was family! They held my hands, patted my cheeks, touched their hearts, and had their grandson take their picture with me.

When they left I was able to enter into sadhana. I grounded, chanted to Ganesh, and then centered in my heart and chanted "Ma". The power in the temple vibrated my bones. I immediately became dizzy and felt myself lifting up through my head. I remembered that a Tantric acquaintance in West Bengal had said "protect your head". I wrapped my scarf around my head and immediately felt more in my body.

When Alex reconnected I told him I needed to go down from the hill to stop being so dizzy. I called our driver to come pick us up. It was early enough that we could fit in another stop. We decided to take our guide's advice and visit the Navagraha Temple. It's not far from Kamakhya Temple but sits on a different hill, the Chatrakar hill.

One of the best things about this hilltop was the view down to the Brahmaputra River. The name means "son of Brahma" and is the only river in India considered to be male.

The temple complex included a main temple building and an open-air courtyard where homa rituals can be conducted – one was in progress when we stepped up. The main temple building had the distinctive Assamese beehive tower or shikhara.

The sign outside the door asked visitors to keep oil lamps and incense out of the main temple and provided a shelf for oil lamps. We didn't see a vendor to purchase these from so we didn't make an offering here.

The temple had an anteroom before the inner sanctum. In the garbagriha there were nine huge stone yonilingas in a circle with ghee lamps the size of birdbaths. Niches in the wall held nine black images of the navagrahas. From our guide and other sources I gathered that devotees could come here to have priests do ritual to one or more of the navagraha to balance out issues in their horoscopes. I stood outside the room and peered in. A couple of men stepped inside. They were quickly shooed away by priests who came and closed the temple doors. Then the shrine shut down for the afternoon altogether.

There is a navagraha shrine in a Hindu temple near my house. A priest there instructed me to circle the navagraha images counterclockwise. Other visitors to report being able to make the circle there at the Navagraha Temple. I might have been able to do it if we'd gotten there earlier in the day.

The Temple

Cave, spring, forest form the sacred ground of the pilgrimage site. Who put the temple over Manobhava cave? Well, that's a story. Juthika Mahanta starts her version with a sigh: "The origin of the Kamakhya temple and the Nilachal hills has been a mystery to everybody." It all started so long ago that it's hard to see the beginning of the tale. One thing is for certain: where the land is a source of power, the temple is a statement of empire, a target for destruction and rebuilding.

The physical sciences help us here. Rajib Sarma is a hereditary Brahman priest at the temple. Sarma tells us that Gauhati University used radio carbon isotope dating to fix the oldest level of the temple at 2200 years old. We can presume that the highest rank of priests have the education and local knowledge to identify the oldest parts of the temple for testing. So it seems that the physical temple at Kamakhya is more than two thousand years old.

The next level of the temple dates to 500 CE. Something happened then – some catastrophe seems to have damaged the temple. A persistent legend attributes the destruction to the Turkish Muslim invader Kalpahar. Sarma and other scholars have come to doubt this story and believe an earthquake is a more likely cause. At any rate there are physical indications that the temple was rebuilt then. There's also an inscription in the Umachal Rock Cave at Nilachal dating to 500 C.E that records the construction of a temple by Maharajadhiraja Surendavarman. Sarma believes this refers to the reconstruction of Kamakhya temple.

The next story comes from a written text. The Kalika Purana was composed in Assam in the ninth or tenth century. It is a collection of myths, a history, and a ritual instruction manual all in one. Mousimi Deka recounts the Kalika Purana's stories of the Danavas and Asuras. Brahma created the stars in the city of Pragjyotisha, ruled by the non-Aryan king Mahiranga Danava. When the Danava dynasty failed the king Naraka took over, and the name of the country changed to Kamarupa, the place where love takes form. Biswanarayan Shastri points out that land grant inscriptions from the seventh to twelfth centuries frequently cite the Naraka story. Deka and Shastri see in the story of Mahiranga and Naraka a record of the conflict between indigenous non-Aryan and settler Aryan peoples.

In the centuries after the Kalika Purana was written, Kamakhya was periodically looted by incursions from neighboring Bengal and Bihar. The temple may also have been damaged by additional earthquakes. We do know that the temple was rebuilt by King Biswasingha of the Koch Behar kingdom early in the 1500s, and again in the mid-1500s by his son Naranarayan. The striking features of the temple today - five beehive domes and fantastically sculpted walls - date to this reconstruction, using materials from the older temples.

The Koch kings imported Brahmin priests to establish a ritual calendar. Historian Edward Gait reports that the temple was rededicated with a massive human sacrifice of some one hundred and forty men. Prabalika Sarma notes that when the Ahom kings took Kamarupa from the Koch they further established categories of priests and temple workers, and granted large tracts of land for temple upkeep. The state of Assam takes its name from the Ahom dynasty.

In the Koch and Ahom eras, the temple rituals were dedicated to the welfare of the kingdom and the ruling kings. Prabalika Sarma tells us that the Burmese invasion broke the connection between the kings and priests and interrupted rituals in the temples. When the British arrived in the mid-1800s, Sarma says, the Assamese people welcomed the change from Burmese rule.

The British government set a policy of non-interference with the temple, which became self-managing at that point. More earthquakes in 1897 and 1950 damaged the temple, which was repaired with steel reinforcements and Portland cement. The state of Assam now provides for the upkeep of the temple, and the rituals are directed for the benefit of all the people of Assam.

Damaged by earthquake and ransacked, the temple has been periodically renewed. Touching the temple walls links the devotee to 2200 years of physical history on the site and the devotion of the people who have loved the land and the goddess.

Thursday

The Journey

When we parted on Tuesday our guide had indicated he might be available on other days of the week. Our adventures on our own had proven that we could handle ourselves, which was gratifying, but also demonstrated that it was easier with a guide. So we asked him to guide us on Thursday. It's Jupiter day, which codes blue in western astrology and jyotisha. Our guide showed up in blue pants, Alex had a blue tunic, I wore a blue dress, and we all smiled at each other, sharing the common secret.

Traffic was tougher for some reason and our driver had to find an alternate route to Nilachal. Our guide had him drop us off farther up the hill and showed us another alley to the main staircase that cut off some of the climb. As he watched us navigate the staircase he nodded approvingly. "Already you are more confident," he said. He picked out the vendor-of-the-day and bought three puja kits while Alex and I stowed our shoes.

Alex wanted to meditate near the Kamakhya garbagriha so we spent a few minutes there. The familiar dizziness hit as I touched my head to the wall. I told our guide I thought you only need to visit the Kamakhya garbagriha once, after that you can feel it through the walls, and he agreed.

Tara Temple

Our first stop was the Tara temple. The archway was beautifully painted and still decorated from Navratri a week earlier. We struggled up the steep uneven steps into the courtyard. The sacrifice yoke here was covered with flowers, no blood. Entering the temple proper, our guide set up our oil lamps. While we lit them our guide saw a priest he knew and went back out to chat with him. I looked around for somewhere to put my incense sticks. I saw our guide had stuck his in the sand next to the sacrifice yoke so I put mine there too.

There was no priest in the garbagriha. As we entered a man was taking advantage of this to conduct a private puja. He did his work neatly and quietly, making rapid-fire mudras with his offerings, then sweeping up as he left. He touched the well and then touched his head. When he was gone I knelt to put my hand in the well and found to my surprise that it was dry, smeared only with kumkum. I touched this to my head. It was so quiet I thought about praying a mala, but a woman came in and I didn't want to hog the small crowded space.

Dhumabati Temple

Our next stop was the Dhumabati temple. The route led along the outer wall. On the way we passed the stair that Google Maps had led me to on Wednesday. I asked our guide if the stair led to the Bhairabi Temple. "Yes, but don't use it," he said. He led us past the goat vendors to the stair leading to Dhumabati. "Use this one," he said, indicating that it would lead me to the Bhairabi temple.

When Alex stepped into the Dhumabati courtyard red-faced and panting, the priest took one look at him and turned on a fan. That made lighting our lamps more difficult. Our guide indicated we should sit on the ground. I started to sit in the corner near the sacrificial yoke and then realized there was blood on the ground, so I scooted away and found a doorway lintel to sit on.

I have been advised not to pray directly to Dhumavati. This Mahavidya made herself a widow by eating her husband Shiva! She is the one who takes everything. As I sat on praying in front of my lamp I wondered how to address her. Our guide identified her as Ketu. I addressed her as the Dhumavati who is Ketu - I offered her respect in that form only.

Inside the temple four men sat cross-legged in front of cloth squares, all performing a grain puja. One of them was a white man I'd seen meditating on the grounds. In the garbagriha two white goat heads perched on the edge of the well. They looked peaceful. I thought to them, have a good next life, little goats! I wondered if they had been sacrificed for the men doing puja.

The priest in the garbagriha engaged in a puja with us. Our guide told us to repeat the mantra the priest gave us; we did not remember it.

The priest indicated to us that we were to throw flowers. I was proud our flowers landed well. Afterwards our guide told me to touch the water in the well. It was so clear I didn't see it until I felt it.

Our guide led us back up the stairs. Then he stopped and delivered a spiritual suggestion. He said praying for only good things isn't a balanced approach. Maybe you ask for something positive but what you actually need is something negative. It is better to ask Ma to give whatever is needed – she would know. I told him that this was an excellent suggestion. Later Alex and I traded notes and found that was pretty much what we were doing in all the small shrines: show up, pray, and release expectations. Put ourselves in Her presence for whatever She chose for us.

Ugra Tara Temple

My internet researches had turned up the interesting fact that there was another Tara temple in Guwahati. This is known locally as a Shakti pith, although I didn't find it on a country-wide list. Our guide was happy to add it to our itinerary on a Thursday. When we arrived I was very glad we'd asked him to guide us; the signs were in Hindi and the puja vendors did not speak English. They also didn't watch shoes, people just left them on the sidewalk at the temple gate.

This temple was more like the others we'd visited, a building in a courtyard surrounded by a wall. Compared to the shrines on Nilachal it had a lot of space. Tourist web sites inform us that the Ahom king Siva Singh built the temple in 1725 CE.

When I stepped through the courtyard I was punched in the heart by a presence. My eye was drawn to an image of Tara above the doorway arch of the garbagriha. Hindu imagery of Tara resembles that of Kali, with blue skin and skull ornaments. This was more in the Buddhist style, white with delicate features. I stopped and said "Oh!" Our guide smiled and said "Ma!"

Our guide had acquired puja kits from one of the two vendors outside and helped us set up the lamps. He set one of the incense boxes on the floor and instructed us to put the lamps on them in a row.

Then we went into the garbagriha. Here there was only a well filled with water, no murti, no stone. A metal framework held a red cloth over part of the basin. At our guide's instruction I touched the water and touched my lip.

The temple was so spacious and peaceful that I felt I could do a practice here. Alex and our guide were happy to wait. I have a White Tara empowerment from the Gaden Shartse monks so I have her mantra. It's generally written "om Tara tuttara ture mama anja punya jnana pushtim kuru svaha", although we received it slightly differently. I sat on the floor and did a mala of that mantra. I strongly felt connection with White Tara in the temple. Internet tourist web sites repeat the idea that there is a Buddhist connection in this temple. I would love to see a more detailed history of this temple.

As we left the courtyard our guide checked our lamps and found them all burning brightly. He was pleased and considered this to be a good omen. Alex and I did too.

Umananda Island

Back in the car our guide suggested this was a good day to see Peacock Island. We were happy to have the chance to do it with a guide.

The British named the island for its shape. Local folk know it as the place where Parvati became happy, Umananda. We had considered trying to visit Peacock Island on our own and we could probably have managed it, but it was a lot easier with our guide. He could explain that we were waiting on the mud bank while workers replaced a bamboo walkway because the river had changed height. Then he got tickets and we all sat in the plastic chairs in the welcome shade of the dock's roof.

The boat waited until enough tickets had been sold before loading. There weren't many seats and we didn't try to compete for them, we stood on the deck hanging onto railings. Even though the boat moved very slowly it only took five minutes or so to reach the island. We were excited to finally be out on the river and eagerly took photos during the whole ride.

Once on the island the boat's passengers flowed up a long flight of stairs. There were actually two routes, our guide led us up the route that was less steep but had more stairs.

Our first stop was a new Ganesh shrine built in 2017. It had a large and rather cute rat statue out front that had its own tray to collect donations. A priest did puja there, but I didn't interact with him, I quietly said my own chant and moved up the hill.

A line had formed in front of the Shiva temple. Someone went to get the priests to tell them that the boat had come in. The delay gave me a chance to memorize the decorations on the tiles around the door: Saraswati, Lakshmi, Krishna on a boat with gopis, baby Krishna on the snake. It seemed to me there was a lot of Krishna imagery for a Shiva temple, but then, there is a Krishna temple tucked within the walls of the main Kamakhya temple too.

Once the door opened and people flooded in the priests worked rapidly to process everyone. A priest tried to turn me aside but our guide insisted I was with him. In the garbagriha we knelt and threw flowers at the murti while a priest chanted a mantra we dutifully repeated. The priest dabbed us with kumkum. Our guide helped me to my feet. Alex was out of my reach but others kindly assisted him to stand.

As we left the temple people starting asking us for photos. This happened a lot; we were the only white people we saw except for one man at Kamakhya and a few westerners at the hotel. Our guide waved them off and started rushing us at this point. I didn't realize it at the time but the ferry was offloading and our guide wanted to catch that one back. He helped Alex navigate the many stairs while I went out ahead. I stood next to the rail anxiously, intending to call out if the boat started to leave before they made it on, but it turned out our guide had asked people to tell the ferry to wait for us. Once Alex and our guide made it we waited for the last two couples, so we were not the last people on the boat.

It was a long day. I recorded everything I could remember every night, but by the time we got to the hotel I had already lost detail about the Tara Temple visit.

The Goddess

The Nilachal hills shelter the yoni of Ma. The stone walls and towers enclose the cave with its yoni and spring in Kamakhya Temple. But who is Kamakhya? How did she emerge from Ma?

Tribal Goddess

Rajib Sarma is a hereditary Brahmin priest at Kamakhya. He starts his description of Kamakhya with the Khasi and Garo tribes in the surrounding hills. Both, he says, are matriarchal, and see the goddess of the cave as the natural creator. Many scholars have referenced the tribes as the original worshippers of Ma since Gait wrote his history a hundred years ago. Today academics question this idea (we note in passing the patriarchal hostility to woman-centered culture), but at least one priest at Kamakhya firmly insists on the tribal history.

Nihar Ranjan Mishra details the beliefs of many of the local tribes. He points out that the Khasis call their grandmother goddess Ka Mei Kha. On the jaimaa.org web page Kulasundari Devi talks about the history of the goddess. She notes that in other places in India the goddess is called "Kamaksha" or "Kamakhya", but the local people in Guwahati still pronounce her name "Ka Mei Ka". After I read this one night in the hotel room I listened closely to our guide and realized that was how he pronounced the name.

The Kalika Purana describes five versions of Kamakhya. Chapter 62 describes the first version, the cave with the spring. Biswanarayan Shastri translates:

> Mount Nila is triangular in shape, low in the middle, which is Sadashiva himself. There on the middle of this stone lies a beautiful mandala, associated with thirty saktis; within that mandala is the cave of Manobhava, which has been created by Manobhava (Kama) himself.
> On this stone the female organ is in the form of a stone, attractive and lovely, which is twelve anguli [fingerbreadths] wide and twenty one anguli long, gradually sloping in a very fine proportionate way going down to the Bhasma mountain; it is as reddish as vermilion and saffron; there

in that pudendum the amorous goddess always amuses in
her fivefold form, who is the source of the creation, eternal,
repose of the universe, and bestower of all desires.

Here is the hill, the Shiva Pahar, with the cave, created by the god
of love, and the yoni on the floor of the cave, in a sacred text composed
a thousand years ago.

Sanskrit Goddess

How did Ka Mei Kha become Kamakhya? Kulasundari Devi notes that
the Aryan people moving into Assam/Kamarupa/Pragjyotisha brought
Hinduism with them and imported the worship of Shiva. The arrival of
the East India Company brought a new wave of patriarchal culture. The
woman-centered Khasis and Garos were pushed to re-focus their leadership and inheritance on men. To some extent the tribes have resisted
this push and women continue to be important in these regions. As one
example, many of the Guwahati graduate students whose theses I have
studied are women, and at least one is coached by a women professor.

Mishra believes the names Pragjyotisha and Brahmaputra have pre-
Aryan roots. The shifting of these names reflect a general movement to
bring the tribal peoples into the Hindu fold. As he sees it, the Kalika
Purana documents this effort. The Koch and Ahom tribal peoples are
re-imagined in the Hindu caste system, coming in as kshatriyas, one
level below the highest Brahman class. New stories frame the goddess
of Nilachal as a Hindu goddess and Sanskritize her name. Now she is
Kamakhya and she has a history.

The story of the Kalika Purana establishes the Shakti piths and maps
the sacred landscape of India as the scattered body of the goddess. In
this story the great goddess Mahamaya takes incarnation as Sati, the
daughter of Daksha. Sati married Shiva over the objections of her father
Daksha who deeply disapproved of the ash-covered ascetic. One day
Daksha held a great fire ritual and did not invite Sati and Shiva. Sati
became very angry at the insult to her husband. She showed up at the
ritual and demanded that Shiva be invited. When Daksha refused, Sati
leapt into the fire and immolated herself.

Shiva was overcome with grief. He picked up Sati's body and carried it everywhere in mourning. Meanwhile his divine duties were being neglected. Finally Vishnu followed him around and threw his discus to cut Sati's body into pieces. Wherever the pieces fell there is a place of power, a Shakti pith. Kamakhya is the place where Sati's yoni fell.

Wherever Sati's body landed, Shiva's phallus touched the ground. At Kamakhya the phallus enters the yoni, and Shiva and Sati are finally united permanently. Mishra makes the interesting observation that the story makes Kamakhya both a place for amorous union and a graveyard.

This story is told in a number of puranas. The story continues: Shiva retreated into ascetic contemplation and withdrew from the world. Mahamaya again took incarnation as Parvati, the daughter of Himalaya. She engaged in severe meditation with the intention to marry Shiva. However Shiva declined to break his ascetic lifestyle. The gods dispatched the god of love Kama to break his meditation. Kamadeva found Shiva in meditation on Umananda Island with Parvati nearby. The god of love cast springtime over the island. When Shiva stirred to see what was happening, Kama loosed an arrow of love. Unfortunately Shiva caught the movement. Angrily Shiva opened his third eye and blasted Kamadeva to ashes. Nonetheless the arrow hit its mark and Shiva fell in love with Parvati.

On Umananda Island Shiva anointed Parvati with ashes and gave her instruction, a blessing which brought her happiness. Kamadeva's wife Rati pleaded with Shiva to restore Kamadeva to life. Shiva relented and permitted Kamadeva to be reborn. In Assam the temple of Madan Kamdev, now an archaeological site which displays erotic sculptures, is held locally to be the place of Kamadeva's rebirth. The statue of a man and woman in amorous union found there is held to be Rati and Kamadeva.

The Kalika Purana casts the ancient kingdom of Pragjyotisha as Kamarupa, the place where the body of Kamadeva took form. I learned this story first as a pan-Indian story about Shiva, Parvati and Kamadeva. It was only when I visited Assam that I realized that one of the sources of the story is a medieval Tantra and roots in the specific landscape of the land of love.

The Kalika Purana lists only a few Shakti piths. Other puranas fill out the full complement of 50, 51 and 52, depending on the source. A few stand out as Adi Shakti or very important Shakti sites. As the site of the yoni and the ongoing union of Shiva and Devi, Kamakhya Temple is usually at the top.

The Sanskritization of a tribal goddess explains why the description of Kamakhya Temple as a Shakti pith did not do the reality of the place justice. Mishra and others point out that bringing Kamakhya into the Shakti pith system connected the temple in Assam with other temples all over India. It gave the temple a context and brought pilgrims from around the country, the region and the world.

The Form of Kamakhya

The cave on the hill is not the only form of Kamakhya listed in the Kalika Purana. Biswanarayan Shastri's English version summarizes parts of the purana and translates excerpts focused on the descriptions of deities. Chapter 62 describes another form of Kamakhya called Kamesvari. This form of Kamakhya has six faces, each of which has a name and a color:

- Mahesvari
- Kamesvari
- Tripura
- Sarada
- Kamesvari
- Candika

- white
- red
- yellow
- green
- black
- variegated

Kamesvari appears twice in this list. Possibly oral instruction would give a different name for one of these. Each of these faces has three eyes, so she has eighteen eyes in total. She has twelve arms holding twelve tools. She stands on a red lotus coming from the navel of Siva, who appears here as a white ghost wearing a tiger skin and lying on the back of a lion.

This six-headed image matches the image I saw in the calanta in Kamakhya Temple. Since photographs are forbidden and I can only rely on memory, I am not certain whether there are differences between the description in the Kalika Purana and the image in the temple.

Buddhist Goddess

Kamakhya also has a Buddhist connection. Mishra points out that the ninth century Hevajra Tantra, a Buddhist text, lists Kamakhya as one of four main sacred centers of the goddess.

The scholar-practitioner Mark Dyczkowski has made a lifetime study of the secret Newar goddess Kubjika of Nepal, culminating in a multi-volume translation of the Kubjika Tantra. Dyczkowski explores her relationship to the Shiva linga. She is the goddess who emerges from the linga, and the goddess who contains the linga within herself.

Dyczkowski gives a translation of the Kalika Purana which discusses the journey of Bhairava and Vetala. Shiva told them:

> ...go to the inner sacred seat (antahpitha) of Kamarupa called Nilacala. This is the secret abode of (the goddess) Kamakhya called the sacred seat of Kubjika; there the heavenly Ganges (flows) (akasanganga). (Bathe there and) sprinkle (yourselves) with its waters, O sons: worship there Mahamaya who is the universe. Pleased, the goddess will quickly bestow (her) boons on you. (p.250)
>
> The goddess answers their prayers by bursting out of a lingam and appearing in a beneficent aspect. She does not appear as a lover, but as a Mother, and feeds them with streams of milk from her breasts, after which they became immortal.

The iconography of Kubjika matches the iconography of the six-headed Kamakhya. How did the goddess Kamakhya end up in Nepal?

Dyczkowski says that the Kubjika Tantras rely on the works of Matsyendranath, the founder of the Kaula Tantric lineage. Kulasundari Devi reports the legend that Matsyendranath was born in Assam and initiated into Tantra by yoginis at Kamakhya; he then Sanskritized the goddess and her teachings and spread them to Nepal.

Kamakhya's transference to Nepal as the goddess Kubjika lifts her into another dimension. As Ka Mei Kha she is the goddess of the cave. As Kamakhya she is a goddess of Tantric practice with an anthropomorphic visualization or dhyana. To become Kubjika, the goddess of the Newar people of Nepal, she transcends country and religion. She becomes universal.

Friday

The Journey

Every trip has a day like Friday, where nothing goes right.

Bhubaneswari Temple

I was excited to visit the Bhubaneswari shrine. My tutelary goddesses are aligned with Venus. I thought this would be the day that I would understand the Mahavidya and connect with her strongly.

This was a day that our guide was not available so we guided ourselves. Our driver knew where he was going and took us straight to the parking lot. The shrine sits higher than the others we had visited. It's on an entirely different hill than the main Kamakhya Temple, on the Brahma Pahar. The walkway up to the temple was flat with no stairs, a real treat.

I bought incense, oil lamps and garlands of flowers from the puja supply vendors. The trouble started when we stepped onto the temple grounds. As soon as we crossed the threshold Alex and I started fighting. This was a surprise and a departure. We had been travelling for nearly three weeks at that point and had been working together as a team. We did a lot of planning and trip preparation, including how to resolve travel irritations, and it had worked out really well. It felt as if we were travelling in a bubble of grace and happiness.

In the shrine of the goddess of love and domestic bliss our team fell apart. Each of us couldn't figure out what the other was doing, resulting in mis-steps in the ritual process. The familiar procedure of lighting lamps and incense was suddenly difficult. The steps into the garbagriha were crowded with eager devotees. The priests hurried us through the offerings and muttered the mantra at us without pausing for us to repeat.

The temple itself was under renovation, with bamboo scaffolding everywhere and piles of dirt in the walks. Alex found what he was looking for, a yogini statue next to an ancient tree. The statue is actually two yoginis back to back, but it was hard to get a photo that captured this.

While he took this photo I wandered down to the vendors and purchased a small image of Bhubaneswari in small glass frames. I took this home in my suitcase, and when I unpacked I found that despite wrapping it well, the glass had shattered, although the paper image was intact.

We had our driver take us down to the main temple walkway. We decided to split up and see if getting some space helped to re-establish our accord. I found a vendor and dropped off my shoes, which later turned out to be a mistake.

With much of the day in front of me I decided to visit the Bhairabi temple. I took the route our guide had recommended, passing the Dhumabati shrine. The stairs were lengthy and steep, but also clean and paved. Down below I saw two men carry a buffalo carcass on a pole. Clearly it had been sacrificed and was on its way to some location to be processed for the priests' families.

I walked through the gate of the temple courtyard. There were two buildings, both with locked doors, and a pond. A bored looking priest loitered in front of one of the buildings. From the lion decorations on the I gathered that one of them was a Durga temple.

Families came down to the pond to admire the large turtles that live there. I leaned against the fence to take pictures and wait for the temple to open. It turned out that I was standing on the buffalo carcass trail. Another pair of men walked briskly by just a few feet from me. The carcass was still twitching. My journal notes "big balls!"

That was, frankly, a little intense. Before another one of those could come by I approached the priest and asked him when the temple would open. "It is open," he said, and led me to a side entrance. It turns out that this is where you need to take off your shoes, and I could have worn them all the way down and back.

Inside the temple was dark and silent; the puja days are Sunday so there was no water in the well, although it did have a metal framework covered with a red cloth. There was no priest on duty either, but the guard priest from outside did follow me in so I didn't feel that I could sit and meditate. I made a quick pranam. Without any other offering I left money. My smallest bill was a 500 rupee note. As soon as it hit the offering tray it evaporated into the priest's pocket.

I decided to walk up the hill along the other route, the one Google Maps had indicated, that I had been warned not to try. The stairs looked clean and even from the temple courtyard. I figured that I would be able to tell people what the route was like. I got a good view of the Bhairabi Temple from the stairway.

Midway up the hill I discovered why I had been warned against the route. The stairs look good from below and above, but in the middle section hidden from view the walkway turned into a runoff channel. The stairs had deteriorated. They were covered with trash. The water that ran down the channel smelled like sewage.

I thought about turning back but I had already come some distance. Instead I talked myself through it, walking barefoot through the squishy bits trying not to breathe.

At the top of the hill I marched into the Kamakhya Temple rest rooms. They have troughs where you can wash your feet which was a real blessing. I sat on a bench outside the rest room to catch my breath. Families came and went, mothers and grandmothers with their children. One small boy walked up to me and stared at my white face. When his Mother noticed she told him to leave me alone, but told her it was okay. I was the stranger there.

When Alex and I met up again I asked to make the hotel our next stop. I wanted to wash my feet, change my leggings, and spray Lysol inside my shoes. Then I thought we could go to the state museum since it was still early in the afternoon. When our driver heard that plan he insisted on going to the museum first. When I checked out the map I realized why, it was not far from the temple, and traffic was building up.

The museum was closed for a special event. With that we returned to the hotel and called it a day.

At dinner we talked about the unnerving experience at the Bhubaneswari shrine. Alex said as soon as he stepped off the temple grounds he stopped being irritated. Both of us were puzzled about what had triggered our discord. Then I remembered what our guide had said, that Ma will give you what you need for balance. If we had been arguing for our entire trip Bhubaneswari might have given us a moment of grace.

Since we were getting along so well She gave us a moment of dispute so we could appreciate our harmony!

The Cradle of Tantra

Priests

When Anjali Pathak showed up at Kamakhya to interview a priest, Jitendra Sarma solemnly assured her Tantra was no longer practiced on the hill. "I learn to my surprise that the legendary tantrics of Kamakhya have all but disappeared," she said. "Since very few had disciples, their knowledge of tantra vidya died along with them. Jitendra is not a tantric or a Sanskrit scholar. He dropped out of college to follow in his father's footsteps as a pujari."

In contrast Ranjib Sarma's web profile tells us he is "Purnabhisheka Sadhaka (full adept) in the Kulacara Tantra Marga (Tantric tradition) of the Kamakhya Temples' Complex" and goes on to list the many scholarly research projects he has undertaken. Maybe Jitendra didn't get the same educational opportunities that Ranjib did. Or maybe Jitendra decided to downplay the Tantric stuff for a random reporter writing for a travel web site.

The priests seem to talk more openly with serious researchers. Parimal Kumar Datta, Nihar Ranjan Mishra and Prabalika Sarma all report on the Tantric rituals conducted by the priests. The overlap in their reporting serves as a verification that the priests are at least saying the same things to different researchers.

The Koch kings imported five Brahmin families to serve at the temple in the 1500s. The same families still live at Nilachal five hundred years later. Mahanta and Sarma both report on the hierarchy of the priests. The hereditary Brahmin priests occupy the highest rank. The non-Brahmin priests fill out the rank of temple workers. Their duties including guarding the temple gates, maintaining temple stores, keeping the temple accounts, making and repairing and cleaning temple gear, bringing water to the main temple and shrines, cooking food, and sacrificing animals. Mahanta noted that when she wrote her thesis, six families provided the balikata priests who perform the sacrifices.

We may recall that the tribal people were brought into the caste system in the class below Brahmin, kshatriya. I wonder how many of the temple worker families have some tribal heritage, if their ritual understandings differ from that of the Brahmins, and if there is some resentment.

This is a fair question in light of the socialist revolution. During British rule, and after Independence in 1947, the Brahmin hierarchy managed the temple. In 1998 a socialist group took temporary control of the temple with a coalition of Brahman and non-Brahmin sevaits. In the second chapter of her thesis Prabalika Sarma describes the events from the point of view of the Brahmin priests: "They attempted to implement a socialistic pattern of management of Kamakhya temple by sharing the control of Bardeori Samaj and the Dolois and giving charge to people who were neither by custom nor by tradition capable of taking such a charge. They even promised to give the voting rights to the females". With all due respect to Sarma, I'm rooting for the socialists!

The revolution didn't last. There were accusations of misuse of funds. The government stepped in and tried a power-sharing scheme that also failed. Ultimately the five hereditary Brahman families regained control of the temple. They have since allowed non-hereditary priests to hold some additional offices, but re-established the procedure that only men can vote and be priests.

Ritual

I found the third chapter of Sarma's thesis to be riveting. "The Calendric Activities Of The Kamakhya Temple Religious Rites, Rituals, Ceremonies, Vratas & Festivals" documents the rituals of the temple. Some stories leapt out in particular.

Secret practitioners. Sarma tells us that there are practitioners doing private and severe meditations who only come out at particular times of year. I've watched videos of Kamakhya at festival times swarming with sadhaks and wondered where they come from. They do come from all over the country, but it turns out that some of them live at Nilachal all year long.

Severe practices. Human sacrifice was performed at the temple until fairly recently. The practice dropped off both because of the outcry and the decline of people volunteering themselves to be sacrificed. People also remember their grandfathers engaging in practices like meditating while sitting on a corpse, worshipping a skull while naked, and erecting altars on human skulls. These practices have reportedly also declined in the modern era.

Animal sacrifice. The balikata priests are kept busy. The main garbagriha gets one goat sacrifice every morning, and the smaller temples and shrines have sacrifices on their open days. Some, like the Kali temple, have larger yokes that can even handle buffalo. These sacrifices are offered by priests at the temples for the common good, but devotees can also offer a pigeon or a goat for their own requests any day of the week, although Sarma notes a buffalo sacrifice requires a two-day notice. On Navratri the priests make so many sacrifices for the main temple they don't even start in on the buffalo until midnight.

Deodhani dances. In August, during the festival of the snake goddess Maa Manasa, a special class of laity enact what Sarma calls shamanistic dances. They identify themselves to the priests and get training. During the three-day festival they drum and dance all night, possessed by the spirits of the Devis and Devas of the various Nilachal temples. As they dance people make offerings of goats, ducks and pigeons, asking to have their future read. The Deodhas sometimes bite the heads off the pigeons and drink their blood. At the end of the third night they immerse themselves in the water of the Saubhagya Kund to cool down and end the trance possession. Once chosen they engage in this ritual role for life.

Cakra puja. During the Rajrajeshvari festival the priests engage in the cakra rituals described in the Kalika Purana and Yogini Tantra. They make the pancamakara or five offerings, one of which is sexual intercourse. The festival goes on for fifteen days, and Sarma lists ten Devis who are offered the puja. The ritual can take place at the Kameswara temple along the main road, or in the Bhairabi temple tucked down by the Durga Kund, Sarma says, "according to convenience."

Daily and Seasonal Puja

Sarma tells us that the elaborate rituals conducted by priests a few generations ago have been somewhat curtailed by the increasing popularity of the temple, as the requirement to open the main temple for darshan has cut into the time available to do lengthy pujas. However slightly shorter forms of puja pujas are faithfully conducted three times a day.

Datta, Mishra and Sarma all agree on the main points of the ritual routine. In the morning the garbagriha is cleaned out and fresh red cloths are stretched out over the yoni. The yoni is sprinkled with water from the nearby Saubhagya Kund and offered a goat head. After that the temple opens for visitors. The garbagriha closes for lunch, at which time the yoni is offered a vegetarian meal. In the afternoon devotees are once again allowed into the enclosure. The garbagriha closes about seven pm for the night when an evening aarti (flame ritual) is offered. Devi is not alone however, at least one priest stays in the garbagriha at all times. This goes on all day every day except for the three days per year that the Devi is menstruating, when no visitors are allowed and she is left alone.

Sarma gives the most complete list of seasonal rituals. There are so many, she notes, that her list is not exhaustive. Once when she went to Nilachal she found the priests celebrating a Chaitra Navratri that no one had previously mentioned.

Viewing the yoni

Prabalika Sarma documents as much detail as she could coax the priests to provide about the morning puja. First, one or two priests called Athporias remove the red saris over the yoni cleft and replace it with new saris. They do this in complete silence. While they do so they cover their eyes with white cloth and avert their eyes so as not to look at the yoni. Once they have performed their duties the Barapujari goes into the enclosure to offer the goat's head and other offerings.

This leaves me with a question. I was somewhat surprised when I visited that my view of the yoni was obscured by cloth and flowers. I thought that the priests must be the only people who see the yoni. Prabalika Sarma tells us that the priests who replace the cloth go out of their way not to view it. By the time the Barapujari conducts the daily offerings the yoni is by concealed beneath the cloth. Does he see it? If not, when was the last time someone saw it?

I notice that some people who visit the temple describe the yoni, while others report seeing only flowers, as I did. I wonder if the people describing the yoni are actually relying on the description in the Kalika Purana.

Texts

Prabalika Sarma tells us, "At Kamakhya the Vamacara Tantra Marg of Puja is followed." Vamacara means left-hand path. As she documents, the left-hand path includes offerings to deity of meat and sexual intercourse. This path can scandalize people not accustomed to thinking of sexuality as a sacred offering. There was a good reason for Jitendra Sarma to downplay the ongoing performance of Tantric ritual to an outside reporter.

Vamacara Tantra is documented in a few texts which were almost certainly composed in Assam. The Kalika Purana specifies some of the rituals, including human sacrifice and the offering of goat heads. I have not found an English translation of the whole text, only the excerpts by Biswanarayan Shastri.

The Kamakhya priests also draw on the Yogini Tantra. This text was written somewhat later than the Kalika Purana, in the 16th or 17th century. Mike Magee summarizes the Tantra on his web site. Biswanarayan Shastri's Sanskrit edition also summarizes the text in an English introduction. The Yogini Tantra identifies Kamakhya as the most sacred site. This Tantra also describes the rituals of pancamakara, the offering of grain, fish, meat, wine and sexual intercourse. The text includes meditation on a seat of five skulls, pancamunda, in which at least one of the skulls should be human. The text notes that no sadhaka can meditate without a Sakti, that is, a female partner. Versions of this meditation include Kumari Puja, worshipping a virgin girl, and yoni puja, worshipping a living female yoni.

Many sources report that the priests draw on the Kalika Purana and the Yogini Tantra for their rituals. Mishra adds the interesting note that the priests perform the kavaca (armor of energy) ritual from the Bhairavi

Tantra. Presumably he is referring to the Vijnana-Bhairava Tantra. Unlike the Kalika Purana and Yogini Tantra, the Vijnana-Bhairava Tantra has been translated into English by numerous scholars, possibly because it is a much shorter text! Personally I refer to the version translated by the woman practitioner Swami Satyasangananda Saraswati. This is a Kashmiri Saivite compendium of meditation techniques.

There is one additional text associated with Kamakhya that I haven't seen any other scholar mention. Parimal Kumar Datta translated the Kamakhya Tantra in 2017. This work begins "The description of the own form or identity of Sri Kamakhya Devi who is in the form of vagina. Aum salutations to SriKalika. SriKamakhya is victorious." Like the Kalika Purana and the Yogini Tantra, the Kamakhya Tantra outlines the practice of Tantra. The text instructs the male practitioner to find a guru, acquire a female partner, and engage in ritual, including sexual intercourse while his partner is menstruating. The text gives mantras to recite along with visualizations of the goddess, and specifies the powers that these rituals impart.

Women at Kamakhya

The legendary founder of Kaula Tantra, Matsyendranath, was said to have received an initiation from a yogini at Kamakhya. We know that a socialist attempt to give women voting power at Kamakhya failed and that only men are priests. We also know that the Tantras are almost always written for the male practitioner. Are there women who practice Tantra at Kamakhya, and do they practice on their own behalf?

In *Kamakhyatantra* Parimal Kumar Datta includes an image among the plates of a "Bhairavini", a woman with matted locks longer than she is tall. She is clearly engaged in some kind of practice. But what does she do?

Sravana Borkataky Varma asked that question. Now with the Department of Religious Studies at Rice University, she was born in Assam and speaks Assamese. She spent a number of years doing field work at Kamakhya. She found that it was very difficult to talk to Tantric practitioners. She was able to find a married man to describe his practice, but it was much harder to gain access to women. She says, "While I hung around in the temple at different times of the day, my contacts would point out the consorts, but I was not allowed to approach them. Since I persisted in asking to be introduced, I was subtly told to drop my requests or I would get into a lot of trouble."

Finally she was able to arrange a joint interview with two wives of Tantric adepts. They came from families at Kamakhya where the girls are raised as Tantric spouses. After they take diksha with their husbands their subsequent duties involve rituals which they perform four times a day. Varma reports that they did not have a meaningful choice in the matter, they were required to take the diksha to aid their husbands, and they found this duty largely burdensome.

Varma notes that she does know women Tantric adepts who have raised kundalini, and that their experiences are similar to that of men. She concludes, "the tradition seems to have tied the awakening of the kundalini to male practitioners. I believe that is merely a bi-product of the socio-cultural narrative that has been driven by men for men's consumption."

Fortunately we do have the direct words of some of the women of Kamakhya themselves. Tracey Wares presented her doctoral dissertation in the form of a film. In this film women conduct puja themselves. They describe Devi, Ma, as the origin of all things. They honor Shiva as her consort and the union of Shiva and Ka Mei Ka as the source of all life. One of the women explains that Ma is everything, in all women, she herself is Ma, she offers puja to herself. One of the men Wares interviewed her required her to repeat to him "I am Ma."

Saturday

The Journey

Kali Temple

"You might want to step over here," our guide said, as the Balikata priest led the goat to the sacrifice yoke.

The Kali Temple is in some ways the most central temple in the complex. It's right on the main walkway. The roofed and open-walled outer courtyard lies at right angles to the inner courtyard. I'd sat there for an hour one afternoon watching a monkey cadge bananas from the crowd while Alex shopped for Kamakhya souvenirs to hand out to the folks back home. Saturday is Kali day and the temple gets a lot more crowded.

While our guide set up our oil lamps I'd seen a goat dragged into the main shrine by the rope around his neck. I knew he was a male goat because only male animals are sacrificed, all females are exempt. (This is why it was such a shock that a woman's headless corpse was found at one of the temples downhill three days before Ambubachi Mela in 2019 - Ma will not accept offerings of any female creature.)

The goat was taken to a priest who perched near the well in the garbagriha. The priest dabbed the goat with red kumkum. Then the Balikata priest dragged the little guy to a nearby water bucket and splashed his head with water. The goat was dragging his heels and protesting all the way. I thought about what a Tantric acquaintance at a Kali temple in West Bengal had told me that his tradition believes: the goat should be taken to the sacrifice yoke and given a choice. If the goat protests he is set free. If he accepts the sacrifice, gives up his goat life, he will be reborn again as a human being. I discovered there isn't time for that kind of nicety at Kamakhya. The devotee has bought a goat, the priest is waiting for the head to continue the puja, and there's a line of people waiting for their moment in the garbagriha.

As the bleating goat's neck was placed down into the sacrifice yoke, I said to Kali, *do you really need this*?

I want you to see what is happening, She answered.

Thwack!

After we lit our candles and incense, our guide led us into the garbagriha. By then the little goat's head had been placed at the well and a candle set on his forehead. It looked so much like a prop on Hollywood B-movie set that I almost laughed. All this was done in accordance with the thousand-year-old Kalika Purana, in a brisk but respectful manner, in a sacred place. It was also the exact image of everything many westerners fear and condemn.

We gave the priest money and touched the well, which was dry. Our guide stepped back against the wall for a moment of private prayer. I realized there was a lull in the busy pulse of the temple day, so I stepped back next to him to spend a moment in the inner sanctum.

Look, She said to me. *I want you to see what is really here.*

I looked up into the round tower. The darkness seemed to be infinite, like the night sky, but without stars. It was the universe, the black womb of the cosmos, and I was floating in it.

I looked down at the well. I realized there was a large black stone in the center of the well. It was covered with red hibiscus flowers which dripped down its sides. With an electric shock I realized that the stone was breathing. As she had instructed I looked, really looked, to make sure I wasn't imagining it. Was it an optical illusion because the flowers were sliding? No. The stone was expanding and contracting with tremendous pulses of power.

There was no part of me that doubted this. Westerners have skepticism built into our outlook, and there are places it is very useful to have. But when we are confronted with experiences outside our worldview we use our skepticism to hide from our fear of what we can't assimilate: that can't be true, there must be an explanation. That automatic this-isn't-really-happening voice was entirely silence by the experience. I was in the Kali Temple at Kamakhya on the day when special pujas are offered and the stone in the garbagriha was breathing.

When we had all finished our meditations we took one last trip around the Kamakhya Temple grounds. I wanted to check the famous image of the crouching nude goddess with the prominent yoni. It was covered with red cloth all the days we were on site. I asked our guide if it was to hide her, and he said it was a decoration left over from Navratri and meant to honor her. But I was disappointed not to see her.

I did get to see a sculpture of Varahi. I'd read there was an image of her on the temple walls. I asked our guide where it was but he didn't know. He asked the priests in the courtyard but they didn't know. Alex found it and happily led me to her.

I located a spot on the walls around the garbagriha where a sculpture of a yogini had been dabbed with red kumkum. I leaned my head against the wall and felt down into the waters of the spring, feeling the golden light in my heart, resonating with the bone-deep devotion of the ages. I was filled with gratitude. As I stood there a man passing by said to me "Jai maa."

I had another photographic mission. I'd been reading Jae-Eun Shin's book on the Mahavidyas and she mentioned there were two sculptures of Chamundi at the Kameswara Temple. I asked our guide to take us and he said it was right at the bottom of the stairway. The temple was closed but the two sculptures were right outside. I was thrilled to have a chance to make the images to share with my kula sisters.

Madan Kamdev

We still had plenty of time in the day. Alex and I had already done our shopping, we had our tea from Assam and beautiful raw silk shawls. I mentioned to our guide that I would like to come back and see Madan Kamdev. He said why don't we go now? It's only an hour away.

As we crossed the Brahmaputra, our guide commented he was so glad we weren't leaving Guwahati without seeing the north side of the river. Our travels in West Bengal had been on rough roads, but here the road was flat and paved, and the green forest and lush fields were a welcome relief from the city.

Our guide had worried about how we would handle the number of stairs from the parking lot to the main site, but the walkway sloped gradually and the stairs themselves were quite low, so Alex and I managed easily. We took our shoes off at the gate. The ancient temple blocks were piled up around a raised dirt platform. The site has one large intact statue, an image of a man and woman conjoined, which was located in the center of the platform. This had been wrapped with red cloth, once again concealing the erotic image. I walked around the blocks taking photos of the famous images of amorous couples that give the site its nickname "Kujaraho of the North".

Then our guide showed up with oil lamps and asked if we were ready to do puja. Where did he get those? It turned out there were puja vendors on site. We stopped first at the Ganesh shrine. Then we climbed up onto the dirt platform where we found a little Brahmin priest tucked down behind the stones! He had a little altar with gold colored status of

Shiva and Parvati. We lit more diya lamps, threw flowers at the statues, and got tilaks. We concluded the visit with a stop at the Shiva shrine on the grounds.

This was the first archaeological site I'd visited which was still in use as a temple, and I found that very moving.

The priests were very excited to have white people visiting the site. One Brahmin priest put one of the beautiful Assamese scarves around our necks. Alex got to keep it, which was fine with me. We signed their visitor register.

Our guide indicated the statue and said to us, "Rati and Kamdev." The Brahmin priest stepped in and corrected him: "Shiva and Uma!" Our guide looked chastised, so I smiled at him and said, "It doesn't matter. They are the same," and he smiled back.

That was how we ended our tour of Kamarupa, receiving a puja asking for the blessings of the entwined Devi and Deva, in the place where love was reborn.

The Mahavidyas

Until recently there were few texts written about the Mahavidyas in English. David Kinsley's *Tantric Visions of the Divine Feminine, the Ten Mahavidyas* is an extensive academic survey of the goddesses. It gave me a lot of information but didn't bring me closer to understanding how to relate to them in practice. I knew Laura Amazzone had visited the Mahavidya shrines at Kamakhya. When I found that Parimal Kumar Datta's book *Kamakhyatantra* listed the days of the week the shrines held special pujas, I thought that visiting during those days would be a good introduction to the Devis.

The Mahavidya shrines at Nilachal

Before I visited Kamakhya I had thought darshan, receiving the energy from a deity, was about looking into the eyes of a statue. This has been true of Hindu temples I have visited in the U.S. and it was true in West Bengal and Varanasi. I found that the Kamakhya Mahavidya shrines don't have statues, they have rocks and water basins. The visitor comes into the energy field of the goddess just by stepping onto the grounds.

The main Kamakhya temple had many murtis, deity images, in the other rooms of the temple. There was the statue of the six-headed Kamakhya and the six-headed Kameswara in the calanta room. It was hidden under flowers but replicated outside in a large sculpture, so I knew it was there and what it looked like. There was also the painting of the six-headed Kamakhya hanging in the calanta over the entrance to the garbagriha.

None of the Mahavidya shrines had statues or paintings that I saw. There was a plate in the Chinnamasta temple but it was completely covered with kumkum and I had no idea what it might have shown. The vendors around the Bhubaneshwari shrine offered little paper images of the Devi. The shopkeepers on the main walkway to Kamakhya temple offered identical versions of the Mahavidyas surrounding the six-headed Kamakhya, and all ten are depicted there. Those were the only images of the Mahavidyas I encountered.

As a practitioner I usually have an image of the deity and a mantra to focus on. I can repeat a seed syllable, count 108 short mantras on a mala, or chant some number of repetitions of a longer mantra. When I went to Kamakhya I had no images or mantras for any of the Mahavidyas. I did chant the Buddhist White Tara mantra in the Ugra Tara temple in Guwahati, and later learned that temple has a Buddhist connection.

Of all the Mahavidyas I had the best understanding of Chinnamasta. Elizabeth Anne Benard's book *Chinnamasta, the Aweful Buddhist and Hindu Tantric Goddess* introduced her to me as the goddess who is the sacrifice, the sacrificer, and the one who receives the sacrifice. She gives visualizations and the thousand names of the goddess. At Kamakhya, of all the shrines, Chinnamasta's was the one that most closely matched the main shrine, an underground rock with a spring.

While I was in Guwahati I found Jae-Eun Shin's book *Change, Continuity and Complexity, The Mahavidyas in East Indian Sakta Traditions.* Shin tells us that the priests at Kamakhya say the Mahavidya temples were founded at the same time as the main temple. Archaeological evidence can substantiate temples in the sixteenth or seventeenth century, with parts of the structures possibly dating to the eleventh or twelfth centuries. She also tells us that at Kamakhya the Mahavidyas, and the

64 yoginis, are all understood to originate from Kamakhya's yoni. They are all connected to the main temple.

At Nilachal the Mahavidyas map out onto the days of the week through their associated planet and are experienced in that sequence. The order depends on the day you start.

Day	Goddess	Temple	Planet
Monday	Kamala	Main pith	Moon
Tuesday	Bagala	Bagala Temple	Mars
Wednesday	Sodasi	Main pith	Mercury
	Chinnamasta	Chinnamasta Temple	Rahu
Thursday	Tara	Tara Temple	Jupiter
	Dhumavati	Dhumabati Temple	Ketu
Friday	Bhubaneshvari	Bhubaneshwari Temple	Venus
Saturday	Kali	Kali Temple	Saturn
Sunday	Matangi	Main pith	Sun
	Bhairavi	Bhairabi Temple	None

Mahavidyas enshrined in the main pith

In practice there are only seven independent Mahavidya shrines. Parimal Kumar Datta tells us that three of the Mahavidyas, Kamala, Sodasi, and Matangi, are held to be enshrined in the main pith. Special pujas are offered to each of them on their respective days, Monday for Kamala, Wednesday for Sodasi, Sunday for Matangi.

We went to the main pith on Tuesday so did not observe whether devotees could participate in the puja offered to these three Mahavidyas. We were able to participate in the pujas offered by the shrine priests to Bagala, Chinnamasta, Dhumavati, Bhubaneshvari and Kali. There was no priest conducting puja at the Tara shrine on the Thursday we visited, and I visited the Bhairabi shrine on another day than its puja day.

Prabalika Sarma describes the daily ritual the priests conduct in the garbagriha: "Then they spread two saris of thirteen hands of length from the yoni peetha to the peethas of Kamala and Matangi to replace the previous day's saris with the new ones." This locates Kamala and Matangi right at the main yoni. It's not clear to me whether there is any physical representation of these Mahavidyas other than the rock itself.

I am also not clear where Sodasi is said to be located. Our guide said her waters are the first ones encountered when entering the temple. When I entered I saw people dipping their hands into a basin of water; I tried to go there but the guards prevented me from doing so. I don't know if that is the pith of Sodasi.

Swami Ayyappa Giri of the Yogini Ashram in California describes a pilgrimage to the Mahavidya shrines at Kamakhya. As Datta does, he places three Mahavidyas physically in the main shrine. He gives additional detail about where they are located. In his description, when the devotees step down into the garbagriha and receive the water of Kamakhya, they turn to the right "where Lakshmi, Sri, and Saraswati reside. Saraswati, too, is in the form of a yoni and Lakshmi is partly represented by a three-dimensional Sri Yantra." Matangi, he says, is the Tantric Saraswati. "Matangi is placed in the innermost sanctum (*garbhagriha*) of the main temple to the east of the Yoni Mudra Peeth, easily visible as one leaves the sanctum sanctorum." He also says, "On the way toward the outside of the temple, there are additional opportunities to pay homage in small alcoves dedicated to Matangi and Kamala." I did not see those during my visit.

He also maps the Mahavidyas onto the yoni. Of Sodashi he says, "Anatomically she resides in the outside upper right quadrant of the yoni lips." Kamala "is associated with the lower left quadrant of the external portion of the yoni." Matangi "is associated with the upper left quadrant of the yoni. Re-mapping the quadrant shape to the triangle usually associated with the yoni, this would give:

Matangi   Sodashi
            Kamala

From the description though it is not clear whether the yoni he describes is the rock yoni in the Kamakhya garbagriha, or any physical yoni, or both.

Mahavidya Practice

I did not have a Mahavidya practice when I went to Kamakhya. At Nilachal I participated in pujas offered to the Mahavidyas. I offered oil lamps, incense, flowers and money. I touched water. I received a tilak. At the Dhumabati and Bhubaneswari temples the priest spoke a mantra at me, and at the Dhumabati shrine I was asked to repeat it, but I have no idea what that mantra was or how it was meant to affect me.

Our guide told us that local people approach the shrines in the same way that they approach the Navagraha temples. They have their Vedic horoscopes cast, then commission pujas from the Mahavidya associated with a specific planet to correct deficiencies. They also approach the Devis for their generally understood powers: Bagala protects against magical attack, Bagala and Dhumavati grant magical power, Bhubaneshvari grants marital harmony and children. People also approach the main Kamakhya temple with wishes for marriage and children.

Since visiting Kamakhya I have found additional references which speak more clearly to practice. In *The Ten Great Cosmic Powers, Das Mahavidyas*, Sri S. Shankaranarayanan presents the Mahavidyas as ten discrete manifestations of the Divine Mother. Each represents a path to Her realization. Kavitha M. Chinnaiyan's book *Shakti Rising: Embracing Shadow and Light on the Goddess Path to Wholeness* maps the ten Mahavidyas as a spiritual journey, exploring dark and light aspects of each, with accompanying exercises and meditations. Madhu Khanna's book *Saktapramodah of Deva Nandan Singh* has an English introduction with some descriptions of practice, although the sixteen texts with visualizations and mantras are given only in the Sanskrit originals.

I am now on the path of experiencing the Mahavidyas through the Tantric practices of visualization and mantra. I am still exploring how this connects with my experience of the Mahavidya shrines at Nilachal. I look at the images of the Mahavidyas and try to relate them to what I felt at the shrine. Scholars, priests and practitioners talk about the Mahavidyas as if they are the same from one place to another. That may be true on a more universal level, but on the hills the experience is so energetically overwhelming, it's very much tied to the feeling of the place. Whatever else they are, like the Devi Kamakhya in the main temple, the first layer of the power of the Mahavidyas at Nilachal is grounded in water and rock.

Ongoing Practice

We visited Assam the week after Navratri in October 2019. Just a few months later Assam erupted in protests of the Citizenship Amendment Bill. The Indian government responded by stopping plane and train travel to Guwahati, shutting down internet access and imposing a curfew. I worried about our guide and his family. When the internet came back up I waited for a day to make sure his urgent message queue was cleared out, and then sent him a WhatsApp message letting him know I was praying for him. He had quite a story – he'd been guiding three European tourists out of town when the trouble hit, and managed to get them to a regional airport and out of Assam safely, before getting himself back home. He truly is an exceptional guide.

Alex and I made the trip thinking that this might be the only time we visit India. It was physically difficult for me, but I am powerfully drawn to return to Kamakhya. I would like to practice Mahavidya sadhanas in their shrines and connect the mantras and visualizations to the energy of place. I didn't get to any of the Durga temples, and there's an entire Shiva circuit I didn't even register while I was there. I can easily imagine spending a month in Guwahati.

Whether or not I return I have made a permanent connection. Even though I live thousands of miles away I continue to feel the power of the temple. Alex, Ted and I are reading through the Kamakhya Tantra together. Alex and I brought a statue of the six-headed Kamakhya home with us and installed it on our house puja altar.

I do sadhana every night and I often revisit Her. I use the visualization from the Kalika Purana of Siddhakamesvari: a young woman with a saffron complexion, seated on a lotus, standing on the ghost Siva. She has three eyes, offers the protection and boon-giving mudras, and holds a rosary. I keep her golden light in my heart as I experienced it at Nilachal, and chant her mantra.

As I chant I place myself back in the garbagriha. This time I am alone in the cave, dipping my hand in the spring welling up from the rock.

It isn't a visualization or imagining; while I am chanting, I see the rock walls, I hear the echo of thousands of years of chant, I feel the power of the Mother surrounding me and filling me.

Jai Maa Kamakhya!

Appendix A: Illustrations

Kamakhya Mandir entrance

Kamakhya stairway

Entrance gate to Kamakhya Temple grounds

Information desk and toilets

Waiting hall

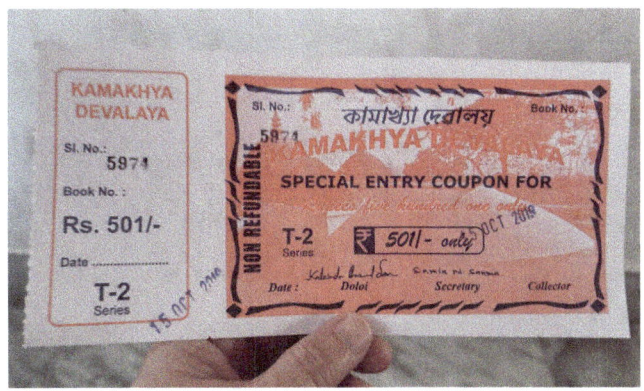

Empty hallway on left, occupied hallway on right

Alex and me

Carved temple walls

Free line

Kameswara and Kamakhya

Temple exit

Buffalo yoke behind priest

Maa Bagala Temple stairs

Left: Shelves for lamps; Right: Brazier for fire offerings

Southern view of forest landscape from vantage above Bhairabi Mandir

Chinnamasta Temple sign

Sacrifice yoke

Chinnamasta Temple entrance

View from Navagraha Temple

Navagraha Temple

Flower garlands on the Tara Temple arch

Overhead view of Dhumabati temple roof

Gate into the Ugra Tara temple

Gateway to Peacock Island

Alex descending the stairs at the Shiva Temple

Walkway to Bhubeswari Temple and vendors

Tree and yogini statue – Photo © 2019 Alex Williams

Small image of Bhubaneswari

Stairway past Dhumabati Temple to Bhairabi Temple

Durga Temple through Bhairabi gate

Turtle pond

Bhairabi Temple

A fouled stairway

Kali Temple alongside the walkway

Crouching goddess, hidden yoni

Chamundi

There's a priest hidden behind those blocks

Bibliography

Amazzone, Laura. *Goddess Durga and Sacred Female Power*. Hamilton Books, 2010.

Benard, Elizabeth Anne. *Chinnamasta, the Aweful Buddhist and Hindu Tantric Goddess*. Motilal Banarsidass, 1994.

Chinnaiyan, Kavitha M., M.D. *Shakti Rising: Embracing Shadow and Light on the Goddess Path to Wholeness*. New Harbinger Publications, 2017.

Datta, Parimal Kumar. *Tantra Its Relevance to Modern Times*. Gauhati University (Doctoral dissertation), sg.inflibnet.ac.in/handle/10603/67811, 2017. Accessed 12/27/2019.

Datta, Parimal Kumar. *Kamakhyatantra and the Mysterious History of Kamakhya*. Puthi Pustak, 2017.

Devi, Kulasundari. "What's in a Name? The Ancient Origins of Ma Kamakhya", *Jaimaa.org*, www.jaimaa.org/articles/kalikapurana-why-is-she-called-kamakhya/. Accessed 12/27/2019.

Devi, Kulasundari. "Matsyendranath (Macchendranath) and the Origins of Tantra", *Jaimaa.org*, www.jaimaa.org/articles/matsyendranath-macchendranath-and-the-origins-of-tantra/. Accessed 12/27/2019.

Devi, Namita. *Landform Dynamics in Greater Guwahati Area (Assam): A Study in Environment Geomorphology*. Gauhati University (Doctoral dissertation), shodhganga.inflibnet.ac.in/handle/10603/69747, 2008. Accessed 12/27/2019.

Dyczkowski, Mark. Mathanabhairavatantrum Kumarikahandah. *Volume One, Introduction: Myth, History and Doctrine of the Goddess Kubjika*. Indira Gandhi National Centre for the Arts, D.K. Printworld, 2009.

Gait, Sir Edward Albert. *A History of Assam*. Thacker, Spink and Co., 1906.

Giri, Swami Ayyappa. "Pilgrimage to Kamakya: The Great Yoni and Mahavidya Shakti Temples of Assam". *Yoginiashram.com*, www.yoginiashram.com/pilgrimage-to-kamakya-the-great-yoni-and-mahavidya-shakti-temples-of-assam/, 2014.

Kinsley, David. *Tantric Visions of the Divine Feminine, the Ten Mahavidyas*. Motilal Banarsidass, 1997.

Magee, Mike. "Yogini Tantra", *shivashakti.com*, www.shivashakti.com/yogini.htm. Accessed 12/29/2019.

Mahanta, Juthika. *Tourism and Associated Development in and around Nilachal Kamakhya, a Geographical Analysis*. Gauhati University (Doctoral dissertation), shodhganga.inflibnet.ac.in/handle/10603/184533, 2017. Accessed 12/27/2019.

Mishra, Nihar Ranjan (2004). *Kamakhya, A Socio-Cultural Study*. D.K. Printworld, New Delhi.

Pathak, Anjali. "For a priest at the famed Kamakhya temple in Guwahati, Assam, work is worship". *Outlook Traveller*, Aug. 26 2014. Web site: https://www.outlookindia.com/outlooktraveller/travelnews/story/45715/assam-a-day-in-the-life-of-a-priest-at-kamakhya-temple. Accessed 12/28/2019.

Saraswati, Swami Satyasangananda. *Sri Vijnana-Bhairava Tantra, The Ascent*. Yoga Publications Trust, 2003.

Sarma, Prabalika (2018). *Mother Goddess Kamakhya and the Role of the Pandas*. Gauhati University (Doctoral dissertation), hdl.handle.net/10603/209147, 2018. Accessed 12/27/2019.

Sarma, Rajib. "A Historical Note on Sri Sri Kamakhya Temple", Jaimaa.org, www.jaimaa.org/articles/a-historical-note-on-sri-sri-kamakhya-temple/. Accessed Dec. 26 2019.

"About Rajib Sarma". *Nilacala Kamakhya, Sacred Abode of the Mother Goddess*, kamakhya.org/about-us/rajib-sarma/. Accessed Dec. 17 2019.

Shankaranarayanan, S. *The Ten Great Cosmic Powers, Das Mahavidyas*. Samata Books, 1975, 2001.

Sharma, Navamallika. Ancient Temples of Guwahati City: Religious activities and Socio-Economic Life Pattern of the Temple Serving People, A Study in Social Geography. Gauhati University (Doctoral dissertation), 2015. Accessed Dec. 27 2019.

Shastri, Biswanarayan. *Kalikapurane Murtivinirdesa.* Motilal Banarsidass, 1994.

Shastri, Biswanarayan. *Yogini Tantra.* Bharatiya Vidya Pradakshan, 1982.

Shin, Jae-Eun. *Change, Continuity and Complexity, The Mahavidyas in East Indian Sakta Traditions.* Routledge, 2018.

Varma, Sravana Borkataky. "The Ancient Elusive Serpent in Modern Times: The Practice of Kuṇḍalinī in Kāmākhyā or The Elusive Serpent". *International Journal of Dharma and Hindu Studies,* Volume 1 Number 2, January 2016.

Wares, Tracey (2001). *Shakti: The Performance of Gendered Roles at Kamakhya, Assam.* Senior Honors thesis of Tracy Wares, Anthropology Department of the University of California, 2001, youtube/9MEgEtpbun8. Accessed Dec. 27 2019.

BOOK FOUR:
VARANASI

Introduction

Kashi, Banaras, Varanasi, city of joy, city of light, city of Shiva. By any name it is one of the holiest cities in India. Alex insisted that we had to go.

When I asked my Tantric teacher for advice on what to see she asked "How long is your stay?"

"Three days," I said.

"Three days! You can't spend just three days in Varanasi!" The trip was already set, there wasn't much that could change, but I shorted our stay in Guwahati and managed four days in the city.

My teacher recommended the book *Banaras Region, A Spiritual and Cultural Guide.* I diligently studied the text trying to make sense of it. So many sacred circuits imprint on the city, how could we choose which one to do? Finally we decided that we were there to connect with the gods, Shiva for Alex and Varahi for me, so we would focus on two temples in particular. I made arrangements in advance for a local guide to give us a tour of the city. We watched YouTube videos of the evening services on the river where young men lifted huge towers of oil lamps to the sacred waters.

It was 2019 and the internet news was all about the demolition and reconstruction project. The area between Shiva's gilded temple Kashi Vishwanath and the Ganges river had silted up with buildings over the centuries so it was difficult for people to approach the temple from the river. Narendra Modi's government decided to relocate the people and bulldoze the buildings. These were both residences and businesses so they had to replace both the housing and the livelihoods. Finally they managed to buy out the residents. When they tore down the buildings they discovered older temples that had simply been incorporated into the new structures, so they left those standing. As I write the residents of Varanasi still bitterly complain that their families were blamed for cluttering the walkway but their homes preserved sacred places that would otherwise have been razed to the ground by Muslim and British invaders.

In all my reading before the trip what stuck with me was the proverb about the four hazards of the city: "Widows, bulls, steps and sannyasis – only if you survive them can you enjoy your stay in Kashi." Cows: all over India female cows are kept to wander but bulls are not killed and eaten as elsewhere in the world. Instead they are released to wander and fend for themselves. Widows: this is a sad addition to the list. In north India women who lose their husbands are chased out of their homes and villages and sent to Varanasi to beg on the streets. Framing them as a danger seems to lack compassion. Sannyasis: this puzzled me, I wasn't sure what made people who have made vows of renunciation a nuisance to be avoided. Steps: of all the hazards listed this worried us the most. Pictures and videos showed large stone blocks without handrails. We read that there could be a hundred steps between the river and your destination. Alex was 70 at the time, I was 63 and just retired from a desk job, and we worried about our stamina and our balance. The year before we left we went to the gym nearly every day and made a point to climb up and down the stairs.

The gym helped us navigate the city physically, but our research in books and videos and news reports did not prepare us for the conflicting emotions we experienced. The romantic image of the city is ossified in the nineteenth century. In the twenty-first century we found a city of contrasts: ancient and new, spiritual and polluted, a place of pilgrimage studded with decidedly modern hazards.

Arrival: A Palace Hotel and Evening Aarati

We flew into the city. We'd chosen to stay at the Brij Rama, a palace turned hotel, partly because the hotel organized our transportation to and from the airport. As the driver navigated the half-hour drive into the city he talked about God, which he said stands for Generator Operator Destroyer, Brahma-Vishnu-Shiva. He said people want moksha, but when you meet God and return and your body is still alive it is too soon for moksha. You have to wait. In my journal I wrote "Varanasi, where the cab driver is a theurgist."

The driver pulled over at Assi Ghat. The stone ghats or docks crowd along the river providing spaces for boats to pull up and for people to step in the river to bathe. This one was a good place to offload passengers to avoid driving through the narrow and dense roads of the central city. It's much easier to transport people by boat up and down the river. The hotel boat had an engine and a roof over the benches which turned out to be a luxury. The boat wobbled and I had to be helped by the staff to make it on safely.

As we motored along the river I scanned the banks eagerly. It was a unique place to take in. Other cities have rivers, other river cities in India have ghats crowded with people, but in Varanasi these are central features. I could make out the spires of temples along the street. We registered the visceral impact of the fires of the crematorium right on the river bank. There was an immediate sense of being at the heart of something. In the west we might call it the spiritual center of Hindu religion and talk about faith, but the experience is not about belief, it's about place. In *Banaras Region* Rana Singh calls it the genius loci of the sacredscape. The river is a goddess, alive and sacred, flowing along Shiva's locks.

We pulled over at Darbhanga Ghat and were admitted by a security guard into the elevator to the hotel lobby. Our arrival there was even more ornate than our welcome at the Oberoi Grand in Kolkata and the Taj Vivanta in Guwahati. Here two young men in hotel livery placed turmeric on our foreheads, gave us sandalwood malas, and sang to us while we checked in.

The Brij Rama started out life as a palace built in 1812. This makes it one of the older buildings of the city. Varanasi is one of the oldest continually inhabited cities in the world, but it was demolished periodically between 1200 and 1770. The buildings are new, it's the spirit and the river that hold the sense of timelessness. The Brij Rama itself exemplifies the story arc of a Varanasi building: bought by a king a century after its construction, it was left to decay for years before the current owners bought it and then spent twenty years in renovation. The sandstone pillars, scalloped archways, and inlaid floors give off an air of an ancient palace, but it's a palace reconstructed, a material expression of impermanence.

A hostess escorted us through the marble lobby and decorated corridors to our room. It had an ensuite bathroom, kettle, television, all the modern conveniences, while the rich draperies, deep red linens, dark wood paneling and desk evoked the era of the Brahmin kings. We pulled back the curtain and looked out onto the river. The holy Ganges! The curtain movement startled a monkey on the window ledge. He wasn't cute, he was threatening, and pounded on the window with anger before jumping off. I thought well, that monkey lives here, I'm just visiting. That immediate contrast, the gasp of wonder followed by an unpleasant poke, was a capsule of our experience of the city.

We were just in time for afternoon tea. The hallway on our floor let out onto a verandah where staff served afternoon treats. We had chai and pastries while we looked out over the river. It was hot for us, even in October. More worryingly the air was a dirty brown, so polluted we could taste it. We hoped it might clear up in the morning or evening but it remained solid throughout the days and nights we were there. We struggled with the dissonance between the spiritual force we sensed and the oppressive pollution we were breathing.

That evening the hotel staff shepherded us back out to their boat to take in the evening aarti or fire service. The shore was crowded with boats and we wedged in at the edge as one of the last. The trumpet sounds of the shankh floated out over the river. Alex and I shared a moment of "we're here!" The service went on for an hour that felt like a floating minute. The young priests offered ghee lamps to the cardinal directions, they lit so much camphor we could smell it from our boat. The crowd on the steps sang and clapped and the young men in our boat clapped too.

Just as the service was ending the young men in our boat pushed away. They said theirs is the nicest boat on the river and they didn't want to get it scraped up like the other boats. They motored down past the Manikarna Ghat cremation ground where the fires blazed up in the dark. The staff warned us against taking photos of the fires. I'd already taken one on the way in from the airport but refrained from taking more for the rest of the trip.

A Heritage Tour

We were up early the next day to meet the guide I'd organized in advance. I thought a local person could help us sort through the bewildering variety of options. We traded emails before we arrived so he could explore what interested us. I had settled on a tour with three parts: a morning boat ride which everyone assured us was essential, a visit to Kashi Vishwanath which was Alex's top priority, and a pre-packaged South Varanasi Heritage Tour so he could show us what he considered important to see in the "city of joy".

Once we met in person we spent some time syncing up with him as we had done with our guides in West Bengal and Assam. We had the shortest time with him, only two days, so we had to get to know each other quickly. Meeting through a web site was so impersonal that we had to start from scratch to figure each other out. Through his choices we learned the city through a series of vignettes that sketched an outline of a complex city and briefly sampled its depths.

City of the River

Our guide led us confidently down to the ghat where he had hired a boat that was substantially more primitive than Brij Rama's. This was one of the traditional bajras, flat bottomed wooden boats with no roof or handrail. I nervously asked where the life preserver was and he laughed. Okay then.

This was touted as one of the must-do experiences in Varanasi, the sunrise boat ride on the Ganges. The deeply polluted air made this a much less thrilling experience than the YouTube videos led us to expect. The boat driver motored down a few ghats and then turned off the engine so our could deliver his lecture. He has a practiced spiel about the fundamentals of Hinduism and Kashi. I kept feeding him information about us to try to get him on the right wavelength. Finally he realized that we were not run of the mill tourists. He asked curiously, "Why did you pick me?" I said liked his local tour approach and that he teaches at a girl's college. That didn't seem to fit for him though. I had the same question, why is he our guide? Why did She pick him for us?

We passed a structure on the bank of the river, a walkway built over twin concrete towers. One of the towers was painted with an image of Shiva with his trishul (trident) and bull, the other had an image of the goddess Ganga sitting on a crocodile. Shiva and Ganga, the patrons of the city.

That early in the morning the banks were crowded with people who waded into the river to bathe, both for personal hygiene and for the spiritual benefit of touching the sacred current. Bottles of Ganges water are packaged in puja (ritual) kits that are shipped all over the world. I confessed to our guide that I didn't understand how the river which was so polluted, which had body parts floating in it, could also be sacred. He explained that the spiritual benefit of the water overcame any material pollution. That explained to me how he navigated the conflict but I wasn't sure it worked for me.

City of Shiva

We docked again at Dashwashmedh Ghat. Our guide led us up the hill and asked us to wait for a minute while he called his priest. I looked around and said "Oh!" He said "ah?" I said "we are in the new corridor!" There were a bunch of little temples standing amidst the rubble of their former houses. He repeated the story that people had taken them in when the Moslem rulers leveled the temples in order to save them. I said I had heard a few people were refusing to sell. "Like this house," he said, pointing to the one I was standing near. It was a shock to find myself suddenly standing in a landscape I had seen in photographs, as if I had stepped from a dream into real life.

The area was cordoned off with barbed wire and guarded by soldiers. Our guide explained that as a licensed tour operator he could be there with his clients. He led us to a shop where he and the shopkeeper told us earnestly that we had to buy new rudraksha beads. The little ones are the best. We dutifully bought two small necklaces. I thought it was a fleece-the-tourist moment like the obligatory papyrus purchase in Egypt and worry beads in Greece but they turned out to be important in ritual later. We also surrendered all of our electronics – cell phones, fitness trackers, watches. The shopkeeper stored them for us as shopkeepers in other temples watch people's shoes.

It turned out that our guide couldn't enter the temple proper, instead he introduced us to a priest who could take us in. This man showed us his certified priest ID. I asked his name and he said "Hari Om". He seemed startled that I asked.

Hari Om led us through narrow allies and across busy streets to the foreign visitor ticket office. The woman who took my passport smiled at me. We sat while Hari Om filled out a form, took it to another desk where he got tickets, and took these to yet another desk where he got scarves and prasadam. Someone trotted out to him some wrist bands which he put on our right wrists. It was 300 rupees but covered in the cost of the tour we'd paid for in advance. When the many steps of the process were finally complete he put scarves on us, gold for Alex and pink for me, marking us as proper pilgrims. People kept saying "Om Namah Shivayah" to us while we wore them.

Hari Om led us to the temple gate. There was a security entrance which separated women and men. The woman who felt my purse asked a question, I said "passport". She said "what country?" I said America. She waved me through.

Alex had a harder time. The guard who searched him didn't seem to like Westerners. He found a box of matches in Alex's pocket from buying a diya lamp and thought about bouncing him for it. Our priest took the matches and tossed them away, so he got through.

While I waited them to navigate this I had a chance to settle myself in the energy. Just as there are Shakti piths, sites sacred to Shakti or Goddess, there are sites across India sacred to Shiva which house jyotirlingas, naturally occurring rocks in the shape of the lingam. Kashi Vishwanath is one of the twelve jyotirlinga temples. Being in the sacred city this temple came in for special attention from the Moslem conquerors who destroyed the original temple and built a mosque on it. There are stories about priests hiding the original jyotirlinga to save it. Eventually Kashi Vishwanath was built and the current jyotirlinga, whatever its provenance, was installed there.

I looked around to try to spot the gold-covered spires but I couldn't see them from below. As I settled into the sacredscape I experienced it as very powerful but a different power than the Shakti piths. The word I had to describe it was "grounded". This makes sense. Shakti is fire, sun, power, while Shiva is moon, cool. When Kali rages out of control he lies down for her to dance on him. He's the stabilizing ground beneath her feet.

When our party reunited Hari Om led us to shelves where we put our shoes in a basket together. Then he led us to a courtyard where people were praying. I was pleased to see a woman reading from a Sanskrit roll. Hari Om found us a metal bench to sit on. Then he went on a scavenger hunt. He collected two silver colored pots decorated with red swastikas that contained milk. He collected another pot filled with water with a spout in the shape of a bull head, a nod to Shiva's animal companion Nandi.

Then Hari Om was ready for the puja. He knelt in front of us and recited prayers. He had us cup our hands and poured the water into them to drink. I touched my water to my lips. He gave us flowers to tip into the milk. He asked our names. As usual he got Alex's diksha (initiation) name Varada but my own name Satya Vani didn't register so I think he just named us Varada and wife in his prayers. Every priest I met in India addressed me in prayers as Varada's wife.

Then we joined the line for the shiva lingam. It was packed. Hari Om pushed us forward to cut everyone in the line. Another family also cut in front supporting a man who was walking as if he had had a stroke. Hari Om tried to move him aside but I said "let him do it" and drew back a bit so the man could pour his milk out. I was deeply affected by his need and by the obvious love of the people who were carrying him.

Then it was our turn. I saw a black Shiva lingam with a pot suspended above it. Alex and I imitated the people around us and threw our milk on the pot. The smell of sour milk was strong. Hari Om leaned over and took a handful of milk from the pot. He led us back to our bench where he smeared the milk on our foreheads.

Then he continued the puja. He had the rudraksha we had purchased and put them around our necks. He told us to wear them inside our shirts. Then he wrapped a red and yellow cord twine around our wrists, Alex's right and my left, and briefly brought our wrists together. I felt a powerful blessing on the two of us as a couple which settled into my heart.

Alex wore his thread for two years before it finally came off. He put it on his altar. I wore mine for most of a year before I carefully eased it off to put on my altar.

Then it was done. We collected our shoes and walked back to the corridor of rubble to the shop where we retrieved our electronics. I gave all my remaining cash to the priest in thanks for his care for us.

Our guide asked us if we'd rather take the boat or walk back to the hotel. Alex and I both wanted to walk as we hadn't yet had a chance to experience the famous twisted galis (alley-streets) of Varanasi. They lived up to their reputation. Even our guide who is native to the town and makes a living as a tour operator had to ask people several times which way to the Brij Rama. We made our way through the dark corridors, stepping gingerly over cow patties and piles of human dung. These are pedestrian walkways but scooters race through them. Several times we had to flatten ourselves against the walls to let them past. A motorcycle collided with a man carrying a pot of milk directly in front of me; fortunately no one was hurt but the physical danger was clear.

In one quiet byway we passed an Aghori who was meditating deeply. Ash coated his naked body from his matted locks to his bare feet. Shiva is the god of outcastes, demons, wild spirits and the dead; Aghoris smear themselves with ash as part of their renunciation of the world and their dedication to him. As Alex passed the Aghori his eyes popped open wide and he saluted Alex with an open palm. I wondered if he did that to prank the tourists or if he genuinely recognized something in Alex. It was impossible to tell.

City of Ghats

Our guide brought us through the alleys of Varanasi back safely to the Brij Rama. I was startled to realize it was 8 am, it seemed like we'd already had a whole day's worth of touring. Alex and I had breakfast and a nap before meeting our guide again in the hotel lobby. He sat with us and chatted for a bit still trying to figure us out. In an effort to bridge the gap I showed him a picture of our teacher. He asked how long we had been practicing. I said we had done practice and reading all our lives but our diksha a few years before changed everything. He brightened and said "Doesn't it?" He explained that he comes from a Brahmin family. His family has been connected with a family of gurus for five generations. His guru is the son of his father's guru, and his guru's son will be guru to his son. He got his diksha at his wedding when he and his wife received the mantra together. Now they both teach their son and daughter. As always in India I wished I could talk to his wife to get her perspective on that life. What did she pass to her daughter?

It turned out that we could use the Brij Rama's boat on demand to travel along the river. I was relieved we didn't have to spend the whole day in the minimalist bajra.

Before the trip I had studied maps of the river trying to make sense of the ghats. When we say "dock" in English we think of wooden or concrete structures jutting out into the water. In India a ghat is a stone or concrete structure on the river bank itself, a place for people get in and out of the river and to stand or sit or bathe. Ghats also have steps leading up the river bank to the street level.

In Varanasi the ghats sit side by side along the river bank. With the steps connecting them all it's hard to tell where one ends and the next begins. Some of them are marked by signs in English, some have signs in Devanagari, some have no signs at all. Guide books say there are a hundred ghats along the river and about twenty-five of them lie along the city center. In our days in Varanasi we motored along the Ganges from Assi Ghat in the south to Raj Ghat in the north, a distance of roughly five miles.

Each ghat has a distinct character. We'd already been introduced to Darbhanga Ghat which led to our palace hotel. At Assi Ghat our guide told us that this is where the Assi River meets the Varana River, thus Varanasi. Dashwashmedh Ghat leads to the temple Kashi Vishwanath and serves as the stage for the magnificent evening aarati or fire offering. Raj Ghat on the north end of the city is an ancient site with archaeo-logical significance and a modern site leading to shops on a busy street. Raj Ghat became my favorite to walk – it had handrails on the steps down to the river.

The most famous ghat in the city is Manikarna Ghat. The crema-torium there isn't hidden away as in other cities but instead is the focal point of the river. All across India people come to Varanasi to die and be cremated so their ashes can be scattered in the Ganges which releases the soul from further rebirth. The fires are tended by the lowest sub-caste of the lowest caste, the Dalit, families who work all day and all night every day of the year. It takes a lot of firewood to consume a body so some patrons take the unburnt bodies and toss them into the river too. The government of Uttar Pradesh installed an electric crematorium at Lal Ghat just alongside Manikarna but people have generally preferred the traditional one. The visible fires are a reminder that Shiva grants liberation.

City of Persistence

I'd booked a tour to discover what a local resident considered important to show us. He focused on the continuity of the culture of Varanasi in the face of deliberate attempts to destroy it. Waves of conquerors had washed over the city wiping out buildings and carrying away treasure, but when the conquerors were pushed out the essential character of the people surfaced again.

Our first stop on the heritage tour was a boy's Vedic school. I asked where the girls were and our guide said they were taught in a separate school. We peeked into a classroom where rows of schoolboys dutifully recited with the teacher. Our guide said his grandfather wanted him to go there but his mother refused to send him so his grandfather taught him at home. Our guide commented that this was his favorite part of the tour because it demonstrated how the people of Varanasi had preserved the sacred language which is so important to their spiritual lives.

As we walked along the street to our next destination we passed an ashram where two monks chanted in a doorway. Our guide told us that they were chanting to Ram and that the monks of the ashram kept the chant going continually all day every day. He pointed out the importance of spirituality in the city.

City of Resistance

We spent a few minutes in a lovely clean courtyard filled with greenery. The centerpiece of the courtyard is a statue of a woman her riding a horse and raising a sword with a child strapped on behind her. This turned out to be a memorial to Rani Lakshmibai, a queen who opposed the British in the early 1800s and was killed in battle. A woman with a sword standing up to oppression seemed to me to be an avatar of Durga. I very much appreciated that our guide put this stop on the tour honoring the spirit of resistance in a woman's form.

City of Death

Walking down the street we passed a hospice. Our guide explained that when the time of death approaches people can do the sannyasin ritual of renunciation and enter the hospice. There they receive meals and other care to allow them to pray all day until their deaths. Then they can be cremated in Varanasi. At the time I thought it made better sense than the American custom of medicating people and warehousing them. Later I learned that these hospices can have a time limit for stays and push people out on the streets again after two weeks which is significantly less compassionate.

One of the times we motored along the river in the Brij Rama boat we spotted a male wearing only a loincloth lying the steps of a ghat. We realized he was dead -there's just something about a spiritless body that is instantly recognizable. One of the hotel guests riding in the boat with us said "Oh, how sad." I was thinking that the man had realized the great good fortune of dying in Varanasi along the banks of the Ganges, he might even have traveled there expressly for that purpose. In the west we react to death with sorrow, but it is also possible to meet death with joy.

City of Holy Men

During our walking tour our guide sprung a surprise on us and introduced us to a baba. Our guide explained that the baba had given up a government job, installed a Ganesh and Kali altar, and taken up asana. He lived beneath a tree in a roofed enclosure with some solid walls and some open to the street. The open walls allowed him to have a fire pit to make offerings. Alex and I were installed against a wall and dutifully admired the baba's ability to stand on one leg for a long time. Alex took photos.

This wasn't an advertised service on the tour but I understood why our guide made it a regular stop. So many people come to India in general and Varansi in particular looking for a guru, and if Alex and I had been seeking a spiritual guide we would have been thrilled to find one. Our guide told us that we could ask the baba anything. He said many of the people he brought to him had found the baba's advice helpful and one had even taken him as his guru. The baba dabbed a kumkum tilak on our foreheads. Our guide, translating for him, said he could tell that there was something wrong with me and asked if I wanted his advice. I smiled and said I have a teacher, a sadhana, and a living husband, so I have everything I need. This was an answer everyone could understand and accept.

As we got up to leave Alex stumbled over a loose tile in the street and fell hard. Our guide and the baba rushed to help him back to his feet. It broke the spiritual-guidance mood and replaced it with normal human care.

City of Modernization

On our second day our guide took us around in a car. He'd purchased the car just the week before after running into trouble renting vehicles. Just as in Kolkata our guide didn't drive himself, instead he hired a driver. That driver guided the car through narrow lanes where there were mostly just motorcycles and people and on one occasion squeezed the car through a passage so narrow the walls couldn't have been an inch off on each side. We all exhaled in relief when we were through.

Out of the old town onto a modern road Varanasi looked a lot like Kolkata or Guwahati. I saw my first traffic light in India which seemed to help traffic a lot. As everywhere we had been traffic snarled the roads and we spent a lot of time jostling in the back seat while our guide and driver talked. At one point our guide asked if that bothered us and I said we were self-entertaining. He laughed and said he guides enough American academics that he understood the phrase. He mentioned he'd visited America himself. I asked what the difference was between America and Varanasi. He thought a moment and said quietly, "In America the streets are clean."

Our guide took us to a weaver's cooperative. The English speaking host said that one shop supports 600 families. Only the men weave in his establishment. He didn't believe me when I said in the West Bengali countryside it is the women who weave.

They had two jacquard looms which can do 5 to 10 centimeters a day. Each of these operated by one man. They also had one handloom operated by two men that could do 1-2 centimeters a day. It takes half a year to do a bedspread. Each weaver knows one pattern that is passed down through his family. The host showed us a stack of wall hangings, mostly of Krishna with Radha. They did have Ganesh as well, all the same image in different colors. Alex chose one of those to take home with him.

Outside our guide explained that there were once many shops where people wove by hand. Today the famous Varansi weaving industry is automated; we passed warehouses clanging with the sound of the machines. The shop we visited survives on tourist dollars.

We ended our sacred shopping spree at a really good statue store. We were able to get all the images we'd been looking for all over West Bengal and Assam: Ganesh, Lakshmi, Durga on a tiger. I was looking for an image of Varahi and found a boar-headed statue labeled Varaha. I asked the shopkeeper if he also had Varahi and he said it was the same, and when I thought about it I agreed with him and took it home. Most were destined for our friends but Varaha/Varahi sits on my personal altar.

City of Temples

Throughout our two days with our guide we visited a number of temples.

Jagannath Temple

The first temple we visited was a small Jaganath shrine tucked away in a courtyard surrounded by houses. I was excited. I explained to our guide that I had felt a call to visit the Jaganath Temple in Puri in Odisha but it was closed to white people. He commented that Varanasi contains all of India, you can come to that one city and experience everything you wish to do.

Jaganath is a form of Vishnu. He actually comes as part of a set with his brother Balabhadra and his sister Subhadra. At this open-air temple all three images were propped up on a platform, wrapped with cloth, wearing masks. With no one around I was able to connect with the deities and felt I had received darshan even through the masks. I asked our guide if I could leave money for the shrine. He pointed to the donation box on the platform. When I took off my shoes to step onto the platform he was surprised and pleased that he didn't have to ask me to do it and explain why. Apparently he gets a lot of pushback from American tourists.

Durga Temples

The major Durga temple we visited was Durga Kund. It's a massive square building topped with a shikhara towers and painted brick red. The image of Durga here is said to be self-created, found rather than crafted. I asked our guide to point out to me the images of Lakshmi and Saraswati I'd heard were on the grounds. They were side by side, both covered with cloth wearing identical silver masks painted with white eyes. I had no idea which was which so I offered a quick set of mantras to both of them.

After paying our respects to the enshrined Goddesses we went down to the large kund or water tank, once fed by the river and now topped up by runoff from the temple. It's fenced off and I didn't see anyone using the kund as I had in other temples. Tourist web sites comment that it's used once a year to float an image of Vishnu sitting on the Shesha Nag, the serpent that remains when everything else ceases to exist.

Down by the pond we encountered two other shrines. The Durga Vinayaka enshrined a massive orange statue of Ganesh which attracted a good many devotees. Our guide also made a point to show us a small shrine for Shitala, the goddess of smallpox, who both sends the disease and cures it. I didn't experience a particular affinity but I offered a small prayer to her. A few months later when the COVID virus swept the world I was glad I'd taken the time to acknowledge her. India has a long memory and a Goddess to handle any circumstance.

Kamaccha Temple

Before the trip our guide had asked what we were interested in and we had mentioned that we were touring Kamakhya Temple in Assam, so he made a point of taking us to the Kamakhya Temple in Varanasi. Here she is known as Kamaccha. The neighborhood around the temple, also called Kamaccha, was highly decorated and I was able to take a few pictures including a wall painting of Durga.

Our guide explained we would begin with Vairav. I asked "Vairav?" and he said "You know, the brother of Durga?" I said "Bhairav?" and he agreed. Bhairav is a form of Shiva who is usually described as Durga's husband, I hadn't heard him described as Durga's brother before this.

The Batuk Bhairav temple turned out to be part of the Kamaccha Temple complex. I was able to take a picture of the Ministry of Housing and Urban Affairs sign. which explained that Bhairav is worshipped in his infant form here. The statue was black and covered with cloth and garlands. Two black dogs faced each other in front of him. Our guide led us on another pradakshina or circuit around the shrine, acknowleding each side view and touching his head to the wall behind the shrine.

Then we approached Kamaccha herself, a black statue of the goddess Kamakhya with intensely staring eyes. I felt the same energy there that I had felt at Kamakhya Temple in Guwahati. We circled this shrine as well and touched our heads to the back of the shrine. The shrine also included a tree swathed in red and gold cloth which I touched in acknowledgement.

This was not a particularly large or prominent temple but it managed to cram a number of other shrines onto the grounds, including several forms of Durga, one of the twelve jyotirlingas or self-created Shivalingas of Varanasi, and another form of Shiva called Krodhan Bhairav which *Banaras Region* names as one of the eight Shiva images protecting Varanasi.

Ten Thousand Temples

By the time we'd toured just two temples, the Durga Kund and the Kamaccha Temple, I was already overwhelmed. Varanasi is said to have ten thousand temples and in our two days with our guide we toured so many that it's difficult to include them all. The city is full of gods. At one point as we walked along the street I touched my forehead to an orange painting of Ganesh on a street corner and our guide commented I had to let up on doing that or I'd be literally bowing to gods all day.

On one of our rambles our guide led us to a temple to Durga that turned out to be closed. He hadn't known that it would be shuttered for lunch, he visited every day early in the morning. He particularly wanted to show it to us as it is dedicated to Durga as Mahishasura Mardini. I said "I chant to her! I chant the Chandi path." He laughed as we had a moment of recognition: that's why we've been brought together! It was Chandi! It relieved both of us to have solved that mystery.

On our last afternoon together our guide said he'd enjoyed guiding us because we have Durga Ma in our hearts. I thanked him for helping us through our physical challenges and he said he treated us as he would his parents. I was struck again that I have met with respect for my age during my travels, but in my own country the elderly are mocked and discarded. I was grateful that Durga Ma brought us together with a guide who took such good care of us.

Watching the River

Our touring days began and ended in the Brij Rama which cushioned us in luxury. We took breakfast and dinner in the dining room. We watched young women perform Barat Natyam dances in the courtyard, stamping their feet onto the stone floor to make their anklets jingle.

From the window of our room I filmed a monkey troupe swarming over the rooftops. That same monkey troupe menaced the terrace where we took tea in the afternoons to watch boats cruise by on the river. A barbed fence shut the troupe out but they worked sporadically to find a way around it.

Monkeys weren't the only hazard on the terrace. One afternoon a kite fluttered down from the sky. A young boy dining with a family crowed with delight and ran to pick it up but was rapidly intercepted by a young man on the staff who explained that the kite was not safe. Kite warfare was a favorite local pastime and the cords are studded with razors and glass shards to cut the cords of other kites. The young staff member carefully took hold of the cords and coaxed the kite up into the air to mollify the boy.

After two days of non-stop touring I was ready for a break from the crowds, the noise, the colors, the pollution, the press of the myriad gods. I spent a day in the hotel room while Alex went out on his own. I sat at the lovely wooden desk looking down the river at the windows of other rooms where famous writers had penned their works and reached for words to capture the moment.

Winged kites and paper kites and dragonflies spin in endless spirals. Sunrise brings the boats onto the river, noon sounds the call to prayer, the lamps are lit at sunset and offered to the river, and the dogs bark all night. Monkeys own the rooftops, bulls own the roads. Stone steps climb from the ghats to stone buildings built on a limestone bank. The walls press so close that only two people can walk side by side, and still the motorcycles manage to pass them.

The air is polluted but healing, the river is polluted but purifies. Garbage is swept into piles and the bulls, goats, dogs, pigs, monkeys live on the piles, an entire ecology. This is the human impact. Without us the skies would be clear, the river would run clean, the animals nourished by a jungle filled with life. If the spiritual depends on the physical, the soul reliant on the state of the body, our urgent task is to craft a way of life that sustains more than destroys. There is more than one reason this is the city of Shiva.

Twelve lakhs of people live in the city, visible in the houses and on the streets and washing themselves on the ghats. Nonetheless there is quiet here, physical and psychic too, as if the people are not actually present, or the city itself half in another dimension, which is what the locals say.

It is said that everyone who lives here is Shiva. There is Shiva covered in ash and meditating, Shiva chanting all night and all day, Shiva teaching children to speak the holy language. There is Shiva soaping up his armpits, Shiva taking a switch to his donkey, Shiva shitting in the street. There is Shiva touching his head to Her temple and saying "Ma," Shiva taking Her hand and smiling, Shiva lying lifeless beneath her dancing feet. Shiva cannot exist without Her, and life spills out from Her boon-giving hands.

The river cradles the city, a guide told me, like a mother cradles her child. Without the river and the limestone bank there would be no city. It seems that there has always been a city here; it is impossible to imagine a world without Kashi. It is aspiration, and failure, and attainment. Without Kashi we would be less than we can be. In Kashi our struggle to live in spirit teaches us that it is necessary to be human.

Alex came back hours later than he wanted somewhat harried by the experience. He had wanted to take photos but wasn't able to stop at all as every step was dogged by touts and beggars. He walked down to Dashwashmedh Ghat and then to Manikarna Ghat to try to get closer to the cremation fires. He found local shrines open for people to go in and make their offerings. On the way back he went to one of the temples of Maa Kali with a three-foot-high icon protected by an active priest. He did get darshan but felt it was snatched as he didn't want to have to fend off the priest.

He did locate a road with shops, Bangla Toda Road right at the top of the steps where he saw a dozen or so other white people. We determined to do our final shopping there the next day. I said I wanted to try to visit the Varahi Temple too. It's only open in the morning. I thought we'd have time to do that before breakfast. He advised me to add an additional two hours to my time estimate to account for getting lost in the alleys. I laughed but it turned out he was right.

Varahi Temple

Of all the goddesses in India Varahi is the one who called to me. I love them all, I chant to Durga, but Varahi had reached into my heart. She doesn't present as a beautiful young thin woman as nearly every other goddess, instead she wears a boar head and boasts a full belly, joyfully embodied. As a warrior she has that blend of male and female that always calls to me. In the stories where the goddess Lalita does battle with demons there are two generals in her army, the female general Shymala and the male general Varahi. That's why the shopkeeper who sold me the statue of boar-headed Varaha said it was also an image of Varahi and why I agreed with him.

I'd been to Kolkata during Durga Puja, visited many Kali temples in West Bengal, visited the shrines of the Mahavidyas in Assam. I very much wanted to have a chance for Varahi's darshan while I was in India. Banaras Region let us know that there is a temple to Varahi in Varanasi that opens for a few hours in the morning. Google Maps placed it within walking distance of the Brij Rama. On our last day in Varansi I was determined to go.

We were up before 6 am to make the attempt. We left the Brij Rama by a door that let onto the uphill side and threaded our way along narrow galis that opened into a market square. There were shopkeepers hawking murtis, stall owners hawking rudraksha, vendors on the sidewalks selling vegetables and puja bowls. Scooters roared through while bulls trotted down the road and we found ourselves having to duck through them.

We fell in with a tour group where I heard an American accent. I commented to them that they were the first Americans I had met in India. They said there were other Seattleites in their group. They were all taking photos so I told Alex quick, here's your chance! We used them as cover to snatch a few shots.

As we walked I asked every older woman if I was approaching the Varahi Temple and they always said yes. We found a sign, missed a turn, circled around, found another sign. An older woman hawking puja supplies sold me a coconut-garland-cloth basket. At the next gali we finally spotted the gate and the line of women. Found it! I told Alex he didn't have to go so he decided to stay on the street and guard my shoes.

The temple is a squarish building housing a huge black stone statue of the boar-headed goddess Varahi standing on her buffalo. The statue is held to be so potent that it can't be seen directly by anyone but the priests who serve her. There are stories of Brahmin families who insist on looking at her and then fainting at the sight. The statue can only be viewed from above through two holes cut into the floor above.

The stairs climbed that whole first flight alongside the temple building. The walls of the temple were painted yellow and fixed with red handprints. The line moved slowly. Nearly all the women carted pots with handles and I wondered what they were carrying. The woman in front of me complained about the wait. The woman behind me pushed me. Two women talked in mixed English and Hindi about visiting the Annapurna temple the day before. "One kilometer line!" I'd had a thought to visit that temple next but scrubbed that idea off the agenda. One of the women was humming a popular tune for the Mahishasuramardini Stotram. When she got to the chorus she sang out "Jaya jaya hey Mahishasuramardini, ramyakapardini shailasute!" I was gratified to learn that I'm not the only person who only knows the words of the chorus.

At the top of the stairs I had some time in the courtyard to look around. The jumble of buildings around the temple made up a variegated tower. I could finally see the temple flag which was supposed to guide visitors to the spot but ended up lost among those rooftops. A tree filled the sky. There was a red pillar, one side carved with a bas relief of a goddess in white wearing blue with four arms holding weapons, the other side with an image wearing a leopard skin which I guessed might be Bhairav. There was also a cage which had a small black stone image I couldn't identify, and a Shivalinga, and an image of Nandi, as if every courtyard in Varanasi had to cram as much sacred statuary as it possibly could.

The line shuffled past a second courtyard where a Brahmin priest sat next to another Shivalinga and a stone triangle which I thought looked like a yoni. He was passing out fennel prasadam. Then there was yet another Shivalinga in a shrine right next to the temple door. This one was a miniature of the one at Kashi Vishwanath setup, a black Shivalinga with a pot hanging above it. The women who carried pots poured water over that Shivalinga, mystery solved.

Through the open door I could see an image on the wall, a picture of the statue of Varahi, clothed, with a painted face and white eyes which darted into me. I felt I had darshan right then. The woman behind me pushed again. My heart pounded as I crossed the threshold into the temple. The line snaked past a priest who took the offerings. The women then bent down to a hole in the floor with a raised lip, then another hole farther along, and then out a door on the far end.

When my turn came the priest didn't bat an eye at the white girl. I gave a 100k note, the going rate, and handed over my coconut. He gave it to another priest who broke it and poured it into the hole, then handed it back to the first priest who handed it back to me.

While this was happening I had my chance to bend over and look into the hole. The hole wasn't directly above the statue, it gave a sideways view so you couldn't see the eyes. The statue was at least as large as a person and had been clothed by the priests. The power knocked the breath out of me. I thought I wouldn't actually want to see her directly, the glimpse of her and the picture on the wall were enough power to handle. I almost missed the second hole but the women in front of me stopped there, so I paused on my way past to glance down and caught a view of her buffalo vehicle.

As I looked down on her I asked her if she wanted me. I got the impression that approaching her would be a process as slow as the line into her temple.

I touched the lintel of the temple door as I left. I noticed the clock on the wall said 8 am. Back on the street Alex gave me my shoes and told me he'd watched the line move with fascination. Only women visited the temple. We couldn't be sure any of them were widows but it was certainly possible.

Just a block from the temple we found ourselves on Bangla Toda Road again. In the street a sadhu tried to tag us with ash but we dodged him. We popped into a couple of shops to buy some statues and walked out with bags in our hands. This turned out to be a mistake as the touts spotted a mark and descended on us. Alex let them irritate him but I've fielded worse in Egypt and I was able to get them to leave us alone by fiercely waving them away.

Our next task was to find our way back to the hotel. I tried using my phone GPS but that got us good and lost among the twisting galis. At one point we found ourselves looking up at our exact hotel balcony with no way to get there over the surrounding walls.

Finally we found an open lane to the river. Alex said we could walk to the hotel because it was just one ghat over. This proved to be the case.

The stairs had no rails but were manageable. I was so focused on fending off a vendor and managing the footing that Alex said "where are you going?" There was our elevator and guard! I marched up to him and gave him our room number with great relief. He looked like he was going to laugh at how happy we were to see him.

The hotel furnished us with breakfast and luxurious showers. Alex said he wanted to have another one, it felt so good to be clean again. We'd accomplished all the things we'd meant to do in Varanasi and we were frankly worn out by the town. We spent the rest of the day in the hotel.

I realized that the day had presented us with all the traditional hazards of Varansi: the bulls we dodged, the pandit who tried to tag us with ash, the woman poking me in the back in the temple line, the steps that led us back to the hotel. I realized too that the traditional hazard list seems quaint in comparison with the contemporary dangers of traffic, touts and trash. And even with modern technology the dark narrow lanes remain as difficult to navigate as they have ever been.

Departure: What Changed Next

From the moment we left the Brij Rama to the moment we set foot in our own house again we traveled nonstop for more than 24 hours. It was the longest day. When we got home we threw away the shoes that had walked India's filthy streets and bought new ones. Taking off your shoes before stepping into a temple makes sense on both the level of respect and of physical cleanliness.

We avidly followed the progress of the Varansi corridor project. It didn't take long for the government to finish it. As I write in 2023 videos show the gleaming new walkways and open courtyards. It's a beautiful stroll to the temple now. We were there after the warren of houses was cleared out but before the new entrance was completed, standing in the rubble. Another lesson in impermanence.

More has changed since our visit than the completion of the new corridor. The temple staff at Kashi Vishwanath have installed a camera above the jyotirlinga which broadcasts a livestream much of the day. I check in every night when I go to bed. Because of the 12 hour time difference that's usually when the temple is in full swing. Generally there are four metal troughs directing a flow of milk, flowers, and other offerings down into the silver well where the Shiva linga sits. I haven't seen milk on the pot as I did when I visited in person.

Sometimes I catch the priests when they are cleaning out the silver well in preparation for the new day's new offerings. Sometimes I catch priests sitting cross-legged near the Shiva linga performing a puja, offering incense, flowers and milk. During Shiva's great holiday Shivaratri the temple operates around the clock and people file past in long lines. Once I saw a group of priests throw red powder on each other. Another Shivaratri I checked in at midnight Varanasi time and caught an unruly band of sadhus with matted hair who were laughing, dancing and hanging from the pot. I rather think they capture Shiva's character.

Of course the world itself changed in 2020. All the temples closed, including Kashi Vishwanath, and when they re-opened everyone was wearing masks. Today the masks are gone, the lines have returned, and everyone has adapted to living with another permanent illness. Shitala added coronavirus to the list of plagues she both causes and cures and her shrines did see an uptick in popularity.

When the tourist business died our guide in Varanasi contacted us to ask us for a donation to support his family, which we sent, but even so I was left with a lingering feeling of guilt. Was it enough? What did I owe him? I wanted to give more than I could.

Alex's fall at the baba's home was in retrospect a portent and the beginning of another journey. A few months later he would receive the medical diagnosis Amyotrophic Lateral Sclerosis, a neurological progressive disease that whittles away the ability to move and is ultimately fatal. It's a story arc of impermanence and his first loss of balance happened in the baba's courtyard. Our teacher gave us the Shiva's great mantra conquering death, the mrityunjaya mantra: "I worship you oh three-eyed Shiva. Like a cucumber falling from the vine liberate me from death into immortality." I chant it for him every night.

Our magical pilgrimage ended in the Sattvic atmosphere of Shiva's city. The city of joy offered us the cremation fires, the sacred river, Shiva's presence in his great temple, the necessity to embrace filth as a requisite for embracing life. Varanasi packs in so many spiritual opportunities that a lifetime would not exhaust them, but the four days we spent there granted us the experiences we needed.

True Journey is Return

The fabulous treasures of the east that once traveled the trade routes came home in our suitcases as souvenirs: embroideries, silk, tea, bronze statues, images of the gods, necklaces, magical tools, and many pounds of books. We distributed these among our friends and cherish them in our home. As precious as they are to us we will leave these physical gifts behind us after we are gone. The most important treasures we brought home with us are the stories. Our Tantric training assures us that knowledge is the treasure we carry with us life over life.

Just a few months after we arrived home the COVID pandemic put a stop to worldwide movement for some months and continues to complicate travel years later. Alex is disabled now and has lost the ability to travel. We made the journey at the last possible moment both in travel conditions and personal ability. We are enormously grateful to have been able to make the pilgrimage in this life and to be able to share our experiences here. They have made us better magicians, better Tantric practitioners, and better people.

Appendix A: Illustrations

Brij Rama

Varanasi Rooftop Monkeys

Varanasi Aarati

Rani Lakshmibai statue

Wrestling ground at Durga temple

Durga Kund

Durga Kund

Batuk Bharaiv Temple

Shiva and Kamaccha

Bibliography

"How a goddess called Corona Devi came to be worshipped in West Bengal", The Hindu.com, June 10 2020, www.thehindu.com/society/a-goddess-called-corona-devi/article31795320.ece

Jacob, Shalin. "Shunned & Neglected, The Widows Of Varanasi Live As Social Outcasts Showing The Ugly Side Of India." Scoopwhoop.com, Jan. 16 2017, www.scoopwhoop.com/culture/widows-of-varanasi/

Kashi Vishwanath livestream, www.shrikashivishwanath.org/.

Shankar, Priyanka. "Doms of Varanasi make a living among the dead". Reuters, October 26, 2017, www.reuters.com/article/india-doms-varanasi-cremation-idUSKBN1CV1K8.

Singh, Ram. P. B. and Pravin S. Rana. *Banaras Region, A Spiritual and Cultural Guide*. Indica, 2006.

"Varahi Devi, A Small Temple with a Powerful Goddess". Varanasi Mirror, Dec. 16 2021, www.varanasimirror.com/varanasi-temples/varahi-devi-a-small-temple-with-a-powerful-goddess/

ABOUT THE AUTHOR

Brandy Williams is a Wiccan high priestess, a Pagan Magician, and a Tantric yogini. She is an elder in Coven of the Mystical Merkabah, founded in 1987, and has worked with the Golden Dawn group Temple of Light and Darkness and with Ordo Templi Orientis. She meets regularly with the Theurgy Forum hosted by Hercules Invictus which brings teachers of theurgy together in public conversation. Currently she studies Shri Vidya with a private teacher. She teaches at magical conferences in person around the country and virtually around the world. She lives with two partners, two cats and a dog. Visit her online at www. BrandyWilliamsAuthor.com.

www.ingramcontent.com/pod-product-compliance
Lightning Source LLC
Chambersburg PA
CBHW061138120626
46546CB00005B/1840